CONTENTS

Introduction: The Age of the Economist 1
  1 *The Journey of Adam Smith* 13
  2 *A Christmas Carol* 28
  3 *The Gilded Age* 54
  4 *The Mistake* 80
  5 *Reap Where They Never Sowed* 94
  6 *Noise in the World* 109
  7 *Tales of Enterprise and Avarice* 127
  8 *Gifts of Science* 138
  9 *The Eternal Sophist* 152
 10 *Father Arizmendi Comes to Mondragon* 169
 11 *Textbooks of the Temples* 190
Notes 207
Index 223

INTRODUCTION

THE AGE OF THE ECONOMIST

Our time has been called the Age of the Economist. The social philosopher Edmund Burke first used this term to characterize the eighteenth century, which was his own century and also the century of Adam Smith, but this expression has since become even more appropriate.[1]

Economists are now key advisors to governments, presidents, prime ministers, and even autocrats and dictators, in addition to their obvious and expected place in the world of business, banking, and finance. The celebrated twentieth-century economist John Maynard Keynes well describes the influence of economics in our time: "The ideas of economists and political philosophers, both when they are right and when they are wrong, are more powerful than is commonly understood. Indeed the world is ruled by little else. Practical men, who believe themselves to be quite exempt from any intellectual influences, are usually the slaves of some defunct economist."[2]

It could well be said that the religious passions of past history have now been superseded by economic ones, so that in this sense our ultimate cosmologies are now economic rather than religious. While in the Middle Ages the beliefs that divided society and set large blocs of people at war with each other were theological in nature, in our time the great ominous divide between peoples is based on differing philosophies of economics.

This is so much the case that when, under the heading of "perestroika," the Soviet bloc began dismantling its centralized authoritarian economic planning in the late 1980s, one commentator described this transition with a certain wistfulness as marking "the end of history"—at least in the sense of the history of ideas.[3] This book, however, should put to rest anyone's concern that the development and challenge of ideas has ended.

The centrality of economics in the major issues of our time is undergirded by its widespread influence in a range of fields and academic disciplines. In the social sciences, economic concepts and models appear often in the work of psychologists and sociologists. In political science, the presence of economic theory is everywhere. An economist has been elected to the governing council of the American Political Science Association. One social scientist noted with some misgivings that "leaks from economics threaten to inundate the compartment of political science." Almost all the best law schools have at least one economist on their faculty. A textbook entitled *The Economic Aspects of Law,* written by Chicago Circuit Court of Appeals Judge Richard Posner, who is a graduate of Chicago law school and who also holds a Ph.D. in economics from the University of Chicago, has been a legal best seller and influenced "an army of recruits."[4] Most notably these recruits include Douglas Ginsburg and Robert Bork, two rejected nominees for the United States Supreme Court, as well as the successful contender Judge Anthony Scalia. Posner himself remains a top candidate for a future position on the Court.

Economics certainly continues to influence philosophy, a field from which, about two hundred years ago, it began its journey to its present prominence. Philosophers John Rawls *(A Theory of Justice)* and Robert Nozick *(Anarchy, State and Utopia)* disagree almost across the board, but they are alike in that each of their arguments has been deeply influenced by the study of economics.[5] Economics has even made its presence felt in medical schools, where decision making is increasingly analyzed economically and taught in terms of cost-benefit. This is the approach, for example, of the ground-breaking book *Costs, Risks, and Benefits of Surgery.*[6]

This is the Age of the Economist; however, there are other grand designations for our time that have caught on because they strike a responsive chord: it has been said that we are living in the Age of Uncertainty, the Age of Anxiety, and the Nuclear Age. And finally, our time has certainly been called the Age of Science and the Age of Technology. We may have a suspicion that all of these characterizations, different though they may be in their particular focus, have a certain underlying something in common which goes to the heart of what the modern world is about—and perhaps indicates what ails that heart. It is one of the theses of this book that economics holds a key to understanding what that "certain something" may be.

When I first went to college I didn't know that the key lay in economics, and I was drawn instead to study psychology and eventually to become a psychologist (after a brief flirtation with engineering in the late 1950s). When I received my doctorate in psychology I never would have described ours as the Age of the Economist. But, as these things have their way of working out, my not studying economics in the beginning turned out be a very fortunate choice. Had I first studied economics and become an economist I seriously doubt that I could have come to realize what I have written in this book.

When we begin to study a discipline, the first things we learn in that first textbook in that introductory course are the foundational concepts or axioms of that field. We imbibe them at that tender time almost like children imbibing the very rudiments of the language and culture that will become the framework for their lives. Later on, when we are learned and credentialed in our particular field, its fundamental concepts and ways of thinking become as deeply rooted as a first language, so that it takes great pain and effort to dig back to these roots in order to critically examine them. And there is the further barrier that at that point there is often little reason or motivation to do so. Had I studied economics first, I don't know whether I would have had what it takes to make such an intellectual return journey. Consequently my hat goes off to all those economists qua economists who have made this journey back through their own efforts; I have drawn on some of their work as background and inspiration for what is presented here. For myself, I went into economics as a psychologist already thoroughly educated in the social sciences, rather than as an impressionable and naive kid taking his first economics course, so I was able to apply a proper degree of critical alertness from the beginning.

My career as a psychologist included working with low income families in their homes through a public health agency in rural Maine. The agency administered programs to mothers or families eligible for state and federal assistance. I should note here that *low income* is itself a bit of social science jargon for the word *poor*. As a psychologist trying to provide psychotherapy and counseling to these poor and "multiproblem" families, I became very aware of the differences in needs between these patients or clients and those that I saw in my private office practice. The analyses and techniques that were developed in regard to the problems of my private patients often had little to do with the problems families living in or near poverty were dealing with—problems, naturally enough, not of the psyche, but of the physical world. They often weren't able to pay the rent, to buy adequate food, to pay for a telephone, to keep the car on the road, or to fix the plumbing (or even to *have* plumbing). I found that psychology could do little to help these people solve their most immediate and pressing problems. In my frustration and helplessness, I came to feel that they should first be informed as to what kind of problems psychology was supposed to deal with, so that they wouldn't trouble me with all their physical world problems. But I tried this and it didn't work. Somehow they were never able to stick to matters of the psyche and function as good psychotherapy patients when their lives in the physical world were under such daily siege.

Up until this point in my life, which was around 1974, I had had little interest in formal economics, but I began to wonder more about things like money, employment, wealth, and poverty, and I became curious as to what the field of economics had to say about all this. As chance would have it, I had a brief acquaintance at that time with Mark Lutz, who lived in the same small town that I did and who was a professor of economics at the University of Maine. As chance would further have it, at around the same time Mark had become increasingly curious about the field of psychology, and how its knowledge might apply to certain questions in economics. So he and I came together in a rather perfect meeting, and we began sharing and exchanging each other's expertise. It was soon apparent that this was a fruitful and exciting interchange, and what started off as a few get-togethers turned into frequent and ongoing meetings. So I began my tutorial in economics, and Mark began his in psychology. Five years later this collaboration resulted in our first book, which was republished in 1988 as a revised version entitled *Humanistic Economics: The New Challenge.*[7] Our collaboration in the field of economics has become ongoing, as part of what is becoming known as the new field of economic psychology.

I said previously that at the time when I obtained my doctorate in psychology I would not have described our era as the Age of the Economist. Instead, like most social scientists, or perhaps like most people trained in the sciences in general, I would have seen science and technology as the dominant and defining features of our modern world. In history I had learned about the period called the Industrial Revolution and how it had helped usher in the modern world. But most of the history I learned was taught as politics and wars. The possibility that our present age came into being through certain critical changes in beliefs, attitudes, and values—in a word, through changes in consciousness—was not something that was conveyed by the teaching of history as I experienced it. Furthermore, I understood the Industrial Revolution to be largely a revolution in science and technology and in the application of these to mass production. Thus its significance conformed to my understanding that the origins of the modern world lay in the development and applications of science.

So it was a jarring and marvelous eye-opener for me when, in the beginning stages of my career in economic theory, I read Robert Heilbroner's great book about the history of economics and economic thought, *The Worldly Philosophers*.[8] In particular, reading chapter 2, "The Economic Revolution," was one of the factors that led me from a mere curiosity about certain basic economic questions to a total immersion in a second academic discipline.

Heilbroner's account began to make evident to me that the making of the modern world was a transformation in values and consciousness well before it was the application of science and technology. This realization was later reinforced and broadened by other classic works in the field, such as Richard H. Tawney's *Religion and the Rise of Capitalism* and Karl Polanyi's *The Great Transformation*.[9] These studies make quite clear that the widespread use of science in economic development did not come into play until at least two centuries after a transformation in values had begun. Further, in the early stages of this transformation—around the middle of the fifteenth century—other cultures such as China and the Islamic world had science and technology that were at least equivalent and possibly superior to those of the West. This discovery began to shatter my long-held belief as a student of the social sciences that science was the linchpin of the change that occurred between the Middle Ages and the twentieth century. Through the study of economics I began to see that the astounding and perhaps overwhelming development of science and technology in our time is as much a result of the economic transformation as it is its cause.

Just what is this change that we can call the economic transformation of society? Is it the pursuit of wealth? Yes, in part it is certainly that. However, I also learned from my economic studies something that I already vaguely knew but without an adequate appreciation of its significance. I was reminded that in the Middle Ages—a time dominated by the Church and its teachings—the pursuit of wealth, at least the naked pursuit, was considered wrong, for it was the sin of avarice. And the increasing interest in the lending of money, which we now know to be the heart of finance, was condemned by the Church as usury. So, between the height of the Middle Ages and the present there had to be a fundamental change in thought that allowed and perhaps even encouraged activities that were once considered wrong.

This shift cannot be adequately explained as merely a new interest in the pursuit of wealth. The tendency toward avarice, if we want to call it that, has always been present in human nature and in fact has been indulged by the princes of all ages. But it seems that rather suddenly—if we take into account the whole span of human history—such a tendency began to emerge in one area of the world on an unprecedented scale. The pursuit of wealth became open not only to princes and monarchs but seemingly to all people.

I use the word *avarice* here for convenience, but certainly we are also talking about something much broader: a democratization of society and a loosening of the exploitative hold of the aristocracy on the common man and woman. This is surely a change we can assent to. In it lies much of what we value in our own culture, such as the ability to write critical analyses of it—including the present study. But if something was gained, something may also have been lost. Or, putting it in economic terms, for our gains we may have paid a considerable price.

Because of my background as a psychologist, I knew, perhaps more than most economists, just how dear a price we have paid. Psychologist Paul Wachtel refers to this price as the "poverty of affluence."[10] Whatever this poverty is in essence—if such an essence can be found—its effects are certainly multidimensional. We can see this price, this poverty, in the social, spiritual, and even economic spheres. We see it too in the damage to our environment, the natural world.

Trying to understand the exact nature of the economic transformation of our culture became a compelling drive for me, and I sensed that an answer could not be found through psychology alone. However, a significant glimmer came when I began to realize the extent to which economists misunderstand basic human processes. Below is a potent example. It is a textbook description of what is known in economics by the somewhat formidable name of *diminishing marginal utility,* but the principle is really quite simple. We could say that it is economists' explanation of why people cease one activity and go on to another.

> Diminishing marginal utility is an expression of the "variety is the spice of life" philosophy of most individuals— that people prefer to have one or a few of a lot of different goods and services rather than a great many of only a few goods and services. For example, diminishing marginal utility suggests that an individual will derive more satisfaction from eating a first apple than a second apple, which in turn provides more satisfaction than a third apple, and so on—where all the apples are eaten at one sitting. . . . Exceptions to diminishing marginal utility are only infrequently observed.[11]

To me it was obvious that this explanation was wrong. The reason a person gradually gets less satisfaction as she continues eating apples is not that somehow the apples become less interesting—"the variety is the spice of life" theory—but that a need has been satisfied. The person is simply less hungry. It turns out that this example is not merely incidental. Economics also denies that people have needs. The layman on first hearing this may find it hard to believe, but here is one economist's very forthright assertion:

> In economics, "need" is a non-word. Economics can say much which is useful about desires, preferences, and demands. But "need" presumably is a moral, psychological, or physical imperative which brooks no compromise or adjustment—or analysis. If we "need" something, we must have it: there is literally no alternative of either substitution or abstinence. But the assertion of absolute economic "need"—in contrast to desire, preference, and demand—is nonsense.[12]

And so we learn that economics talks about *wants* (or *demand*) rather than needs. An important thing about *wants* for the economist is that they are ultimately infinite and therefore unsatisfiable. Again, from an economic textbook, as explained under the heading of "Unlimited Wants":

> As a group, material wants are, for practical purposes, insatiable, or unlimited. This means that material wants for goods and services are incapable of being completely satisfied. . . . Finally, let us emphatically add that the overall end or objective of all economic activity is the attempt to satisfy these diverse material wants.[13]

Does the reader notice something strange about this conclusion? It appears that economics has construed itself so as to attempt to accomplish the impossible: to satisfy that which cannot be satisfied. Wants as a class are insatiable, and yet the aim of economic activity is to try to satiate wants. From this we can start to see that economics, even at the level of its theory, may have something to do with why we are destroying our natural world.

We live on a finite planet. If human beings are defined as being made up of infinite wants, and the task of an economic system is to fulfill that infinity, then such a system will go on endlessly churning out goods in an attempt to reach what is from the beginning an impossible goal. When the infinite production of goods meets up with a finite planet there is bound to be a collision. *Ecological crisis* is the name we have given to that collision.

All through the writing of *Humanistic Economics* I thought that economics' rejection of *needs* in favor of *wants* was as close as we could get to the essence of the problem. But the question still remained as to why this rejection of needs had been made in the first place. Heilbroner, in the conclusion of his chapter "The Economic Revolution," describes how Adam Smith came along in the melee of change that was going on in the latter half of the eighteenth century and wrote his *Inquiry into the Nature and*

Causes of the Wealth of Nations.[14] Heilbroner concludes that in this book Smith "gave the world the image of itself for which it had been searching. After the *Wealth of Nations,* men began to see the world about themselves with new eyes. . . ."[15] Max Lerner traces that impact right up to the present day. He says that Smith's work "has done as much perhaps as any modern book thus far to shape the whole landscape of life as we live it today."[16]

From my acquaintance with Smith's work I knew that he was very much concerned about needs, and when he used the term *wealth* he was not referring to the accumulated possessions of the rich, but to the wherewithal of the common person to meet their necessities and to have a decent life. So how did economics arrive at its present emphasis on infinite *wants?* Did Smith somehow, in his well-intentioned and certainly brilliant efforts, plant a seed that was eventually to bear some dubious fruit? If he did, that seed would seem to be at the heart of the matter.

After ten years the answer finally became clear. Perhaps, as a psychologist, it should have been obvious to me much earlier in my study. But like those who learn economics as their first language, I too had possibly been beguiled by the preachings of the old master. The heart of economics turns out not to be *wants*—that is only a later extension of a more fundamental idea. The heart of economics, as any introductory textbook will tell you somewhere right near the beginning, and as Adam Smith first told us a little over two hundred years ago, is this: The essential nature of the human being, at least as an economic actor, is self-interest, and self-interest is a very good thing.

The melee that Heilbroner referred to was a loosening of the old institutions of authority and along with it the old standards and principles, and what was to come in its place was unknown and undefined. Adam Smith's work was to give this openness and fluidity the stamp that later came to be called economics. The inhabitants of this new society were no longer "man in Christian society," or "man in feudal society," but rather *Homo oeconomicus,* or economic man. Smith wrote about how nations became wealthy and said that it was not a result of the dictates of the aristocracy nor from anyone's benevolence or good intentions, but out of everyone's being able to pursue the interests of his or her individual self.

This is presented to the reader of every textbook in economics. As this introduction tries to show, this fact is of great social importance. Economists at least seem to know very well the power of their discipline. This is wryly explicit in the statement of one of the most eminent of contemporary economists, Nobel laureate Paul Samuelson: "Let those who will write the nation's laws, just so long as I can write its textbooks."[17]

It is good for me to remember my humble beginnings in this work because back at the beginning I barely knew who Adam Smith was. And so today if I happen to mention his name to other psychologists or generally educated people not in the field of economics and they dimly, if at all, know whom I'm talking about, then I should not be shocked, and I should not find it inexcusable that there is such a critical gap in their education.

I

THE JOURNEY OF ADAM SMITH

Adam Smith was born in 1723 in Kirkcaldy, Scotland, a small town of around fifteen hundred people, but one that boasted shippers trading with the Baltic and one or two nail factories, as well as many a good smuggling story.[1] Before he was born, a great tragedy overtook the Smith family: Adam's father, who was a customs officer, died several months before his birth. Perhaps befitting an account of the founder of economics, the historical record gives us a listing of the expenses at the funeral, but does not tell us how or why his father died.

Fortunately for Adam, his mother lived much longer than his father—to the ripe old age of ninety—and died only six years before Adam himself died in 1790. As an only child of a single parent, Adam was exceptionally close to his mother. In fact, he never married, and as far as we know he never had a serious romantic relationship. Adam spent much of his life living with his mother, and it was said by at least one person who knew the household well that his mother was always the principal avenue to his heart.

Adam was quite a precocious child. At age fourteen he became a student at Glasgow College. Glasgow was a flourishing city where trade and commercial practices were well established, and his biographer sees this environment as one of his early "laboratories." At age seventeen Adam received a scholarship to Oxford. Unfortunately, Oxford wasn't then what it has since become, and Adam complained about the frivolity, the drinking, and the overall lack of academic seriousness. Even in his great book *The Wealth of Nations* he discusses this shortcoming and offers suggestions for reform.

Smith had been much more inspired at Glasgow College where he had as a professor the eminent philosopher Francis Hutcheson—someone who was to be a very important influence in his life. Hutcheson was considered to be one of the great teachers of the time. Smith also made the friendship of David Hume, another great figure of what has been called the Scottish Enlightenment. The story is told that while at Oxford, Smith was reprimanded for reading an evil book: Hume's *Treatise on Human Nature*. The spirit of Isaac Newton, who had died just four years before Smith was born, also lay large over all of British thought. At Glasgow Smith wrote an essay in which he described Newton's work as "the greatest discovery that was ever made by man."[2]

After graduating from Oxford, Smith lectured at Edinburgh for a few years; then, at the early age of twenty-nine, he was elected to the professorship in moral philosophy at Glasgow—a position that previously had been held by his teacher, Francis Hutcheson.

Moral philosophy as an academic discipline doesn't exist today. In Smith's day it was a very broad field consisting of four areas: natural theology, ethics, jurisprudence, and political economy. If we were to try to put a label in modern terms on what was then moral philosophy we would be hard pressed to do so. Perhaps the most accurate designation would be to equate it with the humanities, very broadly conceived. What was then evidently a coherent body of thought, today we would see as consisting of the very separate areas of theology; ethics, which is now part of philosophy; jurisprudence, which is now law; and finally political economy, which today we know simply as economics and regard as a social science. One thing this tells us is that in Smith's day there was no field such as the one we now call economics. In fact, this field owes its origin to Adam Smith; he is thus very rightly known as the father of economics.

Smith lived during the time when the old order of the Middle Ages was well along in its process of breaking up, but a new order to replace it had not yet taken definitive shape. Smith's work was to play a central role in defining the new order. The old political and economic system had come to be known as *feudalism,* and it will be helpful for us to know something of its character.

The term *feudalism* comes from the word *fief,* which has the general meaning of "property," as in an estate. Society in the Middle Ages was built around the manor, which was a country estate in a largely agrarian world. The lord of the manor held the fief, at least in theory, at the behest of the king, or of the king as a regent or agent of God. The lord's inheritance of the manor was fixed, and he could no more sell it to someone else than, as Heilbroner so aptly puts it, the governor of Rhode Island could sell off some counties to the governor of Vermont. All transfer of land, and this happened rarely, was either by gift deed or by conquest. The concept of selling land didn't exist, and the present notion of land as a commodity was literally unthinkable. That selling land became first thinkable and then actually practiced marked one of the great and momentous changes from the fuedal world to that of the new economic society.

Feudal rulership of the estate proceeded down from the king, who often had little or no actual influence, to a hierarchy of nobles. Some of these nobles directly administered the estate; others were vice-administrators or vassals who administered in the absence of the principle lord. Vassals could be clergical princes, such as bishops and abbots; relatives of the ruling lord or seignior; members of the military class, such as knights, or even their next-in-command, the squires; and eventually the gentry.

The land of a typical manor was divided into three general portions. One was for the exclusive use of the lord and was called the *demesne,* from which our word *domain* comes. The second was *tenant land,* which was arable or plowable, and this was occupied and farmed by the peasants who were the tenants. The amount of land they tenanted would be determined by whether they were farmers or artisans. The peasant kept a portion of what he or she produced, which was usually at or slightly above a subsistence amount, and the rest was the property of the lord. This was the fee, as again reflected in the word *fief*. Now we note that this was not a contractual or market arrangement. The lord and peasant did not get together and strike up a bargain as to what the fee would be and what would be the conditions of tenancy. Like the status and inheritance of the lord himself, this was an arrangement that came with birth. At the high point of the Middle Ages—say between the years 1000 and 1300—the peasant came with the land and was as much a part of the manor as the land itself. In that sense the people and the land formed an entity. The feudal conception, backed up by the Church, was that the peasants could not be ejected from the land and therefore had a right to it. Furthermore, in the case of a bad harvest the lord had the duty to support the subsistence needs of the peasants out of his reserves or even through his expenditure of coin.

The third portion of the manorial estate was the *commons*, which was generally made up of meadows and some woodlands. As the name implies these properties were held by all on the manor—aristocracy and serfs alike. The estates could be very large, and during the course of the later Middle Ages most of the one thousand or more towns that developed in England had a manor as a nucleus. The town commons that we still know today is a carry-over from the original manorial system.

Peasant artisans, now no longer working on the manorial estates, lived in the medieval towns. But they did not work in a system where they received wages or found jobs. They worked under the direction and according to the rules of *guilds,* which were tightly controlled trade and craft organizations. The guilds determined "fair" prices, specified methods of production, and set standards of quality. Work was forbidden on Sundays and holidays—and also at night, on the grounds that lack of sufficient light would affect the quality of workmanship. Members had to share in any bargains they had received in the purchase of raw materials. All work had to be performed in the front of the shop, where inspectors and the public could watch.

This description of the fuedal economic system is not meant to paint an idyllic picture of pastoral peace and contentment. There *was* peace, and there was order in the Christian-centered world of the Middle Ages. And there was the security of an organically whole society in which everyone had a place and knew what that place was. From our vantage point today this is one of the feudal system's striking features. But there was also a vast chasm between the two distinct strata made up of the aristocracy and the serfs, with approximately ninety percent of the population belonging to the latter.[3] This vast group, despite its traditional rights, was shackled and bound in the "double chains of lordship and labor."[4] Life for these people was hard, often mean, and extremely limited. One writer estimates that most villagers of the Middle Ages saw no more than a hundred separate individuals in the course of their whole lives. Despite the security of the social system, there was scarcity and pestilence, and one's physical existence was extremely precarious. There was the cupidity and violence of the powerful. The obligations of the rulers to their inferiors (the noblesse oblige) was often enough violated by the rulers' power and position (the "droits de seignior"). Although it was a time of sublime spirituality, of the creation of the manigificent Gothic cathedrals of Europe, it was also a time of appalling ignorance and nearly universal illiteracy. It is generally conceded that it was a time of an extreme range of contrasts: from "exquisite gentility" on the one hand to utter brutality on the other, so that we can detect, in the words of the historian Josef Huizinger, "the mixed smell of blood and roses."[5]

By the time of Adam Smith all of this was rapidly changing. The ancient manorial bonds were being broken, and the peasants were being pushed off the land. The English aristocracy had discovered that an overseas trade, particularly in wool, lay available to them, and they were increasingly looking toward commercial and profit-making activity. Religious proscriptions against the seeking of gain (the sin of avarice) were beginning to weaken. Wool demands grazing pastures for sheep. In order to secure these pastures the lords and nobles began enclosing common meadow lands within fences and claiming them as their own. This "enclosure movement" had its first beginnings in the eleventh century and then began accelerating from 1450 to 1640, and again from 1750 to 1860. Enclosure was essentially complete by the late 1800s. In the rest of Europe the enclosure movement made much less headway until the 1800s.

The aristocrats' securing of the common lands exclusively for their own use had an enormously disruptive effect upon the feudal security of generations of peasant farmers and their families. It was by no means willingly that they left the land to become migrating groups of displaced and vagrant poor, eventually to be transformed into the wage laborers and factory workers of the British industrial system. In just one sixteenth-century riot protesting this displacement, some thirty-five hundred people were killed. The people's distress was ironically and bitterly expressed in a popular rhyme of the day:

> The law locks up the man or woman
> Who steals the goose from off the common;
> But leaves the greater villain loose
> Who steals the common from the goose![6]

Within the atmosphere of these changes an intense debate developed in England as to what principles would make for the best new social order. The Church was increasingly losing its authority, and the precepts of Thomas Aquinas, Augustine, and even Jesus himself were seemingly becoming inapplicable.

Richard Cumberland, who entered into the debate, clearly stated its issues in 1672 in his book *On the Laws of Nature,* originally written in Latin. Cumberland, born in London in 1631, had attended Cambridge and then entered the ministry. He had held several positions as a county clergyman and was seen to be a man who combined simplicity with high purpose. Amidst a wide range of churchly duties he still had time for massive reading and scholarly study. In 1727 a translation of his book appeared in English.

Cumberland's book was written as a reply to an earlier claim by Thomas Hobbes, who, in his famous 1651 work *Leviathan*, stated that only force was an adequate guarantee for social peace and order in a malevolent world where individuals were at war with each other and "life was nasty, brutish and short." Cumberland argued that in addition to the selfishness and self-love which Hobbes had recognized and which were becomingly increasingly evident in British society, human beings also had a natural liking for each other and a capacity for benevolence. The expression of these positive tendencies led to the social good. Cumberland took pains, given the increasingly secular spirit of his time, to show that this benevolence could be observed in nature (thus the title of his book) and did not depend on accepting the authority of religious texts. "These propositions seem to me to have the greatest evidence, little different from that of mathematical axioms," he wrote. The nature of the world is such, Cumberland claimed, that there are sufficient "contingent" sanctions in the form of natural rewards for virtue and punishments for vice to make possible a peaceable and tolerable society even in the absence of civil force.[7]

The economic historian Jacob Viner notes:

> Two main lines of development of ethical doctrine stemmed directly or indirectly from Cumberland's argument, although each of them also had much earlier sources. One of these lines stressed the role in social welfare of man's instinctive capacity for disinterested benevolence, and came to be called the "sentimental" school. The other stressed the incidental harmony between behavior engaged in from calculated self-interest and the public good, and acquired the label of the "selfish" school, where "selfish" meant, however, merely calculated self-interest.[8]

This is where Adam Smith enters the picture. As a moral philosopher in the line of Cumberland and his own teacher, Francis Hutcheson, Smith attempted to deal with the same questions they were addressing—questions which had vexed England ever since Hobbes. Smith did this in his first book, *The Theory of Moral Sentiments,* published in 1759. Its title indicated where Smith stood in regard to the two positions that had developed in the debate: the "sentimental" school and the "selfish" school.

The book begins with Smith's observation that "how so ever selfish man may be supposed, there are evidently some principles in his nature, which interest him in the fortune of others, and render their happiness necessary to him, though he derives nothing from it, except the pleasure of seeing it."[9]

The purpose of Smith's book is to explicate those principles in man's nature that allow him a capacity for sympathy despite "how selfish he may be supposed." For Smith these principles lie not so much in a moral sense or reason or prudence or benevolence, but rather in what he sees as the sentiment of sympathy. While all of these other concepts are valid to some degree, they can each be derived from sympathy. For him, sympathy lies in the ability of the individual to put him or herself in another's place by being able to view the other from the standpoint of an "impartial spectator." The same imaginative faculty that allows one to sympathize with another also allows one to view oneself from the objective standpoint of an impartial spectator. "And hence it is," says Smith, "that to feel much for others, and little for ourselves, that to restrain our selfish, and to indulge our benevolent affections, constitutes the perfection of human nature; and can alone produce among mankind that harmony of sentiments and passions in which constitutes their whole grace and propriety."[10]

Smith clearly placed his work in the line of the great tradition of moral teaching, as befits his profession as moral philosopher. This is evident when he describes what it is that corrupts the moral sentiments: "This disposition to admire, and almost to worship, the rich and the powerful, and to despise, or, at least to neglect persons of poor and mean condition, though necessary both to establish and to maintain the distinction of ranks and the order of society, is, at the same time, the great and most universal cause of the corruption of our moral sentiments."[11]

Smith's book enjoyed considerable popularity and went through six printings in his lifetime. It is a book written in his elegant style, well reasoned and thorough, with obvious compassion and humanity. However, it also makes fairly minute and tiresome distinctions between different kinds of sympathies, and the distinctions between his own and other theories of morality are ultimately tendentious. Today Smith's theory, as a theory, has little or no place in philosophy. Had he only written this book, Smith would probably be no better known than Richard Cumberland and no doubt less so than his teacher, Francis Hutcheson. He certainly would not be the father of a new science. This honor is due him for his second book—one which is now ranked among the most important and influential books of all time. This book was to depart in a certain, significant way from his *Theory of Moral Sentiments.* Let us now see how this second book came to be written.

In the 1760s, under King George III, a man named Charles Townshend was Chancellor of the Exchequer (Treasury). He knew of Smith and when he was casting about for a tutor for his wife's son settled upon him. He made Smith an offer he couldn't refuse: three hundred pounds plus expenses and a pension of three hundred pounds a year for life. And he included a trip with the son—a grand tour of the Continent, *de rigueur* for the education of an aristocrat.

In Paris, while on tour, Smith met with the French social thinkers called the *physiocrats,* a group which opposed the main economic ideas of the day, especially in France. These ideas were summarized under the name of *mercantilism,* which held that the wealth of a country largely consisted in the gold and silver held in the royal treasury. The physiocrats—the word meaning something like social physics—disagreed, and they argued instead that the wealth of a nation consisted in the produce of the land.

Smith was impressed by the new economic doctrines of the

physiocrats, and he began working intensely on his political economy lecture notes. Twelve years later these notes became the basis of his second book, *An Inquiry into the Nature and Causes of the Wealth of Nations,* or more simply *The Wealth of Nations,* which was published in 1776. During the same year a certain disturbance was happening in the American Colonies: the war for independence. Ironically, one of the precipitating factors of the war was the enactment of the Townshend Acts, which included the imposition of heavy import duties in America on tea—a hated tax which led to the Boston Tea party. It was the same Charles Townshend who was both the author of the infamous Acts and an early benefactor of *The Wealth of Nations.*

Smith's second book is in effect a compendium of an age—a new age in the dawning—whose eventual shape received a formative stamp from Smith's account of it. The book illuminates a whole landscape of events, particularly the events of change. In the first edition Smith refers to the "late disturbance in The Colonies," assuming they would soon be over. In the second edition he changes this reference to "present disturbances."

In the book's opening passages Smith adopts the straightforward approach that seems to be naturally his. He sets right out to answer the book's central question: What makes for the wealth of nations? The answer is quickly given: It is in the productive power of labor (and not in the nation's accumulation of gold and silver). And what enhances and enlarges the productive power of labor? It is the "division of labor," Smith says, and he then goes into his famous description of a pin factory, where "one man draws out the wire, another straights it, a third cuts it, a fourth points it, a fifth grinds it at the top for receiving the head; to make the head requires two or three distinct operations. . . ."[12] Smith notes in his calculations that ten men working in this factory could make forty-eight thousand pins a day, whereas each one working alone could perhaps make twenty. The example, he admits, is a "trifling" one, but its principles can be applied to any sort of "art and manufacture."

Through this concept of the division of labor Smith has

established several things. For one, he has established that labor is important to the wealth of a nation, and this wealth does not just derive from the activities of the monarchy and the nobility. He later goes on to make a strong claim for the lot and value of those who labor: "No society can surely be flourishing and happy, of which the greater part of its members are poor and miserable. It is but equity besides, that they who feed, cloath and lodge the whole body of the people, should have such a share of the produce of their own labor as to be themselves tolerably well fed, cloathed and lodged."[13]

Through his notion of the division of labor, Smith has also made a case for technology, although this point is not apparent at first sight and requires interpretation. At the time Smith wrote, technology was not yet a significant force in the productive process. James Watts's steam engine had just been patented, in 1769. Eli Whitney, in what was still the Colonies, would not invent the cotton gin until 1793. Therefore, most accounts of the Industrial Revolution point to around 1780 as its beginning.[14] But what Smith saw as the division of labor was later to become technology—the division of labor was a technique, a mechanism as it were, that would increase the powers of production. So the division of labor, as a principle, is one of the discoveries for which Smith is known.

Smith was impressed by the physiocrats' concept of *laissez-faire*. In order to counter the mercantalist economic doctrines of the French monarchy, the physiocrats had proposed what they called a laissez-faire, or "let alone," policy, which suggested that the king and his advisors should allow people to be free in their economic pursuits. While Smith never used this term in his book, he certainly was imbued with this spirit, referring instead to the "simple secret of perfect liberty" and using the general label of *economic liberty* for what he was proposing.

Few economists, let alone noneconomists, have read *The Wealth of Nations* in its entirety. To do so is a daunting task. For one thing it is a very long book—at nine hundred pages in its present Modern Library edition. It is an encyclopedic book:

those nine hundred pages contains a wealth of details which have little relevance to economics today. There is, for example, an account of the wastefulness of student life at Oxford, statistics of the herring catch since 1771, and an assertion that the number of alehouses is not the immediate cause of drunkenness. Smith's themes and ideas reach us through a small number of extracts or short quotes which appear in almost all economics textbooks and many social-historical accounts of the making of the modern world. These are the nuggets which come to us as the substance of what history has deemed to be Smith's legacy.

One such extract is the division of labor statement just discussed. Another apt and perfect phrase refers to England as a "nation of shopkeepers," noting its then increasingly well-developed commercial sphere. But the very core of Smith's work, the idea that is taken to be the essence of his contribution, is as follows:

> It is not from the benevolence of the butcher, the brewer, or the baker, that we expect our dinner, but from their regard to their own interest.[15]

This sentence occurs in chapter 2, as part of an explanation of what gave rise to the division of labor. In that section Smith first contrasts human beings with animals, noting that when the latter become mature they are largely independent and self-sufficient, so that they need very little assistance from other animals. But human beings are different; they need constant assistance from their fellows, such as in the exchange of goods or services; "Give me that which I want, and you shall have this which you want." And then Smith says: "It is not from the benevolence of the butcher, the brewer, or the baker, that we expect our dinner, but from their regard to their own interest. We address ourselves, not to their humanity but to their self-love, and never talk to them of our own necessities but of their advantages. Nobody but a beggar chooses to depend chiefly upon the benevolence of his follow citizens."

This statement is so important that it could fairly well be said that if one were to choose a statement that most characterizes the transition from the thinking of the Middle Ages to that of modern economic society it would be this. It is this statement that represents the epochal significance of Adam Smith as a philosopher and as the father or economics.

The self-interest, or "butcher-baker," quote stands by itself and is often quoted by itself, as has been indicated. However, another one of Smith's nuggets, which is a supplement to the above and is often quoted in conjunction with it, is the "invisible hand" statement. Smith says that in the pursuit of self-interest an individual is "led by an invisible hand to promote an end which was no part of his intention. Nor is it always the worse for society that it was no part of it. By pursuing his own interest he frequently promotes that of the society more effectually than when he really intends to promote it."[16] The "invisible hand" is a striking metaphor which explains how each individual's pursuit of private gain can nevertheless add up to the good of society.

In England, in the early part of the next century, Thomas Malthus and David Ricardo followed up on Smith's work, giving rise to what became known as the school of *political economy*. In the 1870s, yet another Englishman, William Stanley Jevons, shortened the name to *economics*, by which label the field is now known. Jevons defined economics as "the mechanics of utility and self-interest . . . to satisfy our wants to the utmost with the least effort—to procure the greatest amount of what is desirable at the expense of the least that is undesirable—in other words, to maximize pleasure, is the problem of economics."[17]

In some of today's textbooks this account of human behavior is referred to as "the economic way of thinking." In his contemporary text of that very name Paul Heyne gives his account of this way of thinking:

> It is, most fundamentally, an assumption about what guides human behavior. The theories of economics, with surprisingly few exceptions, are simply extensions of the assumption that individuals take those actions they think will yield them the largest net advantage. Everyone, it is assumed, acts

in accordance with that rule: miser or spendthrift, saint or sinner, consumer or seller, politician or business executive, cautious calculator or spontaneous improviser.[18]

Another popular mainstream textbook, *Economics,* puts it this way:

> Capitalism presumes self-interest as the fundamental modus operandi for the various economic units as they express their free choices. The motive of self-interest gives direction and consistency to what might otherwise be an extremely chaotic economy. . . . *Pure,* or *laissez faire, capitalism* is characterized by private ownership of resources and the use of a system of markets and prices to coordinate and direct economic activity. In such a system each participant is motivated by his or her own selfish interests; each economic unit seeks to maximize its income through individual decision making.[19]

In these statements the words self-interest and selfishness are used interchangeably, and this is how these words are often understood in general discussion. However, some economists claim that the two terms do not have the same meaning, and we will return to this claim in chapter 9.

As a final reference to the place of the concept of self-interest in modern life, let us go outside of the field of economics itself. As noted before, the "economic way of thinking" exerts its influence pervasively throughout modern thought. Psychology, the discipline that studies thinking itself, is no exception. In 1987 the newly elected president of the American Psychological Association, Robert Parloff, chose the revisiting of self-interest as the theme of his presidential address. Parloff was responding to the less-than-positive image he felt self-interest had been given by certain of its promoters, such as Ayn Rand, as a result of the "extremes" to which they had taken their advocacy of it. Parloff wished to restore it to its deserved respectability:

> I present myself as a proud and unabashed advocate of self-interest. I do not apologize for it. Although it has its darker side, self-interest (frequently referred to as individualism

and, misleadingly, selfishness) has had an enormous influence. . . . Self-interest is a fruitful though imperfect model for helping science to understand the behavior of humans and of the institutions they build, the values they cherish, and, yes, even of the ways people extend helping hands to others.[20]

Parloff's concern that self-interest had been given a bad image by people such as Ayn Rand may even be unwarranted. Another psychologist, responding to Parloff's address, wrote to *The American Psychologist* to "assure" Parloff and the rest of the psychology audience that such concern was mistaken. As a long-time acquaintance and student of the late Ayn Rand, that psychologist informed the readers that it was she in fact who showed that self-interest is "profoundly moral."[21] If Ayn Rand did indeed do this, then she certainaly is not to be sidestepped; instead she should be praised for putting the final and finishing touches on the work that Adam Smith so singularly and epochally began some two hundred years ago.

2

A CHRISTMAS CAROL

The first mention of *The Wealth of Nations* in the British Parliament was by Charles James Fox, eight years after the book's publication.[1] Fox was a leading Whig member of Parliament who was an advocate of governmental and social reform, and he was perhaps drawn to Adam Smith's message of liberty and the need to enhance the lot of the commoner. A monument to Fox's life was the bill that abolished the slave trade, which was passed a year after his death, in 1807. Fox had avidly supported this cause during his career.

One of Fox's closest adherents—a disciple of sorts—was another member of Parliament, Samuel Whitebread. In 1795 Whitebread introduced a bill to deal with poverty in England, a problem which had become increasingly prominent since the sixteenth century. It was in the context of this issue that Smith's ideas were brought into English parliamentary debate. In order for us to understand how Smith's book, and the new political economy, came to the forefront over this issue we need to know something of the historical background of Whitebread's bill.

At the end of the sixteenth century, Queen Elizabeth, the triumphant and proud ruler of a great and increasingly powerful nation, made a tour of her kingdom. On her return she made a distressing observation: "Paupers are everywhere!" In an attempt to ameliorate this situation, Elizabeth's councils pulled together several previously existing statutes into the first comprehensive Poor Laws, the Act of 1601.

The first part of the laws concerned "rates." The local unit of government, the Church of England parish, was to assess the landholders in the parish and assign rates, or taxes, that were to be used to administer relief to the poor. The administration of this system was to be by a locally appointed overseer of the poor, who would be unpaid and who would serve in this office for one year. If an overseer refused to relieve a pauper, the magistrate or justice of the peace could order the parish to do so. Along with the system of "rates," the Law of Settlement provided the basis for determining which paupers were considered legally settled in the parish: a man should either have been born in the parish or have resided there for three years, while a woman must be the wife of a man who had resident status. Other aspects of the law included the provision of work to the able-bodied, apprenticeships for children, and punishment for those able-bodied but unwilling to work. The law was paternal, befitting a society less than a century away from being a full feudal state. But punishment was also severe: it included whipping, being bored through the ear, and, in the case of repeated offenses, death by hanging.

Any effectiveness the Poor Laws may have had was largely dashed by the English Civil War. In the middle of the seventeenth century, the English monarchy was temporarily overthrown, and in 1653 the Puritans and Oliver Cromwell came to power. By 1660 King Charles II had been restored to the throne. However, with this disruption of royal authority the parishes became neglectful of their responsibilities, and the relief system began to erode. There was a noticeable increase in idleness, vagrancy, and crime. In order to deal with this, "houses of corrections" were built, which were to function as workhouses. In effect they functioned as little more than prisons, and they became dreaded places.

The increasing misery of the poor drew the sympathies and concerns of humanitarian individuals. A strong center of leadership for these reformers was provided by a group known as the Clapham Evangelicals, who took their name from the country home of William Wilberforce in the Clapham district of London. Wilberforce, himself a solid member of the upper class, had been brought into this position of humanitarian leadership through a personal transformation. While a young member of Parliament, a charming bon vivant, and an active member of London society, Wilberforce had once taken a trip to the European continent with a former teacher of his who was involved with the Wesleyan movement. Together they read several religious books. In his diary Wilberforce writes, as usual, of the details of his social life: "Sitting up all night, shirked Duchess of Gordon, danced till five in the morning." But there is also this entry, uncommon for a man of his wealth and apparent tastes: "Strange that the most generous men and religious do not see that their duties increase with their fortune, and that they will be punished for spending it in eating, etc." These sentiments intensify, and he becomes increasingly discontent with his style of life and its values: "How vain and foolish all the conversation of the great dinners: nothing worth remembering. . . . How ill suited is all this to me! How unnatural for one who professes himself a stranger and a pilgrim."[2]

Wilberforce stayed in Parliament, but his interests turned to social reform—particularly reform directed toward the poor and the apparent "miseries of the industrial revolution."[3] Later he channeled most of his energies into the cause that Fox was to take up: the abolition of slavery and the slave trade. The group that eventually met with him and others in his country home for retreats and discussion came to be known as the Clapham Saints or the Clapham Sect of Evangelicals.

The Clapham Evangelicals were motivated by religious principles. They sought to improve the harsh conditions of the vast lower rungs of British society while at the same time reviving a sense of social responsibility among the aristocracy and the privileged. They strove to improve conditions in prison, soften the penal law, improve the condition of the working classes, and eliminate slavery.

Whitebread's poverty bill, which was put before Parliament in 1795, was in this same tradition. It was also in the same spirit as a 1782 reform bill which considered the "wandering of persons," or vagrancy, to be the unavoidable result of a lack of work; it thus recommended the designation of a grace period in which vagrancy penalties would not be enforced, so that vagrants would be able to return to their families. The 1782 bill also recommended repeal of the part of the Poor Laws that required paupers to enter workhouses in order to receive assistance. Whitebread's new bill advocated what we would now call a minimum wage. It proposed that wages bear some relationship to the price of wheat. This was the first time in history that the idea of a minimum wage was put forth and, indeed, the first time in history that such a concept could have any meaning. As we might imagine, Whitebread's recommendations were minimal and related to subsistence. For justification, Whitebread harkened back to the power of the magistrates under Elizabeth's Poor Laws to regulate wages. In the past the magistrates had used their power to prevent workers from combining to raise wages. Whitebread's bill proposed that that power now be used in the opposite direction—to keep wages at a subsistence level.

George III was still king at that time, and his prime minister was William Pitt. Pitt was somewhat reform-minded himself, but in his allegiance to the king he was a political enemy of Fox and in turn Whitehead. Fox had earlier earned the king's dislike when he became an outspoken opponent of the king's repressive policies in the American Colonies.

Like Fox, Pitt had also read Adam Smith, but he was impressed by a different message there—Smith's *natural law* argument. In regard to labor, Smith had advanced the idea that since the "price" of labor (that is, wages) varies with its supply and the demand for it, labor is in that sense a commodity.[4] So like all commodities it has a "natural" price. Arguing from these principles of political economy, Pitt claimed that to interfere with the market by regulating the price of labor was to interfere with labor's natural price. Pitt presented this, in his criticism of Whitebread, as if his political opponent were ignorant of the first principles of the new science. Whitebread, who was abashed, could only reply that although the laws of supply and demand might in theory operate in connection with the price of labor, in practice, "the deductions of reason" were apt to be "confuted by experience."[5] What position Smith himself would have taken in this debate we can only conjecture, since he had died five years before.

The outcome was that Whitebread's bill was defeated. However, to show that he was no enemy of the poor, Pitt himself advanced a new reform bill incorporating a number of humanitarian measures, but without the minimum wage provisions. But the voice of the new political economists was to be heard further, and with even more authority. This time it was heard through the person of Thomas Robert Malthus, the next great proponent after Smith of the new science.

Thomas Malthus was the son of Daniel Malthus, a country gentleman who was an enthusiastic adherent of the ideas of the Enlightenment, especially the concept of the perfectibility of man as proposed by his friend William Godwin. The Malthus home was also host to such famous Enlightenment figures as David Hume and Jean-Jacques Rousseau. Daniel, who was described after his death as "an eccentric character in the stricktest sense of the term," often used his bright son as an opponent in his penchant for debate.[6]

Thomas went to Cambridge for his college education and then took holy orders. However, he did not remain long as a curate, though he presumably remained celibate until he married his cousin, at age thirty-eight. They had three children. In 1798 at the age of thirty-two, Malthus anonymously published *An Essay on the Principle of Population*. Five years later he published a much expanded version under his name. The work has a pessimism that clearly represents an abandonment of the unlimited optimism of the Enlightenment. This was a reflection of the fear felt by many Englishmen after the French Revolution—that apparent fulfillment of the ideas of the Enlightenment—began to unravel and turn to terror.

Although Thomas Malthus's original motivation for the *Essay* was a wish to refute the account of human perfectibility championed by his father, he eventually came to place his work within the developing social science tradition of political economy:

> It would indeed be a melancholy reflection that, while the views of physical science are daily enlarging so as scarcely to be bounded by the most distant horizons, the science of moral and political philosophy should be confined within such narrow limits. . . . And although we cannot expect that the virtue and happiness of mankind will keep pace with the brilliant career of physical discovery; yet if we are not wanting to ourselves, we may confidently indulge the hope that to no unimportant extent they will be influenced by its progress and will partake of its success.[7]

According to Malthus, this new science had discovered what separates civilization from savagery: "To the laws of property and marriage, and to the apparently narrow principle of self-interest which prompts each individual to exert himself in better-ing his condition, we are indebted for all the noblest exertions of human genius, for everything that distinguishes the civilised from the savage state."[8] Furthermore, this science had found that man, with his inherent self-interest, is "inert, sluggish and averse from labor unless compelled by necessity" to be otherwise.[9]

One of those compulsions is the sex drive: "Plants and irra-tional animals . . . are all impelled by a powerful instinct to the increase of their species, and this instinct is interrupted by no doubts about providing for their offspring." Man has an equally powerful sex drive, but he is also equipped with reason: "Im-pelled to the increase of his species by an equally powerful instinct, reason interrupts his career, and asks him whether he may not bring beings into the world for whom he cannot provide the means of support."[10]

But the voice of reason in regard to sex produces a dilemma. If man attends to this voice "the restriction too frequently produces vice." Vice includes "promiscuous intercourse, unnat-ural passions, violations of the marriage bed, and improper arts to conceal the consequences of irregular connections." For Mal-thus the outcome of indulging in these vices is "misery." On the other hand, if man does not hear and heed the voice of reason "the human race will be constantly endeavouring to increase beyond the means of subsistence." This in turn will bring the miseries of overpopulation, which Malthus enumerates as "unwholesome occupations, severe labor and exposure to the seasons, extreme poverty, bad nursing of children, large towns, excesses of all kinds, the whole train of common diseases and epidemics, wars, plague, and famine."[11]

Malthus's dilemma appears to be strangely unsolvable. To heed reason leads to vice and misery, and to ignore reason also leads to misery. Reason, therefore, presents no solution to the problem of the sex drive. These considerations lead Malthus to put forth what he calls "the problem of population," which is that the power to procreate outstrips the ability of the earth to provide subsistence. Malthus somehow deduces that population when unchecked increases in a geometrical ratio, while the produce of the land can only increase arithmetically. He presents this basic proposition in easily assimilable form:

Population Growth:	1	2	4	8	16	32	64	128	256
Food Growth:	1	2	3	4	5	6	7	8	9

These ratios are simple; they are striking; and to the people of his time they looked scientific. They provide almost irrefutable proof of the problem of population.

The problem of the poor, Malthus believed, was the problem of population: there were too many poor; they were "redundant." The reason for this, he claimed, was the fault of the Poor Laws. Not only did they keep alive those who had no means of subsistence but, even worse, they allowed those who thus survived to also multiply. And as Malthus had scientifically shown, this multiplication was indeed geometrical.

In the second edition of his *Essay*, Malthus expresses his beliefs most forcefully—even with a certain poetical force:

> A man who is born into a world . . . if he cannot get subsistence from his parents on whom he has a just demand and if the society does not want his labour, has no claim of

right to the smallest portion of food, and, in fact, has no business to be where he is. At nature's mighty feast there is no vacant cover for him. She tells him to be gone, and will quickly execute her own orders, if he does not work upon the compassion of some of her guests. If these guests get up and make room for him, other intruders immediately appear demanding the same favour.

This passage was expunged from later editions of the *Essay*, but the message was still present and quite clear: the poor have no right to subsistence, and to attempt to provide this for them is to "reverse the laws of nature." In society's attempt to reverse these laws, "the poor who were intended to be benefited should suffer most cruelly from the inhuman deceit practised upon them."[12]

So, the Poor Laws were an "inhuman deceit" practiced upon the poor, and such misguided moralists as the Clapham Saints, in trying to help the poor through their benevolence, were actually hurting them. For Malthus, an analysis of the problem from the scientific position—that of self-interest—would lead to results that would actually help the poor. The only way to eliminate pauperism was to eliminate the humanitarian reforms that permitted the poor to maintain themselves and to propagate:

I should propose a regulation to be made, declaring that no child born of any marriage . . . should ever be entitled to any parish assistance. . . .

With regard to illegitimate children . . . they should not be allowed to have any claim to parish assistance. . . .

The infant is, comparatively speaking, of little value to the society, as others will immediately supply its place.[13]

Malthus was careful to distinguish between the worker or laborer who was able to maintain himself and his family, and the pauper who was without work. He did not want the latter to impinge upon the subsistence of the former. What then about plans to provide work for the paupers so that they could support themselves and become members of the laboring classes? This had been proposed by several reform-minded Whigs in Parlia-

ment, especially in consequence of the depression that followed
England's participation in the Napoleonic Wars in 1815. But
Malthus disagreed: "The want of employment must furnish no
claims on society; for if this excuse were to be admitted, it would
most probably be attended with the most pernicious consequences."[14]

Malthus saw the "want of employment" as an "excuse,"
because he was convinced that the cause of the problem lay in a
failure to contain the sex drive. This was where the problem
needed to be attacked—at its root—and well-intentioned public
policies that avoided this root only encouraged profligate reproduction and ultimate disaster.

Was contraception the answer? Or at least *an* answer? No,
said Malthus again, and he was a staunch opponent of such
measures: "A promiscuous intercourse to such a degree as to
prevent the birth of children seems to lower, in the most marked
manner, the dignity of human nature."[15] The only answer to
what he saw as a moral problem was moral restraint.

Despite the fact that Malthus's arguments, which appeared
under the banner of self-interest and the new science of political
economy, had considerable impact, they certainly also had their
opponents—particularly when the second edition of the *Essay*
appeared under Malthus's name. Whitebread himself, although
at least politely accepting Malthus's intentions as well-meaning,
and impressed with his apparently scientific argument, warned
anyone reading Malthus "to place a strict guard over his heart."
In his famous *Letter to Samuel Whitebread*, Malthus defended
himself with a denial of the need for a defense: "To those who
know me I feel that I have no occasion to defend my character
from the imputation of hardness of heart."[16]

Also among Malthus's critics was the essayist and literary
critic William Hazlitt. In 1807 Hazlitt described the effects of
Malthus's influence on the poor:

> His name hangs suspended over their heads, *in terrorem*,
> like some baleful meteor. It is the shield behind which the
> archers may take their stand, gall them at their leisure. He

has set them up as a defenseless mark, on which both friends and foes may exercise their malice, or their wantonness, as they think proper. . . . The poor labour under a natural stigma; they are *naturally* despised. Their interests are at best but coldly and remotely felt by the other classes of society. Mr. Malthus's book has done all that was wanting to increase this indifference and apathy.[17]

Hazlitt had already had occasion to be familiar with Malthus's work. Back at the time of the first anonymous edition of Malthus's *Essay*, William Godwin had responded to various critics of the perfectibility thesis, knowing that the son of his friend, the elder Malthus, was its author. Having no wish to do battle with the son of a friend, he instead singled out his contribution for praise. Yes indeed, agreed Godwin, the action of vice and misery was one influence holding down population; he added, however, that this was no limitation on human perfectibility because of the specifically human factor of moral restraint.

The fact of the matter was that, in his first essay, the young clergyman Thomas Malthus had surprisingly not addressed the possibility of moral restraint. In the second edition Malthus corrected this critical and embarrassing oversight. However, he neglected to attribute this correction to Godwin, instead using it to reinforce his criticism of Godwin. Malthus challenged Godwin "to name to me any check that in past ages has contributed to keep down the population to the level of the means of subsistence, that does not fairly come under some form of vice or misery, except indeed the check of moral restraint, which I have mentioned in the course of this work."

Hazlitt detected Malthus's fudging and brought it to light in a series of articles on Malthus's *Essay*. "What are we to think of a man," he asks, "who writes a book to prove that vice and misery are the only security for the happiness of the human race, and then writes another to say that vice and folly are not the only security, but that our only resource must be either in vice and folly, or in wisdom and virtue?"[18] Nevertheless, the commentary of a literary man proved to be no match for the apparently irrefutable logic and presumed facts of the political economist.

The arguments of Arthur Young, William Pitt's first secretary of the Board of Agriculture, were no more successful. After taking an enlightening tour of the countryside Young concluded that if each poor family of three children were given a half acre of land for potatoes and enough grass to feed one or two cows they would be able to feed themselves and would thus not be dependent upon charity. But this was a proposal that ran directly counter to that of the economist. Young, who earlier in his life had been a very strong believer in political economy, had been chastened in this belief by his practical experience amidst the poor, and he had come to reject the principles of the new science. Now, in 1800, he had little doubt that his plan would go a long way toward solving the problem of growing British pauperism. "But," as he wrote in his journal, "Adam Smith prevailed; political principles were thought more nourishing."[19]

Malthus was successfully able to carry the political economy banner forward because he also carried a secret weapon which was eventually to break the back of the humanitarian reformers. In addition to his scientific standing, he was also, we recall, a man of the cloth. Accordingly, he presented his principle of population as being not only consistent with the laws of self-interest, but as also on the side of morality. Indeed, those who out of the mistaken goodness of their hearts had supported measures such as poor relief, the building of cottages for the poor, and the provision of plots of land and foundling homes were, according to Malthus, the unwitting promoters of vice. For his *Essay* was laden with strong messages for the Christian theologian, and especially for the Puritan preachers of a stern morality. God was revealed in nature, as well as in the Bible, said Malthus, thus affirming the influential natural theology tradition. And nature's teaching was the *Principle of Population*: unless there was moral restraint of the sexual urge, vice and misery would surely follow. In their misguided Christian charity, explained Malthus, the Clapham Evangelicals had actually become the supporters of vice and immorality. Thus, anyone who supported the Poor Laws was actually supporting moral degeneracy.

At first the Evangelicals and those influenced by them resisted Malthus's message, but eventually they gave way. The important Evangelical magazine the *Christian Observer* had been established to support the Society for Bettering the Condition of the Poor, an organization founded by Wilberforce and modeled after an earlier society dedicated to abolishing the slave trade. An 1817 issue of the *Christian Observer* reviews the fifth edition of Malthus's *Essay*. The review begins by apologizing for the magazine's earlier rejection of Malthus's principles. It then goes on to praise Malthus's work as one "which has taken such a firm hold of the public attention and, which in the judgement of its partisans, is likely to effect a greater change in public opinion than any which appeared since *The Wealth of Nations*."[20]

The implications for a political stance of laissez-faire—of not trying to change, ameliorate, or otherwise interfere with the workings of natural economic laws—were more pronounced in Malthus's work than they had been in Smith's. According to Malthus:

> [Even] under a government constructed upon the best and purest principles and executed by men of the highest talents and integrity, the most squalid poverty and wretchedness might universally prevail from an inattention to the prudential check to population. And as this cause of unhappiness has hitherto been so little understood, that the efforts of society have always tended rather to aggravate than to lessen it, we have the strongest reasons for supposing that in all the governments with which we are acquainted a great part of the misery to be observed among the lower classes of the people arises from this cause.[21]

Malthus brought additional weight to his argument by contrasting his views with those of Thomas Paine. Paine claimed that much social evil had resulted from the government's unfairly supporting the wealthy and powerful at the expense of the rights of the poor.

Paine was a good target for Malthus. After leaving the mother country for the Colonies in 1774, Paine wrote the pamphlet *Common Sense*, in which he argued against the dominance of the king in the affairs of the Colonies and for independence from England. In 1787, after the heat of the American victory in the war for independence had somewhat abated, he returned to England, and in 1791 he published *The Rights of Man*; but this again alienated him from the English aristocracy, and he was forced to flee England for France.

In the section of his *Essay* that deals with government Malthus writes:

> The circulation of Thomas Paine's *Rights of Man* it is supposed has done great mischief among the lower and middling classes of people in this country. This is probably true; but not because man is without rights or that these rights ought not to be known; but because Mr. Paine has fallen into some fundamental errors respecting the principles of government, and in many important points has shown himself totally unacquainted with the structure of society, and the different moral effects to be expected from the physical difference between this country and America.[22]

In America, Malthus explains, there are few people without property and therefore "mobs" as exist in England could not exist there, and thus the notion of rights does not occasion any "mischief." Malthus goes on to say that "there is one right which man has generally been thought to possess, which I am confident he neither does nor can possess—a right to subsistence when his labor will not fairly purchase it." Malthus concludes: "I cannot help thinking therefore that a knowledge generally circulated that the principal cause of want and unhappiness is only indirectly connected with government and totally beyond its power directly to remove, and that it depends upon the conduct of the poor themselves."[23]

But as great an advocate of laissez-faire as Malthus was, he was not consistent. This was pointed out by David Ricardo, the next great contributor after Smith and Malthus to the new science of economics.

Ricardo entered English history in the debate over the Corn Laws. These laws placed a tariff on imported wheat (the English call wheat "corn" and corn "Indian corn") and thus kept the home price high. This was important for the domestic growers of wheat—the gentry and the landlords—and was welcomed by them. The logic of laissez-faire, which Malthus had fervently interpreted as an argument against the protection of the poor, should certainly also apply to the Corn Laws, which were passed to protect the interests of another class, the landowners. But somehow Malthus could not see this parallel. It is hard to avoid the connection between Malthus's support of the Corn Laws and the fact that his own background was in the country squire and landholding class of British society.

Ricardo's commentary in an 1815 essay was direct and stinging: "The landlord is always opposed to the interest of every other class in the community. His situation is never so prosperous as where food is scarce and dear, whereas all other persons are benefited by procuring food cheap."[24]

Now Malthus suddenly came to believe that there ought to be exceptions to the general application of laissez-faire principles. In 1819 he published his *Principles of Political Economy*, following on the heels of Ricardo's *Principles*, published two years earlier. In his book, Malthus wrote that the "great principles" of political economy should not be accepted in all cases and without exception, since the science of political economy really bore a closer resemblance to "morals and politics" than to mathematics. While Malthus did not take the acute material suffering of the poor to be such an exception, he nevertheless felt that it was necessary for the government to step in to protect agricultural incomes. Here things could not be left to take their natural course: "It is obviously, therefore, impossible for a government strictly to let things take their natural course; and to recommend such a line of conduct, without limitations and exceptions, could not fail to bring disgrace upon general principles, as totally inapplicable in practice."[25]

It is startling to now see Malthus aligning economics more closely with politics and morals than with mathematics, when the essential thrust of his argument against the Poor Laws in his *Essay* was the stark and seemingly inescapable mathematical logic of the Principle of Population. But such were the curiosities of this bold and brave new science of political economy.

Although Ricardo forced Malthus into compromise and inconsistency in their debate over the Corn Laws, Ricardo was entirely one with him in his stance toward the poor and the Poor Laws. If anything, Ricardo was even more harsh here than was Malthus, although he had no inclination for being pious and theological about it. For him it was all a matter of science and natural law, and that provided justification enough: "Whilst the present laws are in force, it is quite in the natural order of things that the fund for the maintenance of the poor should progressively increase till it has absorbed all the net revenues of the country. . . ."

For Ricardo, the certainty of this was equivalent to the relentless determinism of the "principle of gravitation."[26]

And so in 1834, after much heated debate, the so-called reform bill of the Poor Laws, which essentially repealed all humanitarian reform legislation of the previous forty years, became the new law of the land. Thus, thirty-six years after the anonymous first publication of Malthus's *Essay*, the new science of economics, which by that time had become a coherent doctrine of social and political philosophy and had gathered an increasing number of influential and persuasive adherents, achieved a major legislative victory.

The new Poor Law Reform Bill abolished relief through outdoor employment for all able-bodied persons and their families. Henceforth, all the poor had to enter workhouses to obtain relief. The conditions of the workhouses were to be based on the principle of "less eligibility," which meant that they had to be less pleasing than the conditions of the lowest-paid labor. The new workhouses were to be constructed according to economist

Jeremy Bentham's design of the "Panopticon," thus embodying the concepts of "classification, separation, and seclusion"—terms which described the treatment of families, parents, and children respectively.[27] It was confidently expected, as had been scientifically argued and apparently proven, that the new reform law would cause paupers to become independent laborers; in consequence the amount paid in aid to the poor would significantly drop; wages would rise; improvident and perhaps licentious marriages would be reduced; workers would become more content; and, naturally, crime and vice would diminish.

The Poor Law Reform Bill did not fulfill the predictions and promises of its advocates. With the benefit of hindsight we can see that two fundamental and ultimately tragic errors underlay the conclusions of Thomas Malthus. One was in regard to the impressive accumulation of census data that Malthus and others used to show that the rise in the tax rates for the poor and the increase in the number of the idle were related. Here was one of the first instances of empirical data being used to supposedly prove a point derived from the principles of economic theory. The economists said that aid for the poor, either as subsistence welfare or as supplement to wages, would cause indigence in an ever-increasing and vicious cycle which would threaten to impoverish and overwhelm society. And didn't the data (those hard-and-fast Newtonian numbers) actually show this? Aid increased and so did the number of the poor. However, in the conclusion of his masterly study of this period in English history, Raymond Cowherd makes this sobering analysis of the recommendations that came from the political economists: "The great fallacy of the natural law reformers was to attribute the increase in relief expenses to the Poor Laws themselves rather than to the unemployment that came with the end of the Napoleonic Wars."[28]

The second of Malthus's errors is contained in his deduction that the original Poor Laws were destructive because their provision (meager as it was) allowed the poor to "marry early" and procreate when they otherwise would have to wait. Applying Malthus's logic, we would expect that the wealthy, being amply provisioned, would not have to wait at all and would thus far outproduce the poor in numbers of children. Observation, however, shows the opposite to be true: the poor have almost universally higher birth rates than the middle or wealthy classes. Why this is in fact the case is well known to any modern student of population. Quoting from resource and population theorist Lester Brown: "Demographers have long known that with sufficient economic progress, as in Europe and North America, high birth rates fall sharply. Demographers also have generally recognized that widespread poverty tends to sustain high birth rates for the obvious reason that families without adequate employment, education, or health care have little security for the future except for reliance on their children."[29] But this was apparently not obvious at all to Malthus and the political economists.

Studies show that countries that have sharply reduced their birth rates—which are as socially and economically diverse as China, Barbados, Sri Lanka, Uruguay, Taiwan, Cuba, and South Korea—have done so because their populations have acquired access to basic social and economic services. Birth rates dropped in these countries even before the introduction of family planning programs. It has similarly been found that the introduction of family planning and birth control methods has been much more successful in those countries that have "assigned a high priority in their development programs to a more equitable distribution of income and social services."[30]

The failure of the early political economists can now be seen to be even greater and more bitterly ironic than we might first suppose. Their policies were not only inhumane, but essentially 180 degrees wrong. By opposing poor relief and social programs of various kinds—to say nothing of Malthus's adamant opposition to the use of contraception—the economists effectively assured that the "poor rabble" of England would continue to grow in number and to fester in their misery—and this in the name of the new scientific teaching which said that this apparent cruelty was really a kindness, and that to think or practice otherwise, as the humanitarian reformers had tried to do, was an "inhuman deceit."

It is possibly true that in the whole history of social science, from Adam Smith onward, no single policy has ever been more wrong than the one derived from the political economists' scientific prophecies about the deleterious effects of poor relief. This is quite an impressive statement, given that this is a branch of science already noted for the imprecision of its predictions and the ambiguity of its positions in regard to social problems. The equivocal nature of most social science policy recommendations, while probably unavoidable, makes them notoriously hard to completely refute. So we need to stand in some awe at the rather complete erroneousness of Malthus and the political economists.

A new puzzle now awaits us. If Malthus was so wrong and his theories so destructive, why is he still so admired by economists? As already stated, he is seen as one of the field's great progenitors—to make a slight pun. All economics textbooks refer to him with reverence in this regard.

Malthus is recognized as one of the great economists because, right or wrong, he *is* a great economist in terms of the historical role he played in the development of economics as the major and powerful discipline that it is today. And Malthus was not *all* wrong. Even though nearly every one of his basic facts, his main logical premises, and, most importantly, his conclusions regarding the Poor Laws may have been wrong, in the most general sense in which his thesis can be taken he was certainly correct. Population *can* outstrip the available resources, and too large a population for the resource base does of course lead to widespread misery. Malthus's Principle of Population, then, was also about resources, an issue very much alive and ever more vital today. Malthus can be seen as one of the first writers in history to call attention to the problem of limited resources and, by extension, a finite earth. It is thus sometimes said that Malthus "was an economist who was years ahead of his time."[31]

We now have a partial answer to our puzzle. However, this image of Malthus as a thinker ahead of his time is at the least ironic. It conveys the notion of a visionary who was not accepted by the people of his age and whose truths have had to wait until the present to be recognized. In fact, as we have seen, Malthus was enormously influential in his day. Furthermore, his "truths" have not been substantiated by time: in the West we find ourselves with triple the population that existed in Malthus's time; nevertheless we have a much higher standard of living.[32] In addition to this and other errors, Malthus completely missed one of the most significant features of the new economic order: the power of science and technology to enormously expand food production and productivity in general (something which Adam Smith, writing earlier than Malthus, already had an inkling of). Thus, we find that today's recognition of the problems of overpopulation and diminishing resources has very little if anything to do with Malthus, and almost all of our accepted solutions would have been opposed by him.

The serious moral failure of Malthus is generally obscured in most textbooks because his attack on the Poor Laws and the humanitarian reforms is given little prominence; instead it is relegated to a minor role in the Malthusian legacy. However, a closer look at Malthus's career reveals that the abolition of poor relief was the major thrust and almost the raison d'etre of all his work. His Principle of Population served merely as the theoretical superstructure upon which he campaigned relentlessly against any humanitarian sentiments in regard to the poor. Not all Malthus enthusiasts and commentators, it must be pointed out, have missed this. Philip Appleman, who is the editor of the Norton edition of Malthus's *Essay on Population*, and certainly an admirer of Malthus, has to admit that "stripped of their context of 'long-range benevolence,' these notions have the odor of barbarity about them."[33]

Malthus died in 1834, in perfect coincidence with the passage of the Poor Law Reform Bill in which he played so central a role. The bill's passage achieved a seminal political victory, establishing its influence first in Britain and subsequently in the rest of what we have come to know as the modern world. Let us now see what developments followed the passage of this bill. We know that the abolition of poor relief had no effect on restraining the English population, which grew enormously. Many segments of English society opposed the new law. The poor themselves rioted in several areas of West Riding and Lancashire. Many clergy were upset and, along with various gentlemen, doctors, and professional persons, took an active part in agitating against the law, proclaiming it as harsh and unjust.[34] Charles Dickens disliked the bill so much that he contemplated standing for Parliament in order to oppose it; he became the chief chronicler of English life in the wake of the political economists' attack upon social legislation.

In one of his earliest works, *Oliver Twist*, Dickens writes movingly of the life of the hordes of street urchins—those vagrant children who had been cut loose from the bonds of family life by the new factories, the workhouses, and the basic inability of poor families to provide for the needs of their children. Many of these children took to various tasks that more well-to-do families found arduous and dangerous, such as sweeping out the chimneys that were in constant use during the cold London winters. Reports of injury and death to these chimney sweeps were made to committees that had been established in both Houses of Parliament. Sydney Smith, a somewhat humanitarian minister, gives a bitterly satiric example of some of these stories, which were to form the background for Dickens's work:

> We come now to burning little chimney sweepers. A large party is invited to dinner—a great display is to be made; and about an hour before dinner, there is an alarm that the kitchen chimney is on fire! It is impossible to put off the distinguished personages who are expected. It gets very late for the soup and fish—the cook is frantic—all eyes are turned upon the sable consolation of the chimney sweep— and up into the midst of the burning chimney is sent one of the miserable infants of the brush! There is a positive prohibition of this practice and an enactment of penalties in one of the Acts of Parliament with respect to chimney sweepers. But what matter Acts of Parliament when the

pleasures of genteel people are concerned? Or what is a toasted child, compared to the agonies of the mistress of the house with a deranged dinner?[35]

To show the power that economic theory had on even some of the more morally sensitive people of the time, we note that this same Sydney Smith could not bring himself to support a bill before Parliament that no child under fourteen years of age should be apprenticed to a sweeper. This would have virtually prevented the use of "climbing boys," since children over that age would have been too big to fit into the chimneys. Smith instead urged that new chimneys be built wider so that children could not get stuck in them. As historian Brian Inglis notes, "Smith concluded lamely that there was little which could be done without infringing the principles of political economy."[36]

In 1843 Charles Dickens wrote *A Christmas Carol*, the first of what he called his Christmas books.[37] In this beloved work he was drawn to set his story, which dealt with the meanness of the new wealth-seeking merchant, against the background of England's poverty. Most presentations of this classic story only vaguely, if at all, touch on Dickens's explicit theme of the evils of political economy.

In chapter 1 two visitors come by Scrooge's office to ask for Christmas donations. One says:

> "At this festive season of the year, Mr. Scrooge, it is more than usually desirable that we should make some slight provision for the poor and destitute, who suffer greatly at the present time. Many thousands are in want of common necessaries; hundreds of thousands are in want of common comforts, sir."
>
> "Are there no prisons?" asked Scrooge.
>
> "Plenty of prisons," said the gentleman, laying down the pen again.
>
> "And the Union workhouses?" demanded Scrooge. "Are they still in operation?"
>
> "They are. Still," returned the gentleman, "I wish I could say they were not."

"The Treadmill and the Poor Law are in full vigour, then?" said Scrooge.

"Both very busy, sir."

"Oh! I was afraid, from what you said at first, that something had occurred to stop them in their useful course," said Scrooge. "I'm very glad to hear it."

Shortly afterward Scrooge is visited by the ghost of his former partner, Jacob Marley. The ghost is in agony in the afterlife. Scrooge is puzzled and implores, "But you were always a good man of business, Jacob."

"Business!" cried the Ghost, wringing his hands again. He tells Scrooge what his business should have been:

> "Mankind was my business. The common welfare was my business; charity, mercy, forbearance, and benevolence, were all my business. The dealings of my trade were but a drop of water in the comprehensive ocean of my business."

The second of the three spirits that visit Scrooge takes him to the home of his assistant, Bob Cratchit, and his crippled son, Tiny Tim.

> "Spirit," said Scrooge, with an interest he had never felt before, "tell me if Tiny Tim will live."
>
> "I see a vacant seat," replied the Ghost, "in the poor chimney corner, and a crutch without an owner, carefully preserved. If these shadows remain unaltered by the future, the child will die."
>
> "No, no," said Scrooge. "Oh no, kind Spirit! say he will be spared."
>
> "If these shadows remain unaltered by the future, none other of my race," returned the Ghost, "will find him here. What then? If he be like to die, he had better do it, and decrease the surplus population."
>
> Scrooge hung his head to hear his own words quoted by the Spirit, and was overcome with penitence and grief.
>
> "Man," said the Ghost, "if man you be in heart, not adamant, forbear that wicked cant until you have discovered What the surplus is, and where it is. Will you decide what men shall live, what men shall die? It may be, that in the sight of Heaven, you are more worthless and less fit to

live than millions like this poor man's child. Oh God! to hear the Insect on the leaf pronouncing on the too much life among his hungry brothers in the dust!"

Before this spirit departs from Scrooge it withdraws two scrawny children from under its robes. The text says:

> They were a boy and a girl. Yellow, meagre, ragged, scowling, wolfish; but prostrate, too, in their humility. Where graceful youth should have filled their features out, and touched them with its freshest tints, a stale and shrivelled hand, like that of age, had pinched and twisted them, and pulled them into shreds. . . .
>
> Scrooge started back, appalled. Having them shown to him in this way, he tried to say they were fine children, but the words choked themselves, rather than be parties to a lie of such enormous magnitude. . . .
>
> "Have they no refuge or resource?" cried Scrooge.
>
> "Are there no prisons?" said the Spirit, turning on him for the last time with his own words. "Are there no workhouses?"
>
> The bell struck twelve.

In these excerpts we can see that Scrooge is not just the wealth-seeking miser he is pictured to be in Christmas renditions of *A Christmas Carol*; he is also a bitter caricature of the political economist.

What Dickens rendered in his stories was reported with equal pain and outrage in the new penny journalism that arose to carry the voice of the sufferers. One publication, *The Pioneer*, touchingly describes their plight:

> The poor starved eye has no green spot to look upon; the weary sameness of its range is in some loom or lathe or vice or swift-revolving mechanism; midst dust and grease and smoke, and all the rudiments of nausea. Is this an atmosphere for free-born souls? And yet they tell us we must love our country. To love a thing we never see, save when necessity, hard pinching want makes our thin shanks go tramp the road for provender; and then our free-born neighbours call us vagabonds.[38]

Another journal, *The Crisis*, expresses a distinct awareness of the theoretical background that has affirmed that this should be the state of things:

> The political economists in Church and State are the real high priests of the realm. They have set us the golden calf. . . . Impious, dissatisfied people, say they, you men without property, mob and scum of the earth, with minds born to inferiority and hands made for our service. Why if you are still discontented do you not seek to accumulate wealth and so become respectable like ourselves?[39]

This increasing cry eventually made its way into the minds and hearts of a sufficient number of Parliament, and some of the most flagrant abuses—such as child labor in the factories—were curtailed with the passage of the famous Ten Hour Bill, in 1847. This bill built on and shored up an earlier act that had limited the hours of work for apprentice children to twelve a day, six days a week, and forbade children under the age of nine from being employed in cotton mills. As its name implies, the Ten Hour Bill prohibited persons from working more than ten hours a day. John Bright, one of the founders of the Manchester School of political economy argued vehemently that the Ten Hour Bill, despite its apparent kindness, was actually against the best interests of the worker. He said that it was based upon a "vicious principle."[40] Dickens, however, was relieved to see that there was something in human common sense that would not ultimately abide the philosophers of economics: "I am convinced that its philosophers would sink any government, any cause, any doctrine, even the most righteous. There is a sense and humanity in the mass in the long run that will not bear them."[41]

Despite the productivity boom of the early Industrial Revolution, the lot of the English working class did not improve until around the 1860s. Malthus's Principle of Population to the contrary, the beginning of the rise in the laboring person's standard of living occurred alongside an incredible one-hundred-percent increase in the British population between 1800 and 1850 (by comparison, the population growth between 1700 and

30560 Geneva High School Library

1750 had been only eight percent).[42] Historians J. L. Hammond
and Barbara Hammond attribute the gradual development of
modern civilized society since the dark days of the early 1800s
to the growth and reestablishment of the spirit of social reform
and not to the invisible hand of competitive self-interest. In
regard to the "experiment," as they call it, of laissez-faire
political economy, they comment that "the experiment failed.
Though individuals made fortunes, and poor men became dea-
cons, aldermen, members of Parliament and country gentlemen,
this method did not produce a stable society. Discontent was
widespread and acute. It was discovered that there was something
wanting in this philosophy, and a series of reforms passed
through Parliament making town life more attractive."[43]

As noted, this failure received widespread voice. We have
already referred to the new journalists. In literature, besides
Dickens, there were Shelley, Pope, Coleridge, Wordsworth, and
other figures of the Romantic movement. One of these, Thomas
Carlyle, described economics as "the Dismal Science"—a phrase
which has stuck. The Romantic protest was against the cold,
materialistic, mechanistic, and scientific Zeitgeist of that early
Age of the Economist. In politics there were Cobbett and Dis-
raeli, as well as others already mentioned.

There was also a certain merchant who was involved in the
textile trade in Manchester. In his youth he had rather concerned
his businessman father by showing an interest in poetry. Now, as
a young entrepreneur following his father's profession, he observed what he believed to be two Manchesters. The first had
pleasant streets lined with bustling shops, and green suburbs
with gracious estates. The second Manchester was geographically
positioned so that for the most part the residents of the first
Manchester never had to see it. This Manchester harbored a
population stunted in stature; the people lived in a state of filth
and despair while assuaging this condition of life by turning to
whiskey and evangelism in various combinations, and by doping
their children with preparations of opium to achieve their passiv-
ity. The merchant had already seen similar conditions in the

factory towns of his native home in the Rhineland of Germany. In 1845 he published what has been described as "the most terrible verdict" that has ever been passed on the world of the industrial slums: *The Condition of the Working Class in England in 1844*.[44] He noted in this account that the great British economists seemed little more than apologists for the existing state of things. The businessman's name was Friedrich Engels.

Engels's writing greatly impressed the young German journalist Karl Marx, and they soon met and began writing together. At the beginning, Marx, although a radical of the philosophical left, somewhat disapproved of the brash Engels's communist ideas. In 1847 Engels took part in the first congress of the Communist League, in London. Marx then joined him in the second congress later that year. The failures of the political economists had unknowingly set loose a spectre that was to haunt the world of enterprise for generations to come—much as Marley's ghost had returned to pass a terrible judgment on his mean-spirited former business partner.

3

THE GILDED AGE

We have just looked at the period in British history that followed the publication of Adam Smith's *Wealth of Nations*. This period saw the establishment of the discipline and tradition of economics. In their attempt to allow the "natural" law of self-interest to operate and to produce its expected beneficent effects, the economists set forth the doctrine of laissez-faire. For them laissez faire meant eliminating laws assisting the poor and continually opposing any social welfare legislation, such as laws restricting child labor and the length of the working day or laws that regulated working conditions in general.

The doctrine of self-interest was taken to mean that the working person would naturally avoid the "pain" of labor and would only work when he or she was goaded into it by the spur of hunger and want. But there was also the pleasure side to this doctrine. Thus Jeremy Bentham described what he thought was the mainspring of human behavior as the "pain-pleasure calculus." Following Smith, Thomas Malthus had proposed that the poor laboring classes produced their offspring literally as commodities, in accordance with the laws of supply and demand. When there was need in the economy for workers or the means available for sustaining children (in effect the same thing), such as provided by Poor Law assistance, then the poor would indulge all the more in their sexual pleasures and produce children. These implications drawn from the work of Smith made for the first social policy applications of the new science.

Smith's essential presentation of the doctrine of self-interest had been in the context of the employer (shopkeeper or businessman) rather than the employee. This we might see as the "entre-preneurial" or employer side of the self-interest doctrine. Out of his own self-interest, the entrepreneur would also promote "the interest of society," even though that was no part of his intention. Therefore the condition of laissez faire, as previously discussed in the context of the employee, was also seen as beneficial when applied to the employer: Don't hinder him and don't aid him; just let him pursue his own self-interest and all of society will be better off.

Perhaps the best historical laboratory in which to observe the pure workings of entrepreneurial self-interest is not England after the Industrial Revolution, but America following the end of the Civil War, in 1865.[1]

In America, with its huge westward abundance of land, land-less poverty was not a problem. As we have seen, the landless masses of industrial England had been thrust between the politi-cal economists' workhouses on the one hand and the new indus-trialists' prison-like factories (described by English writer Wil-liam Blake as "dark Satanic mills") on the other. By contrast, in 1862 the Lincoln government passed the Homestead Act, which provided for the transfer, at a nominal fee, of 160 acres of unoccupied public land to each homesteader. The reality that the Native Americans, or Indians, did not see the land as "public" in the same sense that the U.S. government did is another matter, and another story.

Also in America, the success of the North in the Civil War marked a sharp and sudden break between the previous domi-nance of feudal-like economic interests, as embodied in the agricultural estates of the South, with their serfs or slaves, and the new dominance of the industrial and entrepreneurial business interests represented by the North.[2] Thus, a process which developed in England slowly and at times ambiguously, over a span of at least two centuries, happened much more quickly and clearly in America, with a major demarcation between the two kinds of economic orders occurring in the mere five-year period of the Civil War.

Although in the North there was certainly legitimate humanitarian and moral interest in the abolition of slavery, following the earlier lead and inspiration of William Wilberforce and the English reformers, the major impetus for the war was a clash between two economic orders. Only in 1863, after the war was well under way, did Lincoln, under abolitionist pressure, issue the Emancipation Proclamation formally abolishing slavery. Until the Civil War the U.S. government had been dominated by the economic interests of the large southern plantation owners, just as in England the feudal estates had dominated the economy and overridden the newly rising urban industrialists.

In England the transition from the dominance of one economic order to the other was symbolized by the eventual repeal of the Corn Laws. In America it took a war between two clearly defined sectors—defined both by region and by economy—to accomplish this change. Of course, the North's moral position against slavery dovetailed with its economic interests in that the cheap labor provided by slavery was the mainstay of the southern landowners' source of wealth. This has led some observers to question the apparently humanitarian motives on the part of the North.

With the war bloodily but decisively settling the issue of which type of economic order would prevail (and wars have a way of definitely deciding such things), America became a hothouse environment for the growth of an entrepreneurial self-interest economy. Very few of the feudal and religious restrictions that had lingered on in England remained in America after the war. America was America almost precisely because it didn't have these traditions. The new America was ready to stretch its young muscle and reach out across its expanse, utilizing the new powers of coal, steam, mobile finance, and the large-scale manufacturing that these facilitated. The problem of the newly freed slaves haunted the country in the following period of Reconstruction, but this was largely viewed as a racial issue—and continued to be seen as such right up until the civil rights movement of the

1950s and 60s. The issue never entered the mainstream of economic debate until the 1960s, and even then not adequately.

In order for this national stretching out to occur, there had to be sinews tying together the far reaches of a great continent, especially since the nation's unity had been so recently and so violently threatened and continued to be fragile in the aftermath of the war. The needed sinews came in the form of a transcontinental railroad—an iron and steel highway that linked the blue waters of the Atlantic with those of the Pacific.

About the need for such a railroad there was no doubt. The question was, what form of enterprise should this mammoth national project take? When and if completed it would easily be the longest railroad in the world, spanning more differing and difficult terrain than any railroad heretofore attempted. Earlier, Senator Thomas Hart Benton, who was a longtime advocate of Western development as well as an early opponent of slavery, had urged Congress to build the railroad "as a national work, on a scale commensurate with its grandeur." However, by 1853, Senator Stephen Douglas had convinced Congress that the Pacific railroad should be built by private enterprise, rather than nationally. (Douglas was later to unintentionally boost Lincoln to national prominence in their debates over the slavery issue.)[3]

The implications of the principle of laissez-faire in this issue were unclear. Huge amounts of public lands needed to be made available. These lands constituted an American "commons," to draw a parallel to the public lands in feudal England, but this time there were no landlords to impose a policy. An economic history textbook notes the confusion and contradictions that a simple laissez-faire philosophy produced in this situation. On the one hand we find out that "at a time when the traditional American view insisted upon the separation of business and the state and upon the maintenance of laissez-faire, the railroads invariably needed to invoke the governmental power of eminent domain in order to secure their rights of way, and they usually appealed for governmental aid in the costly projects that they undertook. These appeals were based upon the premise that the completed roads would perform a public service and would be of value to society as a whole."[4]

So the railroad companies wanted government aid on the basis that they were performing a public service, and not just a private one. Didn't that then mean that the government should be entitled to keep a watchful eye on the proceedings to make sure that the interests of this same public were protected? Not according to laissez-faire. The textbook goes on to say that the thesis that the public welfare ought to be closely safeguarded by governmental supervision of the railroad companies was countered by the "philosophy of Laissez Faire [which] stood in the way of such considerations."[5] With no clear guidance from economics, nor from the statesmen of the times, the public directed most of its attention to the fascinating saga of the picturesque and heroic aspects of the construction of the road beds, largely ignoring the matter of whether it was getting its money's worth in terms of the land grants and low-interest loans made by the government to the private construction companies.

Two railroad construction companies were originally chartered and granted to take on the project. The Union Pacific was to start at the end of the trunk lines that already existed out to Nebraska, at Omaha on the Nebraska-Iowa border, and build westward. Building eastward from the West Coast was the Central Pacific Company. The two companies were to eventually meet and join together, thus completing the great coast-to-coast highway that would win the West and unite the country, its manifest destiny achieved.

The Union Pacific was granted land ten miles deep on either side of the road bed to be constructed, along with full mineral, timber, and land use rights. The total land involved amounted to 13 million acres. In addition, it was given thirty-year government bonds at six percent, for a total of twenty-seven million dollars in capital. The Central Pacific was similarly granted 9 million acres and twenty-four million dollars in bonds. Soon afterward, enthusiastic lawmakers donated another 18 million acres to a group that proposed to build a route along the Mexican border, and another 47 million acres to a group proposing a route along the Canadian border. Further land donations were to double the size of the original 76-million-acre grant; the eventual total has been conservatively estimated at around 131 million acres. This is an area about four times the size of England.[6] President Andrew Johnson, who took over after Lincoln's assassination, was quite disturbed, and he warned in 1866 that "an aristocracy based on nearly two billion and a half of national securities has arisen in the northern states to assume that political control which the consolidation of great financial and political interests formerly gave to the slave oligarchy. The war of finance is the next war we have to fight."[7] But Johnson was from Tennessee and more sympathetic to the defeated South than were the Radical Republicans of the North—those "wearers of the bloody shirts." He was eventually hounded out of office, to be replaced by the victorious Union general, Ulysses S. Grant, in the election of 1868. It seemed that everyone in the North had worked for Grant's election, and it was confidently asserted that Wall Street business would boom.

The public followed the newspaper reports of the day-to-day progress of the railroad builders with great interest. As the workers arrived in each town along the route they were welcomed with music and public orations, and the event was treated as a holiday. Certainly among the heroes of the day were the laborers on the line, who worked virtually nonstop through all kinds of weather and terrain, and who had to fend off periodic attacks by the native tribes through whose territory they put down those iron bands. The workers included some three thousand Irish and ten thousand Chinese (the latter worked for a dollar a day, half the wages of the Caucasians). When the Union Pacific from the East and the Central Pacific from the West finally met, the faith of the backers in the automatic beneficent social effects of private self-interest seemed well justified. The two rail lines were joined with a gold and silver spike at Promenitory Point, Utah, on May 10, 1869. The whole country—from President Grant in the White House to the newsboys who sold extras—celebrated.

The accomplishments of the project were truly on a heroic scale. The western route went over a precipice in Nevada that had a perpendicular drop of a quarter of a mile, while in the central Sierras the road bed ascended nearly 7,000 feet from water level at a steep gradient of 116 feet per mile. The company coming from the east had marched ahead, winter and summer, for four years, with the army of workers laying an average of five miles of track a day. In addition to those who died at the hands of the Native Americans, who occasionally would capture a whole train and slaughter its crew, hundreds more workers fell to intense heat of the desert and the icy cold of the mountains. The construction battalions who thundered across the "great American desert" of the interior heroically sacrificed their lives to build the industrial foundation of a new economic order.

Being savvy businessmen, the major partners of each of these railroad-building companies decided to set up holding companies that were parallel to the railroad corporations themselves. This enabled them to pool the securities of each construction company with those of the many other small companies who supplied the enormous needs of the construction companies. In addition to laying down rail, the railroads were also land companies, selling building rights and town rights along the way. The holding companies for the two railroads were named the Crédit Mobilier and the Crédit Foncier, acknowledging the original development of such an idea in France. The holding companies seemed to make sense from an organizational standpoint because they served a coordinating function for all the subsidiary companies that were involved. In the midst of the glorious success of it all no one seemed to mind very much that the holding companies also served to tie up and draw off from the contracts of the other providers, and even to expand or "water" the value of the stocks and bonds of the principal railroad company. Announcements such as the following were inserted in newspapers throughout the country:

Paris to Pekin in THIRTY DAYS.
Passengers for China this way. . . . The Rocky Mountain excursion of statesmen and capitalists pronounce the Pacific Railroad a great fact. . . the Crédit Mobilier a national reality, the Crédit Foncier an American institution.[8]

However, by 1873 the public's view of the whole railroad enterprise had changed. The name Crédit Mobilier has since gone down in history in a different light from that presented in these early newspaper advertisements.

The first revelation was that Crédit Mobilier had contrived to divert most of the existing assets to itself, and it had achieved this by bribing congressmen with shares of stock so as to avoid government scrutiny. The level of these expropriations was well beyond what anyone would have imagined. A congressional committee was convened to investigate the matter, and the news that came out of the investigation became almost as big as the news of the railroad's construction. The committee's report expressed its disappointment and sense of betrayal: "Congress relied for the performance of these great trusts by the corporators upon their sense of public duty; upon the fact that they were to deal with and protect a large capital of their own which they were to pay in their money . . . upon the certificate of the chief engineer, to be made upon his professional honor. . . ."[9]

The total profit from the construction was estimated to be between forty-four and fifty million dollars. The actual amount that was put at risk by the investors was estimated to be a maximum of two to three million dollars. The dividends paid to stockholders between July 1867 and January 1869 amounted to more than 341 percent in terms of cash value. The committee's report comments further:

> It is also said that it is unjust to look at the question in the light of the present; that we should go back to the condition of things before the road was built, when the whole scheme seemed, to the prudent capitalists of the country, visionary and perilous. This is true; and if these gentlemen assumed

great risks from which others shrank, and thereby great benefits inured to the public, they should have all due credit. But we think they differed from other capitalists, not in taking a risk, but in having discovered that the road could be built at vast profit without risk, the resources furnished by the government being more than ample for the purpose.[10]

In the headlong rush to build the railroad and reap the windfall of "profit" ("if that is the proper word to be used in such a connection," the committee acidly commented), the railroad, it was later discovered, had been built with great waste and inefficiency. The spectacular construction over steep grades and precipices was found to have been substantially unnecessary. An alternative route forty miles to the north, with a rise two thousand feet lower and half the grade per mile, was ignored. Sometimes a whole section of the mountain line was shifted from one side of a valley to another after it had been laid. The rails had been built of soft American iron and soon had to be replaced by the Bessemer steel already in use in England. All of this resounded to the considerable profit of one Andrew Carnegie. The government eventually estimated that the costs of construction were seventy to seventy-five percent over what they should have been. The vast amount of these costs were borne by the public, and the "profits" were estimated to have been about forty-eight percent above these greatly inflated costs.[11]

The roster of businessmen involved in the railroad scandals were among the most prominent and enterprising of their time. In the western company, the Central Pacific, were Collis P. Huntington, Charles Crocker, Mark Hopkins, and Leland Stanford. In the eastern Union Pacific and the other companies were August Belmont, Thomas Durant, Cornelius Vanderbilt, Jim Fisk, Jay Gould, J. Edgar Thompson, and the aforementioned Andrew Carnegie. Among the implicated stockholders were the political figures Rutherford Hayes, Schuyler Colfax, James G. Blaine, and James Garfield. Among the journalists and promoters

were Horace Greeley and the "big business preacher" Henry
Ward Beecher.

These men, along with some others who had made vast profits
during the Civil War, formed the backbone of the American
industrial community at the time when it sat poised, ready to
leap forward after the war. They soon earned the sobriquet of
"Captains of Industry," and the distinctly less flattering appella-
tion of "Robber Barons." For example, among those who made
substantial profits from the war was Philip Armour, who returned from the California goldfields of '49 to become a whole-
sale butcher in Chicago. He supplied the Union armies with a
great deal of pork of various qualities. Then, with financial
acumen, he sold pork futures short before the end of the war.
When the commodity markets crashed after the peace of Appo-
mattox, Armour made trades which, it is said, made thousands
of farmers poorer, to the accompaniment of a large overnight
profit in 1865 of two million dollars. At around the same time,
in Wisconsin, James Mellon, the eldest son of Pittsburgh banker
Judge Thomas Mellon, wrote to his father asking for money for
speculation. He reported that people were making millions in
wheat: "They continue growing richer and don't care when the
war closes."[12] These industrial captains were somewhat dubi-
ously saluted by Walt Whitman for their "extreme business
energy, and . . . almost maniacal appetite for wealth."[13]

Ten years before the Crédit Mobilier scandal, during the war,
a committee on government contracts had investigated James
Pierpont Morgan, the young son of New York banker Junius
Morgan. It seems that the son had presented a bill to the
government in the amount of $109,000 for carbines which were
so defective that the government had to dump the lot for $17,000.
That committee's report bitterly comments: "Worse than traitors
in arms are the men who pretending loyalty to the flag, feast and
fatten on the misfortunes of the nation, while patriot blood is
crimsoning the plains of the South and bodies of their country-
men are moldering in the dust."[14]

It is truly startling to observe the number of prominent industrial figures of that time—from the Civil War to the end of the century—who were eventually implicated in a great scandal of manipulation and fraud. In addition to Pierpont Morgan, there was Jay Cooke, who first became known in history as the major northern financier of the Civil War. In 1873 he tried to use his influence in Washington to block the Crédit Mobilier investigation, but to no avail. The "railroad congressmen" were by then frightened and chastened. His lobbyist brother, Henry Cooke, wrote to him: "The House seethed like a cauldron. You cannot imagine the demoralization in Congress."[15] Cooke was even having Indian trouble. He had to call out the troops to cover the workers along the extended line of the Northern Pacific. With the known Indian fighter General George Armstrong Custer at their head, they advanced as a protective force with the workers and engineers behind them. All this, along with the election of Grant in 1872, was costly to Cooke. He found many of his bonds and securities selling at discounted rates. To combat this, he—the man the newspapers had dubbed "the consumate master of speculation"—attempted to create a bull market in his securities by funding the new government to the tune of fifty-three million. He discussed these plans with President Grant, in his home outside of Philadelphia—"Cooke's Castle." Outside were armed guards; inside were fifty-two rooms decorated with frescoes, three hundred paintings, statuary, and glass works. But by now Cooke was weakened.

Earlier Pierpont Morgan had joined forces with Anthony Drexel, the largest banker outside of Cooke in Philadelphia, to attempt to wrest the monopoly position in government financing away from Cooke. They used the *Philadelphia Ledger*, a newspaper they controlled, to circulate the story that the sole purpose of Cooke's new funding plan was to bolster up his sagging credit. The Drexel-Morgan attack was effective, and in February of 1873 the government loan effort failed. However, the challengers didn't have much time to take cheer in their victory. Bad financial news piled upon bad financial news, and in September of that year the storm broke, sending the nation into the greatest economic crisis in its history up to that time. The depression of 1873 was to last until 1879. The first winter was the most severe, with tens of thousands of people on the verge of starvation. According to accounts, many committed suicide, while hundreds more were driven into bankruptcy and then insane asylums. Out of a total national population of forty million, three million were unemployed; the equivalent in terms of today's population would be at least twenty million unemployed.[16]

In 1873 Mark Twain published *The Gilded Age*, a novel coauthored with Charles Warner which describes the period that followed the end of the war, including its rampant speculation, frenzied drive for wealth, and political corruption. Twain and Warner wrote *The Gilded Age* in the boom years preceding the Panic of 1873 (as depressions were called then). When its publication occurred after the Panic, Twain worried about this timing; the new depressed environment certainly didn't match the gaudy, empire-building climate he had so pointedly described. However, Twain needn't have worried. The public immediately saw in the novel's pages a well-rendered account of the kind of doings that had brought on the economic panic they were now experiencing. The book was a best seller and one of Twain's earliest successes. It also established a tradition of journalistic and literary exposés of business and political corruption, paving the way for later "muckrakers," as they were disparagingly called by President Teddy Roosevelt in 1906. Roosevelt's term stuck, but without his sarcastic spirit. The exposés gained a large audience, and the works of Upton Sinclair on the beef industry and the railroads, of Thomas Lawson on Amalgamated Copper, and of Burton Hendrick on life insurance companies did much to create public demand for regulation of the great industrial combines. Twain's label "the Gilded Age" also stuck, to become the popular designation of that era.

The 1876 centennial of United States independence was observed in the midst of the panic begun in 1873. The concerts at the Philadelphia celebration were so poorly attended that they were eventually closed, and the conductor's music library was sold to pay the performers. The connection between self-interest economics and political corruption was sadly reflected in James Russell Lowell's sarcastic ode to William "Boss" Tweed, the friend of enterprise:

> Show your State Legislatures; show your rings;
> And challenge Europe to produce such things
> As high officials sitting half in sight
> To share the plunder and to fix things right;
> If that don't fetch her, why you only need
> To show your latest style in martyrs—Tweed.[17]

This was from the same Lowell who eleven years earlier had sung, "O beautiful! My Country!"

Other great business figures who became notorious for their corruption were Jay Gould and Jim Fisk. Although their dealings and behavior eventually became so lurid that they are best remembered today as figures of low farce, they were major movers in the industrial scene in the last quarter of the nineteenth century. Together they controlled the Erie Railroad; they almost cornered the gold market in 1869, leading to the "Black Friday" scandal; they had major interests in steamboat and ferry lines; and Gould controlled the Union Pacific and two other railroads, which together formed the four railroads of the Gould System. Fisk was eventually shot by his mistress's new lover, the gilded youth Ned Stokes. Gould was hunted by an angry mob which marched on the offices of the Western Union Telegraph Company, which he controlled, shouting "Hang Jay Gould." (They didn't hang him; he died a more natural death in 1892.)[18]

Of all the great entrepreneurs of the postwar period, probably the most significant, and perhaps the most talented, was John D. Rockefeller, the founder of Standard Oil. In contrast to some of his contemporaries, Rockefeller's life-style was a model of personal discipline and moderation. His significance for us lies in the fact that his procedures and goals became a standard for American industry of that period. Glenn Porter, an eminent contemporary business historian, states, "The pioneer enterprise in the story of industrial combinations was, of course, Standard Oil. The importance of the rise of that firm was succinctly summarized by Ida Tarbell in her *History of the Standard Oil Company* (1925): 'It was the first in the field, and it has furnished the methods, the charter, and the traditions for its followers.' "[19]

Like many other entrepreneurs of the time, Rockefeller had made his first profits during the war, although not nearly to the same extent as Armour, Fisk, or Cooke. His business had been the sale of grocery provisions to the government. Following the war he bought a share in a small oil refining company in Cleveland, which was one of thirty such companies in Cleveland at the time. In order to expand his capital base he invited in as partners two wealthy acquaintances. In no more than two years the firm had become the biggest in Cleveland; in 1870 it was incorporated as the Standard Oil Company of Ohio. How was this status so quickly accomplished?

One of the factors was the quality of the company's product, which the firm had developed with its own staff of chemists. However, Rockefeller's firm was also amazingly able to undersell its competitors by a small yet critical margin. And herein lay a major key to its success. The company had a secret arrangement with the railway lines, whose shipping charges represented one of the important costs in the final product of refined oil. Demonstrating early the force of his steel will and personality, for which he was to later become well known, Rockefeller played one railroad off against another, as well as against the canal carriers, in extracting "rebates" on the official and publicly stated freight rates. This was not an ordinary contract with the railroad for cheaper rates, but a secret agreement which was illegal. As publicly chartered institutions the railroads were required to make all rates public; however, through the rebate device they in effect were posting a false rate. In a subsequent New York State investigation of the railroads, the attorney for the merchants of New York declared that in their relationship with Rockefeller's company, the railroads exhibited "the most shameless perversion of the duties of a common carrier to private ends that has taken place in the history of the world."[20] The prose was a bit purple, but the indictment was accurate.

Now in a very strong position in the Cleveland oil business, Rockefeller took the next step in establishing dominance. An inlaw backer of one of his partners had been involved in the "Michigan Salt Pool"—an attempt by the salt producers of Saginaw Bay to control the competition by creating a pool to fix prices. This was perhaps the first plan of industrial combination in America. Although the pool was successful for a while, doubling the price of salt, some of the participants couldn't resist the opportunity to undercut their partners and get a bigger share of the market—which was perfectly permissible since the pool itself was strictly voluntary, with no legal standing. This eventually weakened and broke the pool.

Rockefeller felt that the same principle might work in the oil refining business, especially since Standard Oil had successfully coerced the railroads and become the leading company. By forming a pool they would be able to even out prices and protect themselves against what Rockefeller repeatedly referred to as "ruinous competition." As a matter of fact, during these formative years one rarely heard industrialists use the term *competition* without the modifier *ruinous*.[21]

The Standard Oil group looked toward Pennsylvania, where the major oil fields were. They obtained a charter to a deficient Pennsylvania corporation and renamed it the South Improvement Company. Then Rockefeller approached the other Cleveland refineries asking them to join in, threatening that they would be crushed if they didn't. Those who didn't already know that Rockefeller had special railroad rates were told. To one potential but reluctant member Rockefeller made this now-famous cryptic remark: "I have ways of making money that you know nothing of."[22] A congressional inquiry into the operations of the South Improvement Company led Rockefeller to abandon it. This inquiry, though weak, was nevertheless an early stigma against Standard Oil.[23]

Rockefeller was not content to rely on those early forms of

pools or cartels, which he accurately described as "ropes of sand." In 1882 he pioneered the organizational form to be known as the *trust*, in which a group of trustees would give trust certificates to other business owners in exchange for their common stock. This was an attempt to get around the common law prohibiting one corporation from holding stock in another without explicit chartering by the state. In setting up such a trust Rockefeller had the advantage of a new form of competition, which this time he approved of.

At the same time that competition among businesses was being increasingly avoided by business owners through trusts and similar combinations, a new kind of competition came along that laissez-faire theorists hardly would have dreamed of. This was competition among states to attract business by legislating lax corporation laws. New Jersey was the leader in this new competitive race, and in 1889 Standard Oil reincorporated in New Jersey as a *holding company*. A holding company was legally distinct from a trust, but the effect was similar; it allowed corporations chartered in New Jersey to legally hold stock in other companies.

By this time the vast monopolistic power of Standard Oil, which had attained almost complete dominance of the oil industry, began to arouse public and congressional anxieties. In 1878 Standard Oil was refining ninety percent of the country's output. In 1887 Standard Oil expanded its sphere of dominance; as well as refining it also became a producer in the oil fields, so that by 1898 its holdings amounted to a third of all production.[24] In addition, the New Jersey move option was being readily adopted by other companies and industries, following the lead of Standard Oil. The Wall Street reporter C. W. Barron, who was to become well known as the founder of a financial information service, related how two lawyers "transferred the Southern Cotton Oil Trust into a New Jersey Corporation in a single night. They locked their doors at six o'clock, drew up one hundred and seventy-five agreements, and landed the Cotton Oil Trust under

a New Jersey charter before daylight. They must have got at least
$50,000 for this night's work."[25]

The New York Chamber of Commerce had already issued a
report, in 1880, that expressed the fear of the rest of the business
community over the voracious appetite of the trusts:

> What has happened in the case of the Standard Oil Com-
> pany may happen in other lines of business. With the favor
> of the managers of the trunk lines, what is to prevent
> commerce in the rest of the great staples from being mo-
> nopolized in a similar manner? Already it is taking this
> course. One or two firms in Baltimore, Philadelphia, New
> York, and Boston, with their houses in the West, are, by the
> favor of the railroads, fast monopolizing the export trade
> in wheat, corn, cattle, and provisions, driving the competi-
> tors to the wall with absolute certainty, breaking down and
> crushing out the energy and enterprise of the many for the
> benefit of the favored few. . . .[26]

The growing call to address this trend moved one of the
Republican leaders in the Senate, John Sherman of Cleveland,
Ohio, to propose, for the first time, antimonopoly legislation in
the form of what came to be known as an *antitrust bill*. With the
bill's passage in 1890, the political era of pure laissez-faire in the
industrialized Anglo-Saxon world, which had begun with Adam
Smith, came to at least a formal close. In England it would be
some time before similar legislation was passed. The doctrine
that self-interest, when operating as the only motive and with no
interference or assistance from government, would lead to the
unalloyed public good seemed again in this context to be called
into question.

In his speech to the Senate, Sherman stated that his antitrust
bill did not intend to interfere with the corporation law of the
states, but since the state courts were limited in their jurisdiction
to their particular state, they were "unable to deal with the great
evil" now threatening the public. This "great evil" was the fact
that certain large corporations stretched across states, and indeed
across the whole country, and had controlling power over foreign

trade as well. Sherman, of course, was well aware that his bill had strong opposition, but he expressed determination to do something about the problem: "And for one I do not intend to be turned from this course by fine-spun constititutional quibbles or by the plausible pretexts of associated or corporate wealth and power." He dealt with objections and outlined the bill's purpose:

> This bill does not seek to cripple combinations of capital and labor . . . but only to prevent and control combinations made with a view to prevent competition, or for the restraint of trade, or to increase the profits of the producer at the cost of the consumer. . . . The sole object of such a combination is to make competition impossible. It can control the market, raise or lower prices, as will best promote its selfish interests, reduce prices in a particular locality and break down competition and advance prices at will where competition does not exist. Its governing motive is to increase the profits of the parties composing it. The law of selfishness, uncontrolled by competition, compels it to disregard the interests of the consumer. It dictates terms to transportation companies, it commands the price of labor without fear of strikes, for in its field it allows no competitors. Such a combination is far more dangerous than any heretofore invented. . . . If the concentrated powers of this combination are entrusted to a single man, it is a kingly prerogative, inconsistent with our form of government, and should be subject to the strong resistance of the State and national authorities. If anything is wrong this is wrong. If we will not endure a king as a political power we should not endure a king over the production, transportation, and sale of any of the necessaries of life.[27]

However, despite Sherman's vigorous rhetoric and the bill's eventual easy passage, the new law had little success in limiting the monopolies. From the standpoint of the development of antitrust legislation it was a grand gesture, but mostly a ceremonial one. Standard Oil had already abandoned the old trust form, against which the Sherman act was directed, in favor of the holding company structure. Thus, Rockefeller continued to demonstrate his early ability to stay at least one step ahead of the law, and in so doing he showed others the way.

The new economic environment was recognized by John Moody, who was editor of several investment journals and, along with Barron, one of the most prominent Wall Street analysts of the time. He recognized the development of business monopolies as "a perfectly natural evolution." He drew this significant conclusion: "The old economic axiom has been reversed in the past twenty-five years. Competition has not been the life of trade; it has been the death of industry in the United States. Monopoly has been built up on its ruins, and it is built to stay."[28]

Despite the fact that Rockefeller and Standard Oil were the impetus for the antitrust law, the company was not brought to court under it until 1911, in the antitrust climate supported by an increasingly concerned Teddy Roosevelt. Roosevelt eventually earned the title of "trust-buster," although historians generally believe that this was undeserved. Standard Oil had continued to capture and control markets and sources of supply in Russia and China. It had also acquired the largest known iron deposits in the world. Heilbroner, in his well-known *The Worldly Philosophers*, describes how Rockefeller purchased Anaconda Copper without the expenditure of a single dollar. Then Heilbroner notes, "Of course, this free-for-all involved staggering dishonesty."[29]

Standard Oil became the biggest investor in National City Bank, and through banking it became a major figure in many other industries, such as gas, railroads, and steel. And finally, Standard Oil became a partner in the United States Steel monopoly and a member of the board of Northern Pacific, after gaining entrance to Pierpont Morgan's empire by engaging him in a huge stock-bidding battle. It was during this battle that Pierpont Morgan uttered his own set of memorable words: "I owe the public nothing."[30]

Throughout the 1890s Standard Oil stock paid out an average annual dividend of forty percent. In the successful antitrust suit against Standard Oil, a great irony occurred. As Joseph Pusateri tells it, "The investing public, through the information disseminated during the lengthy legal struggle, gauged for the first time the enormous real wealth of the various Standard entities and began to bid for the stock accordingly." When it was ordered that thirty-three companies were to be severed from Standard Oil of New Jersey, the parent holding company, the price of all their shares separately increased. Pusateri reports the result: "The principals holding the greatest interests in those companies, and most notably Rockefeller, found that the Supreme Court of the United States had made them even wealthier than they had been before."[31] In 1972 Standard Oil changed its name to the Exxon Corporation.

But the strangest and perhaps most bitter irony of the Sherman Antitrust Act was its effect on labor. Although the act was clearly and obviously directed against the great industrial combinations, the United States court system decided that it pertained to all "combinations" in the economic environment, including those of labor and especially labor unions. Under the antitrust act, from 1890 to 1897 the federal courts ruled in only one case against a business combination, and twelve times against attempts to organize labor unions.[32] The use of antitrust laws to oppose labor organization was only ended with the passage of the National Labor Relations Act in 1935.

The same factors that had brought on the Panic of 1873 caused another severe economic downturn in 1893. Overproduction for an underpaid population and the gyrations of feverish speculation are widely accepted as causes of this "rich man's panic," as it was called. William Jennings Bryan began taking up his banners against the "goldbugs" in Washington; and Jacob Coxey organized his "army" of industrial unemployed who, clothed in their tatters, marched in Washington for the redress of their grievances. A depression of five years followed the 1893 panic. Moody reports the effects on the economy: "In the long depression which followed, manufacturers everywhere were forced into bankruptcy. Capital was scarce, the demand for goods was small, and thousands of plants remained in total or partial idleness for several years. This was particularly true of the steel and iron industry."[33] The crisis ended when Republican William McKinley was elected president in 1897 and, in the name of big business, jettisoned the hallowed economic doctrines of free trade and competition, and enacted new high protective tariffs. Moody notes:

> When the Republican party returned to power in 1897 and immediately enacted a new tariff law, with high protective duties, and when at the same time certain court decisions were handed down which seemed to limit the scope of the Sherman Act, a wave of reviving prosperity swept over the country, and capital returned with new confidence to the industrial field. Several of the earlier trusts besides Standard Oil survived the panic and had been reorganized to conform to the law, notably, the American Sugar Refining Company and the American Tobacco Company. The new industrial combinations were modeled after these. Instead of placing the control plants in the hands of "trustees," holding companies were formed, which acquired all or a majority of stocks in certain competing plants and merged these plants under one control, often by exchanging the stock of the holding company for the stock of the plant."[34]

What followed next has been called the "great merger movement" in the American economy. As Glenn Porter describes it:

> During the decade after 1895, the great merger movement flourished, and nothing like it was seen before or since in the history of the nation's economy. Approximately 300 separate firms disappeared into mergers each year during that time. By 1910, many of the nation's most influential big businesses had been created either through vertical or horizontal growth, or through a mixture of the two. Just a partial list of modern industrial giants already born by 1910 included: petroleum companies such as Standard Oil and Texaco; rubber producers such as U.S. Rubber (now Uniroyal) and Goodyear; metal firms including U.S. Steel, Bethlehem Steel; . . . the electrical manufacturers, General Electric and Westinghouse; food processors such as American Sugar, Nabisco, United Fruit, Swift and Company, and Armour; as well as scores of others including American

Tobacco, duPont, Pittsburgh Plate Glass, American Can, Allis-Chalmers, International Harvester, Singer, and East-man Kodak. It is no exaggeration to say that the structure of the twentieth century American economy had been re-shaped by the end of the century's first decade.[35]

Porter's statement that nothing like the merger movement of 1895–1905 has been seen since needs to be updated by recent developments, as we will see shortly.

The prosperity that followed the recovery was not long-lived, and in 1909 another panic hit. President Theodore Roosevelt, who in one of his "progressive" phases had derided the "malefac-tors of wealth," now humbly called upon Pierpont Morgan to bail out the United States government. He asked the financier to import gold from Europe and to lead Rockefeller and others to guarantee dividend and interest payments on investments. Pier-pont Morgan agreed; money was poured into the stock ex-change, and he ordered the obedient bears not to sell. The operation worked, and another deep and serious American eco-nomic depression was abated.

Congressman Arsene Pujo of Louisiana, who had been a member of the National Monetary Commission investigating the banking system, pressed for an investigation of a reportedly vast "money trust."[36] The Pujo Committee found that such a trust had indeed been brought into existence through consolidations of banks and trust companies. These companies had used their financial resources to establish a system of interlocking director-ates to manage insurance companies, railroads, public utilities, and manufacturing corporations. Morgan and Company was found to have a dominant role in thirty-two transportation systems, thirty-four banks and trust companies, and ten insur-ance companies. Supreme Court Justice Louis D. Brandeis spelled out the implications of this concentration and control in a series of articles in *Harper's Weekly*, and these were later published as *Other People's Money*. His writing's played an important role in stimulating the reformist era that eventually followed.

The tariff weapon that had been so effective against the Panic of 1893 completely backfired when used again after the stock market crash of 1929. Tariffs are widely credited with having turned that panic into the Great Depression. It was then, in fact, that the word *panic*, which had become so associated in the public's mind with the terrors of severe and prolonged economic downturns, was replaced by what was felt to be the milder *depression*. However, as that catastrophe wore on, becoming longer and deeper than any previous downturn, the word *depression* lost all power to pacify, and in time it loomed even more ominous in the public's mind than the abandoned term.

The Great Depression was only effectively ended by the advent of World War II—which in turn was ended with the use of science and technology's greatest discovery thus far: the atom bomb. Following the recovery after the war, economists generally assured the public that the lessons of the Great Depression had now been learned, and the repetition of such an event was not likely. Later, in 1984, an article in the *New York Times* discussed the possible end of an "era of shocks."[37] Nevertheless, in 1987 the stock market once again suffered a crash—with a magnitude rivaling that of the 1929 crash.

The 1987 crash has been attributed to the U.S. budget deficit, which in turn resulted from unprecedented peacetime military expenditures. This occurred against a background that included insider trading scandals, "junk bond" financing (high risk, high yield), "me-first" executive management, and hostile takeovers, as well as a merger movement that drew comparisons with that at the turn of the century.[38]

The major technical factor, and the most likely immediate precipitant of the crash, was the growth and power of trading in financial futures, which is conducted by the Chicago Mercantile Exchange—the Merc. Although there had at first been much skepticism about the safety and sense of trading intangible commodities, such as the future prices of stock indices, the leadership of the Merc had been able to persuade a skeptical financial community. Among their ammunition was a study they had commissioned for five thousand dollars from University of Chicago economist Milton Friedman. This study, which supported the idea of trading in financial futures, was widely read. The Chicago school, with Friedman as its leader, is well known in the world of economics for its staunch advocacy of pure Smithian economics. The chairman of the Merc, who utilized Friedman's study, has been described admiringly as a man who has "an uncanny ability to persuade people to do something right by persuading them it [is] in their self-interest."[39]

The stock market crash in 1987 was quickly followed by the massive failure of the savings and loan (S&L) banking industry, ironically sometimes known as *thrifts*. Estimates of the cost of these failures to the public have constantly gone up from a first official figure of fifty billion to a later, probably still underestimated, cost of five hundred billion. One of the major precipitants of the failure was overzealous deregulation which is now widely recognized as having opened the banking doors to extensive greed, reckless investing, and outright fraud and corruption. To those who believe that the thrift banking industry was already a long-gone casualty of high interest rates in the 1970s (which played their part) the following news statement in 1986 should prove telling: "Already, profit at thrift institutions around the country is greater than ever. Considered a dead industry only months ago, thrift-unit stocks today are outperforming even the soaring market."[40] This is also testament to the fact that an apparently high-flying economy may be resting on a flimsy understructure, very near the point of giving way. *Newsweek* caught the nexus of forces making for this disaster in an apt phrase, adapted from writer Tom Wolfe: "The Bonfire of the S&Ls."[41]

On the two-year anniversary of the 1987 crash there was another precipitous stock market fall; the Dow index fell 190 points in just ninety minutes. It is generally acknowledged that the speculative nature of futures trading on the Chicago Merc was directly responsible for these precipitous drops. The chairman of the Merc defended the establishment of futures trading:

"You and I know, and the world knows, that when there is a strong enough need, the necessary instruments are created to meet that need."[42] In perfect economic logic, wants are equated to needs, and as needs they are unstoppable.

Meanwhile, the national political and legislative process has become dominated by huge sums of special interest money, with significant payments in various forms going to legislators. Political campaigns from the presidential level on down have become increasingly conducted as advertising campaigns with political "debate" taking the form of the candidates' TV commercials and thirty-second soundbites on news programs, sometimes themselves taken from the commercials. As the 1980s closed a whole range of public media, from the *New York Times* to *USA Today*, began characterizing the decade as an "age of greed and excess."[43]

The economic history of the United States since the Civil War represents the world's most sustained attempt to radically apply the principles of market self-interest and political laissez-faire, in a laboratory that could hardly be more perfect—a huge abundance of land, rich with resources. Following are two perspectives on this endeavor, offered by two men who had run for the presidency of the United States—one in its early, highly enthusiastic period, and one at a later, more sober time.

In 1877, only a hundred years after the publication in Britain of *The Wealth of Nations*, many of the fabulously wealthy business leaders of an economically unrestrained America gathered for a testimonial dinner for Junius Morgan (John Pierpont Morgan's father). The dinner speaker was Samuel J. Tilden, a lawyer for the railroad interests, who had just been narrowly defeated by Rutherford B. Hayes for the presidency. Tilden addressed the assembled eminent guests with the following words:

> You are, doubtless in some degree, clinging to the illusion that you are working for yourself, but it is my pleasure to claim that you are working for the public. [Applause.] While you are scheming for your own selfish ends, there is

an overruling and wise Providence directing that the most of all you do should inure to the benefit of the people. Men of colossal fortunes are in effect, if not in fact, trustees for the public.[44]

Sixty years later, in 1937, when Franklin D. Roosevelt gave his second inaugural address, he spoke to a different audience—a nation that found itself deep in the Depression:

Old truths have been relearned, untruths have been un-learned. We have always known that heedless self-interest was bad morals; we now know that it is bad economics. Out of the collapse of a prosperity whose builders boasted their practicality has come the conviction that in the long run economic morality pays.[45]

Could it be that Adam Smith had made some mistake?

4

THE MISTAKE

The central statement of Adam Smith's *Wealth of Nations*—for history, and certainly for economics—is that which affirms the value of self-interest: "It is not from the benevolence of the butcher, the brewer, or the baker, that we expect our dinner, but from their regard to their own self interest." The lines that follow this "butcher-baker" statement are often quoted as well: "We address ourselves, not to their humanity but to their self-love, and never talk to them of our own necessities but of their advantages. Nobody but a beggar chooses to depend chiefly upon the benevolence of his fellow citizens."[1]

In this famous passage Smith seems to be telling us that, within the range of human motives, those in the category of *self-interest*, and not those classed as *benevolence*, are chiefly responsible for our being adequately supplied with provisions for living and the other goods and services that an economy should provide. Economists often debate what, exactly, self-interest means: is it selfishness or something different, perhaps more enlightened? In a while we will give further attention to this debate. But let us first recall that when Smith's predecessors, such as Richard Cumberland and Francis Hutcheson, divided the middle range of human motivation into two categories they were quite clearly talking about "moral sentiments" on the one hand and selfishness on the other. Smith himself takes this division as the starting point of his refutation of selfishness in the opening lines of his *Theory of Moral Sentiments*: "How selfish so ever man may be supposed, there are evidently some principles in his nature, which interest him in the fortune of others, and render their happiness necessary to him, though he derives nothing from it, except the pleasure of seeing it."[2]

With the quickening eclipse of the influence of religion in the eighteenth century, social writers and moral philosophers were constantly occupied with the question of how society could continue to be held together without the traditional guidance of religious teachings. Many even wondered whether society *was* being held together. Smith himself, in the passage quoted from his *Wealth of Nations*, could hardly make it clearer that by *self-interest* he means a concern with the self to the exclusion of a concern with the other: "We address ourselves not to their humanity but to their self-love. . . ."

Indeed, what makes this passage so striking, and what has given it its claim on the modern imagination, is its shock value. Certainly this was true in Smith's day, when the traditional religious conception of morality was still closely adhered to. That which had traditionally been seen as a bad thing—selfishness or self-interest—was advanced by Smith as a good thing, a social benefit. It is not the traditional social benefit of benevolence, says Smith, that nourishes us and sustains us (and note the same linguistic root in *benevolence* and *benefit*), but its essential opposite—selfishness. What a startling revelation was offered to the world in Adam Smith's impressive and distinguished tome!

We now come very close to the point of being able to discern Adam Smith's mistake. It is brought into view when we ask a question of the self-interest passage that is usually not asked: According to Smith's own logic, what would an economy look like if in fact benevolence were the determining motive?

Adam Smith is telling us that the economy in his day, and by extension in our own, is guided by self-interest and not benevolence. How do we know this to be correct? Is Smith a master psychologist capable of probing the minds of people and observing their motives? Perhaps this is the case; Smith has been praised for his keen psychological insight. But Smith's passage seems to carry a definitiveness that precludes any further discussion as to the motives of economic actors in the marketplace. The power of its conviction does not seem to reside so much in its psychology as in its logic. We can see how this is accomplished in the passage when we answer the question that we have posed to it.

An economy based on benevolence would be quite different from our own, as Smith tells us. What, then, would it look like? How would generosity, kindness, and so on translate into the economic sphere? Smith, in his passage, gives us the answer most directly and categorically. In his terms, for benevolence to be operative in the economic sphere, goods would have to be given away, for free. If people have to pay for what they receive then this means self-interest and not benevolence is operating on the part of the butcher, the baker. It is only the beggar (one who is without means of payment) who depends on benevolence. The "appeal" to the self-interest of the butcher and baker that Smith refers to is precisely the exchange of money for their goods. To appeal to their benevolence would be to ask them to give away their goods without exchange—as a free offering.

So we find that Smith is telling us in this passage that in any economy based on exchange—which certainly includes any market economy, and perhaps *any* modern economy—it is only self-interest operating and not benevolence. Thus we can see that, knowingly or not, Smith is being categorical; his logic lies beyond psychological probing, questioning of motives, or any other empirical argument. That is why his passage carries such conviction and power—and why it has been one of the transforming forces in shaping the modern mind and the modern world.

We now are ready to see Smith's mistake. It becomes clear when we go to the second part of his thesis, which says that self-interest, rather than benevolence, promotes the social good and that, in fact, self-interest is *more* effective in promoting the social good than benevolence. Herein lies the big surprise revealed by political economy: the economic actor "intends only his own gain, and he is in this, as in many other cases, led by an invisible hand to promote an end which was no part of his intention. Nor is it always the worse for the society that it was no part of it. By pursuing his own interest he frequently promotes that of the society more effectually than when he really intends to promote it."[3] But here is a problem, a deep problem indeed, and one that goes to the heart of the matter. For we can ask, what about honesty?

If the butcher or baker can cheat us (say by using short weights on his scale), and he can get away with it, isn't it in his self-interest to do so? The answer must be yes. There is nothing in self-interest that rules out cheating, especially if one is good at it. It is not self-interest that prevents someone from cheating. Self-interest only dictates that they not get caught. As we have seen, history is full of accounts of people deceiving, defrauding, coercing, and essentially stealing from others in their economic dealings. And we only know about those who were caught. Even among them, some have been seen as heroes; they did quite well, with their penalties hardly matching the gains of their crimes. In fact, we will see that economists came to conclude that from the standpoint of self-interest it would be *irrational* for someone *not* to cheat if they could be reasonably sure of getting away with it. "Honesty is the best policy" is not an economic doctrine.

Smith himself, throughout his second book, gives many acute descriptions of these tendencies on the part of entrepreneurial economic actors, and he doesn't mince any words about it. For example, in discussing merchants and dealers, he says it is they "who have generally an interest to deceive and even to oppress the public, and who accordingly have upon many occasions, both deceived and oppressed it."[4]

Smith's forthright talk of businessmen cheating and oppressing the public seems to stand in direct contradiction to his advocacy of self-interest as the sole principle necessary for the achievement of the public good. The saving grace was supposed to be the "invisible hand" of competition. It was competition that would keep these instincts and "expensive vanities" of the merchants, dealers, and landlords in line. Smith would hardly have been surprised at the motives of Rockefeller, but he certainly would have been chagrined at his success. Smith had essentially overlooked the possibility that self-interest would work to under-mine and eliminate competition and thus to tie up the invisible hand. It is this outcome of unrestrained self-interest that is the fundamental flaw in any absolute policy of laissez-faire. This was not even adequately recognized by the early advocates of antitrust. When Senator Sherman spoke on behalf of the first antitrust legislation, he said, "The law of selfishness, uncon-trolled by competition, compels it to disregard the interest of the consumer." Implicit in Sherman's statement, but seemingly not recognized by him, is the deduction that the law of selfishness also compels it to eliminate competition. For competition to continue to exist as a restraint on the rapacity of self-interest, it would have to be supported by a force or principle other than economic self-interest.

As we have seen, when taken by itself, self-interest naturally leads to cheating and dishonesty. The example of the merchant who cheats the consumer illustrates the problem of self-interest in the interpersonal or social context. But "cheating" also occurs in relation to the physical and natural context—the environment. For the principle of self-interest dictates that the individual seek self-benefit by imposing costs on the natural environment. From the Industrial Revolution and continuing down into the present, self-interest has produced pollution, depletion, and the progres-sive destruction of the natural world. The evidence begins with the foul streets, sewers, and air of Adam Smith's London and extends to the acid rain, ozone depletion, and "greenhouse effect" of today.

Now, approximately two hundred years after *The Wealth of Nations*, society is just beginning to recognize the destructive consequences of economic self-interest; however, it does not as easily recognize that this state of affairs is implicitly supported by economic theory in its pure Smithian form. For example, in *The Economic Way of Thinking*, Paul Heyne tells us that we don't really *need* such a thing as clean water, because there really are no needs; there are only *wants*, and these are backed up by purchasing power, or *demand*. Demand can always find substitutes, says the economist, for there are "substitutes everywhere." "Who needs water?" Heyne asks. He explains: "People are creatures of habit, in what they think as well as what they do. Perhaps this also explains why so many have trouble recognizing the significance of substitutes and hence such difficulty in appreciating the law of demand. Water provides an excellent example." Heyne goes on to say that "we have confused the issue for ourselves by identifying pollution with environmental damage."[5] So pollution is not environmental damage after all?

What then is pollution? Simply a disagreement over property rights, the economist tells us. Again, Heyne: "Pollution exists when people's expectations about what they can and may do come into conflict. Pollution is eliminated when disagreements about property rights are resolved—when those who formerly protested the actions of others consent to those actions."[6] In other words, pollution is not an objective reality. It is only a question of protest on the part of some about what others are doing. In the economist's world of self-interest, all is indeed self, including the environment; there is nothing objective. If the price system can be adjusted so that those who are unhappy about what they believe to be pollution can be paid enough to keep them quiet, then the so-called pollution will disappear. Following this logic, we can presume that at some point the polluter would find it too expensive to pollute and would therefore cut down on environmentally destructive acts. This assumes, of course, that there really is an environment separate from the self, a fact that economic theory fundamentally seems to deny, as we have just seen.

Heyne concludes: "There may be no more important lesson for us to learn about pollution than that pollution so thoroughly permeates our society that we cannot realistically hope to eliminate it. Pollution exists when teenagers play their transistor radios and thereby infringe on the right of other bus passengers to enjoy peace and quiet; pollution still exists, though in a changed form, when the other bus passengers infringe on the teenagers' right to hear music by enforcing their own desire for peace and quiet."[7] So from the standpoint of economic theory, peace and quiet is pollution for the teenager. And so it goes. Logically, then, pollution must be a constant. Thus we should not be surprised to find that in forums held to discuss the problems facing the natural environment, economists are generally the most resistant to proposed solutions. For example, in a 1988 discussion of the consequences of the warming of the earth as a result of the greenhouse effect, environmental and resource scientists sounded the alarm. Irving R. Mintzer of the World Resources Institute warned, "We are talking about changing the entire fabric of nature." The economist quoted in this discussion, however—a professor at Carnegie-Mellon—is the voice of doing less rather than more: "There is no way to justify spending tens of billions of dollars a year to prevent the greenhouse effect."[8] The economist had studied the law of demand and knew the "real values" involved. More accurately, he or she knew that there are no real values, just as there is nothing objective; there is only personal demand.

Smith's doctrine of self-interest is quite a remarkable one. The celebrated critical economist Joan Robinson is succinct and incisive in this regard: "This is an ideology to end ideologies, for it has abolished the moral problem. It is only necessary for each individual to act egotistically for the good of all to be attained."[9] And there we have the essence of Adam Smith's mistake.

Our review of several periods of history has shown that the good of all is not attained by pure self-interest or egoism. There must be another principle operating in people, a principle that moderates self-interest in favor of the general good. We indicated above that a sense of honesty could be one such moderating tendency. Honesty follows a standard that is outside of self-interest, and this is precisely the definition of morality. Other such principles are fairness, integrity, reasonableness, and a sense of justice.

As a matter of fact, it is according to Smith himself that justice is necessary for the good to be attained. He says this at a point in his book that is far removed from the butcher-baker statement, which occurs on page 14 of the Cannan edition of Smith's work. On page 651, Smith reviews his "obvious and simple system of natural liberty," which is the central idea of his entire text. In fact, his call for liberty, or freedom from the restraints of a mercantile and aristocratic ruling system, and for the just treatment of the working person still rings down through the centuries. It is this call that aligns Smith with the liberty that the American nation was pursuing, coincidentally, in the same year as the publication of his book. Smith says, "Every man, as long as he does not violate the laws of justice, is left perfectly free to pursue his own interests in his own way, and to bring both his industry and capital into competition with those of any other man, or order of men." *As long he does not violate the laws of justice.* This qualification is critical, yet it is missing from his earlier statement, which has become the hallmark statement for economics and for the place of self-interest in the modern world.

While a respect for justice is not necessarily equivalent to benevolence, it is certainly *closer* to benevolence than to self-interest, and that is why Smith counterbalances self-interest with justice in the grand concluding statement quoted above. Although, in his earlier work, *The Theory of Moral Sentiments*, Smith draws a fine distinction between justice and "beneficence," he clearly classifies both as "the virtues."[10]

We turn now to a final elucidation of the butcher-baker statement. Adam Smith made a mistake. He said, "It is not from the benevolence of the butcher, the brewer, or the baker that we expect our dinner, but from their regard to their own interest." We should now be able to see that Adam Smith left out just one little word—a word which has made a world of difference. And if this mistake is not corrected, then the absence of that word could threaten to unmake a world. That word is *only*. What Adam Smith ought to have said was, "It is not *only* from the benevolence. . . ."; then everything would have been all right.

I said before that we would eventually view the butcher-baker statement in an even larger context, and now is the time to do this, because in so doing we will find intriguing confirmation for our account of Adam Smith's mistake. For it turns out that four sentences before this statement we find the missing *only*. Smith, in attempting to explain the origin of the division of labor, contrasts the behavior of animals with that of humans. Animals, he says, are largely independent and have little need for the assistance of other animals. But man, on the other hand,

> has almost constant occasion for the help of his brethren, and it is in vain for him to expect it from their benevolence *only*. He will be more likely to prevail if he can interest their self-love in his favor, and shew them that it is for their own advantage to do for him what he requires of them. Whoever offers to another a bargain of any kind, proposes to do this. Give me that which I want, and you shall have this which you want, is the meaning of every such offer; and it is in this manner that we obtain from one another the far greater part of those good offices which we stand in need of. It is not from the benevolence of the butcher, the brewer, or the baker, that we expect our dinner, but from their regard to their own interest. (italics added)

Of course, we don't mean to imply that Smith *intended* to insert the word *only* before *benevolence,* and that he mistakenly left it out. He intended it to be just the way it is; but in his intention he made a mistake. And what is so fascinating about this analysis of his text is that we can see how close he was to putting it differently. He almost might have said that self-interest wasn't everything, that some measure of benevolence was also needed for society to be benefited. But in the end, and just at the margin of his thought, he made the fateful decision to write on behalf of self-interest to the exclusion of benevolence. What contributed to this, as we have pointed out, is that Smith saw benevolence as operating only in the donation of free gifts or charity, and he did not realize that it also needed to play a part in exchange as well—in the form of honesty, integrity, or fairness. The significance of the omission of *only* in the butcher-baker sentence is clear when we remember that this statement became the basis of the counsel of self-interest in respectable and academic thought.

As we have just seen, Smith's sanctioning of self-interest without any qualifying or restraining force completely eliminated the moral problem in human action. Morality is always a matter of choosing, and situations of moral relevance always involve conflict of interest. One has to choose between the interests of "rightness" (which can be taken to mean honesty, justice, fairness, the concerns of the other, the public, society) and the interests of the self in disregard of rightness. The nature of the latter choice was rather clearly expressed in the now immortal words of John Pierpont Morgan: "I owe the public nothing." Smith's statement equating the pursuit of the interests of the self with the public good completely eliminated the need for choice: Just do what's good for you alone, and the good for all will be attained. There is no more moral problem because there is no conflict of interest. There is only one interest, and that is self-interest.

It is quite striking, and still another confirmation of our analysis of Smith's mistake, to find in the famous "invisible hand" passage almost the same conceptual and moral slippage. In this passage, which appears on page 423, Smith says that the individual

> intends only his own gain, and he is in this, as in many other cases, led by an invisible hand to promote an end which was no part of his intention. Nor is it always the worse for the society that it was no part of it. By pursuing his own interest he frequently promotes that of the society more effectually than when he really intends to promote it. I have never known much good done by those who affected to trade for the public good. It is an affectation indeed, not very common among merchants, and very few words need be employed in dissuading them from it.

Smith states that in the pursuit of self-interest the individual is "led by an invisible hand" to promote the social good, although that is no part of his intention. Furthermore, by pursuing self-interest he will be more likely to promote the social good than if he intentionally sets out to do so. It should be noted how truly remarkable this statement is. Smith would seem to be telling us that if we want to find people who will best promote the public good, we should choose those who are essentially pursuing their own interest. Before the reader has been given the opportunity to realize just how strange this statement is, Smith goes on to say, "I have never known much good done by those who affected to trade for the public good. It is an affectation, indeed, not very common among merchants, and very few words need be employed in dissuading them from it."

We immediately appreciate Smith's dry wit when he says that "very few words" are needed to dissuade the merchant from trading for the public good. It thus appears that Smith is referring to the hypocrisy, perhaps thinly veiled, of those who pretend to trade for the public good. So, the whole passage might then be taken as an ironic invective against such hypocrisy, and we can understand Smith as saying that one who honestly pursues his own self-interest does a lot better for society, or at least does it no harm, than one who deceptively claims to be pursuing the public good. Well and good, and we accept this caution against the ill effects of hypocritical claims in the public interest. But in the previous phrase Smith refers to those who "*really* intend" to promote the public good. Well, if these people really intend to do so, they cannot be the same hypocritical persons that Smith then seems to refer to. Therefore, Smith's adjective *really* is misused and misleading. To be consistent Smith would have had to have said something like, "those who *apparently* intend to promote the public good." To say it as he did leaves the whole passage as a contradiction, and as a remarkable condemnation of truly benevolent intentions.

In both the butcher-baker statement and the invisible hand passage we see that Smith came within a hair's breadth of not slipping into a philosophy of moral failure; the mere use of the right modifying word in each passage would have prevented immorality from finding its intellectual and theoretical justification in the name of economics. The tragedy of all this is that Smith was not a bad man at all. Indeed, Smith was a good man, and all of his intentions were highly honorable, as we will see further on. But in promoting his good ends through the means of justifying self-interest he made a fateful mistake—a mistake which allowed people of much more dubious intentions than Smith, beginning with Thomas Malthus, to find justification for their own self-interests in Smith's name and work.

We have said that in his economics Smith was dealing with the "middle range" of human motivation. This is necessarily the case because economics as a field concerns this middle range. The full range of human motivation involves the *passions* as well as the *interests*, to use Albert Hirschman's delineation of these forces in economic history.[11] We can see human motivation as very simply consisting of a bipolar dimension, with love on one end and hate on the other. These two poles represent the passions.

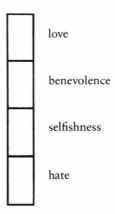

The Vector of Human Motivation

In the middle range of motivation are the interests, and these can be classified as benevolence and self-interest (or selfishness), to use the Smithian terms.

The conflict of interests that we have been discussing is the conflict between the upward and the downward directions on this continuum (or, more accurately, vector). To put it very starkly, but accurately, the choice between these directions corresponds to the choice between good and bad, or virtue and vice.

While it is easy to make a distinction between the two ends of the vector—between white and black—it is always more difficult to make such moral distinctions in the middle, or gray, area, of the continuum. But a distinction in the middle range is still the same *kind* of distinction; it is a distinction between good and bad.

In his doctrine of self-interest, Smith made what can be called a *transvaluation*. That is, he reversed the poles of the continuum of motivation, at least in the middle range. In effect he said that bad was good and good was bad. We will see shortly how Smith was influenced by a predecessor, Bernard de Mandeville, to make this transvaluation. Mandeville's famous utterance that "private vice is public benefit" was to leave its fateful mark on Smith.

We have seen, then, that transvaluations become the root of moral confusion when the polarity is mislabeled. The economic doctrine of self-interest has introduced just this confusion into modern life, and in an intellectually acceptable form. Modern society has been struggling with this problem ever since the inception of the science of economics in the late 1700s.

Transvaluation is not just a product of economics, of course, and people of ill will in all spheres inevitably use transvaluative language to justify their vices and evil intentions. Perhaps the most well-known literary portrayal of this is in George Orwell's satire *Nineteen Eighty-four*, where mechanistic man, living in a totalitarian regime, talks in the language of doublespeak or even "newspeak." Here war is called peace, and lies are called truths.

The misuse of language, or mislabeling, is an important aspect of transvaluation. For Confucius, the path back to morality lay, at least in part, in what he called "the rectification of names." Immorality flourished, according to the Confucian perspective, when things and actions were not called by their correct names.[12] The most serious instance of such mislabeling is when what is bad is called good, and vice versa.

We also need to be clear, however, that immorality is not just or primarily a problem of mislabeling. It is not only a language problem. Immorality flows from the unchecked ill will of the lower self, or lower pole of motivation. It is unchecked because the counterbalancing force, the higher pole, is overpowered or held in abeyance. Language enters the picture because unchecked ill will inevitably distorts language; transvalued language is then used to render the lower pole, or lower self, dominant over a higher self that has been linguistically disclaimed. It is the central thesis of this book that in its self-interest doctrine economics has served precisely this purpose.

It is the task of the present work, then, to affect a rectification of names in the area of economics, and in social action and policy in general. We want to show that self-interest in essence means selfishness, and selfishness cannot produce the social good because in fact it is the very force that destroys the social good, despite the claim of economics to the contrary. As a matter of fact, this claim provides one of the deep mystifications that bedevil what we call the modern world.

5

REAP WHERE THEY NEVER SOWED

The curious thing about Adam Smith's self-interest doctrine is that, when applied to actual economic behavior, it is at the same time too cynical and too naive.

It is too cynical because Smith could not see the operation of benevolent motives in the commercial economic sphere. To him, all was self-interest, and it was "vile," "despicable," and "vicious." As indicated before, he had virtually nothing at all good to say about the merchant or the businessman.

Smith's cynicism is noted by John Rae in his classic biography of Smith. He recounts Smith's impression of Robert Turgot, the reform-minded comptroller general of finances who had also worked on the French *Encyclopédie*:

> Smith, for all his admiration for Turgot, thought him too simple-hearted for a practical statesman, too prone, as noble natures often are, to underrate the selfishness, stupidity, and prejudice that prevail in the world and resist the course of just and rational reform. . . . Tugot made too little account, he thought, of the resisting power of vested interests and confirmed habits. He was too optimist, and the peculiarity attaches to his theoretical as well as his practical work. Smith himself was prone rather to the contrary error of overrating the resisting power of interests and prejudices.[1]

After registering this comparison between the two, the biographer goes on to make this interesting comment: "It is curious to find the man who has spent his life in the practical business of

94

the world taking the more enthusiastic view we expect from the recluse, and the man who has spent his life in his library taking the more critical and measured view we expect from the man of the world."

In his cynicism Smith misleads us. From the self-interest doctrine we inherit the picture of the businessman or -woman as only greedy. This is exemplified by Dickens's portrayal of Scrooge, which is just one among scores of such portraits that exist in literature and in the popular imagination. The real story, particularly recognizable today, may be rather different. Although we certainly continue to have our corporate scandals and our modern versions of Robber Barons, business literature increasingly looks to models other than those of self-interest as guides to business conduct. For example, in a recent interview study of sixteen chief executive officers (CEOs) of major firms, "integrity and competence" emerge as the major values held in common.[2] Integrity, a term that is a prime exemplar of morality, hardly squares with the Smithian description of self-interest.

A modern corporate leader who represents at least a segment of contemporary business leaders is William C. Norris of Control Data Corporation. Norris is legendary for his concern for community and social values, and he has been described as "a manager with an almost obsessive interest in serving society."[3] That is an obsession that is at a far remove from those that seemed to drive the earlier leaders of the United States industrial scene following the Civil War.

The trend toward recognizing the virtues of the businessperson, as well as the economic value of those virtues, was given great impetus by Douglas McGregor's landmark management book, *The Human Side of Enterprise*, published in 1960.[4] McGregor's work can legitimately be seen as the foundation of modern business management theory. All contemporary business texts (which are distinguished, ironically, from economics texts) of any influence reflect the same humanistic values that McGregor recognized and advocated. This is clearly the case in Tom Peters and Robert Waterman's *In Search of Excellence* and in

Kenneth Blanchard's development of the idea of the "one-minute manager" in his book of that title. Significantly, in 1988 Blanchard teamed up with religious and inspirational writer Norman Vincent Peale to write *The Power of Ethical Management.*

Adam Smith's doctrine is at the same time too naive. He believed that, through the invisible hand of competition, motives that he had no trouble labeling as despicable would inevitably lead to the social good. Yet we have seen in our review of business in the United States after the Civil War that such a belief was sadly mistaken. The very same forces of self-interest that Smith was so properly wary of worked to undermine the competition in which he put so many of his hopes. For, as we saw, an economy in which self-interest motives largely predominate does not rest in "stable equilibrium," as certain neoclassical economists in the Smithian tradition tried to postulate. Rather, such an economy takes on the form of something more closely resembling a war, the specific nature of which can be described as a battle for monopoly. John Kenneth Galbraith made a significant contribution to modern economics by advancing the notion that this battle for monopoly is the nature and consequence of unfettered competition.[5] The life and times of John D. Rockefeller and his business enemies and co-conspirators fit Galbraith's account almost to a T.

Smith's cynicism and naiveté account for something very important which so far we have not had occasion to mention. We have described the miseries brought about by the application of the Smithian self-interest doctrine in England during the Industrial Revolution. We have described as well how primitive laissez-faire conditions gave rise to the growth of monopoly and the domination of predatory big business in the post–Civil War American economy. Both of these historical descriptions were tales of rampant selfishness, duplicity, and greed, and of the social evils they brought in their wake. It is necessary for us to be aware of these aspects of Western history. This, however, is not the whole story. If it were, then the whole development of modern economic society would be nothing but a story of unrelieved darkness, grief, and woe. Some, indeed, would claim that this is so, and up to this point the present author may have appeared to be in that company. However, in the face of the evidence, it would be absurd—a displaced romantic flight of fancy—to not recognize the deep good that is also part of the modern economic heritage. Adam Smith may have made a mistake, but he was not all wrong. In very important ways he was quite correct, and we are going to look further at this side of Smith, which we hope will in time assume its proper place in his legacy.

It is well recognized, and a fact that we moderns are justly proud of, that the market-driven economic system has produced an economy of abundance which has raised the standard of living of vast numbers of people and given many others at least the hope that they too could share in this abundance. Along with this abundance, and as part and parcel of it, has come the end of slavery and many other less gross forms of serfdom; the provision of basic political, social, and human rights; and numerous scientific and cultural achievements. So the story of the modern world is not just a story of moral and social decline. It is also a story of moral and social upliftment. Which side of the story is taken to be the predominant one, we leave to the reader to decide according to his or her tastes and preferences (as the economist would put it). What we wish to claim here is that the gains and achievements of the modern economic world have not come about because of the operation of self-interest, but precisely to the extent that self-interest has been moderated by the class of motives that Adam Smith labeled as *benevolence*.

We have referred to the deep mystification that has resulted from Adam Smith's mistake. By this we mean that the penetration of this mistake, this transvaluation, into the roots of our culture has affected our basic modes of perception and understanding. To put it very simply, as a result of this transvaluation we don't see things right. Economics teaches us to attribute the gains and achievements of the modern economic world which we see about us to self-interest. What this book is trying to show is that this is one the deepest and most fundamental misperceptions of our culture; to the contrary, whatever good is in society and economics has comes about through the forces limiting self-interest, as expressed by such words as excellence, values, caring, compassion, honesty, fairness, integrity, and so forth. The extent to which we see social and economic achievements as due to self-interest is the extent to which we have been misled at the perceptual level by Adam Smith's mistake.

The mystification began with Smith himself, which turns out to be a tremendous irony. Smith's intentions were always of the highest order, and whatever he proposed came out of nothing less than a sincere search for the truth which was without a trace of his own self-interest. But where he faltered seems to have been in his cynicism, to which he subtly gave way somewhere between *The Theory of Moral Sentiments* and *The Wealth of Nations*. The historical record shows that Smith became aware toward the end of his life that there was a more serious problem with unmoderated commercial motives than he was aware of earlier. Unfortunately as we shall see, late efforts he made to correct for this were directed toward an ineffective target.

Our understanding of Smith's mystification comes about by once again turning to the feudal system, which lay in the background as Smith began his work. Feudalism justified itself by its paternalism. Feudalism began to develop in the waning days of the Roman Empire, around 300–400 C.E., when the Empire's increasing weakness and the impact of the barbarian invasions had left various groups of scattered communities at the mercy of general hostility and brigandage. In order to seek protection those without defense—who were, of course, in the vast major-ity—grouped around the consuls, dignitaries, and great proprie-tors in the provinces. A natural exchange developed: the weak and unprotected masses declared allegiance and fealty to the majordomo, offering their services as soldiers and farmers; in turn the lord granted protection to the people and provided land and materials for their sustenance.

The word *paternalism* comes, of course, from the Latin word *pater*, which is "father." The old Roman consul and strongman now became a father figure to those gathered around him in fealty—but he was unlike an ordinary father in one significant way. The "children" of this father would never outgrow their dependency on him. The serfs and vassals received protection and succor from the lord, but in turn they were subject to his dominance, his whims, and his potential for exploitation and abuse. Christianity served as both a philosophical framework which encompassed this system and a leavening or softening agent in the form of a sense of conscience.

The paternalistic nature of the English social system was carried through in the mercantalism that Adam Smith, in the spirit of the Enlightenment, set out to attack. The English aristocracy justified their highly privileged position in regard to the yeoman masses by the duties and obligations that they provided for the well-being of those masses—and this was part of the mercantalist's concept of the "wealth of nations." By Smith's time, though, the aristocracy's sense of responsibility to carry out these duties and obligations had worn quite thin, and more and more their privileged position resembled a paltry excuse for exploitation. The actuality of this exploitation, and the Enlightenment outrage at it, are evident throughout Smith's own *Wealth of Nations*.

In *The Wealth of Nations* Smith identifies three economic classes in British society. Ranging from the most privileged and powerful to the least, these are the landlords, the newly rising merchants and tradesmen, and the vast majority of the landless and propertyless, the old serf class. He has nothing good to say about the landlords, and he is also quite critical of the motives and interests of the businessmen—even "pathologically suspicious," according to economist and Smith scholar Nathan Rosenberg.[6] But in regard to the laborer and worker he never utters a harsh or hostile word, and in this sense he is very different from Thomas Malthus and David Ricardo. Smith expresses allegiance to the workers whenever an opportunity presents itself, as the following examples show:

○ Smith proposes a system of tax reform in which taxes should be "distributed more equally upon the whole," and in which luxuries would be taxed at a higher rate than necessities. With such a system, Smith says, "the labouring poor would thus be enabled to live better, to work cheaper, and to send their goods cheaper to market. . . . This increase in the demand for labour, would both increase the numbers and improve the circumstances of the labouring poor."[7]

○ Smith speculates on the conditions of society before wealth accumulation and the "appropriation of land," a harkening back to Rousseau's paradisiacal original condition. He then says, "In this state of things, the whole produce of labour belongs to the labourer." As soon as accumulation of wealth or stock develops, "the whole produce of labour does not always belong to the labourer. He must in most cases share it with the owner of the stock which employs him. . . . As soon as the land of any country has all become private property, the landlords, like all other men, love to reap where they never sowed, and demand a rent even for its natural produce."[8]

○ In discussing the contract established between the employer and the employee, Smith notes that their interests are by no means the same. He says, "The workmen desire to get as much, the masters to give as little as possible. The former are disposed to combine in order to raise, the latter in order to lower the wages of labour. It is not, however, difficult to foresee which of the two parties must, upon all ordinary occasions, have the advantage in the dispute, and force the other into a compliance with their terms. The masters, being fewer in number, can combine much more easily; and the law, besides, authorises, or at least does not prohibit, their combinations, while it prohibits those of the workmen. We have no acts of parliament against combining to lower the price of work; but many against combining to raise it. In all such disputes the masters can hold out much longer."[9]

○ Smith discusses the passage of laws as they differentially favor either employees or employers. He states his position as to which government regulation is justified and which is not: "Whenever the legislature attempts to regulate the differences between masters and their workmen, its counsellors are always the masters. When the regulation, therefore, is in favour of the workmen, it is always just and equitable; but it is sometimes otherwise when in favour of the masters."[10]

○ Smith expresses different sympathies for the producer and the consumer: "It cannot be very difficult to determine who have been the contrivers of this whole mercantile system; not the consumers, we may believe, whose interest has been entirely neglected; but the producers, whose interest has been so carefully attended to; and among this latter class our merchants and manufactures have been by far the principal architects."[11]

When we take *The Wealth of Nations* as a whole, and not just as represented by the self-interest quotes made famous in economics textbooks, it becomes quite clear that the essential thrust of the book is against the avarice of the wealthy and the exploitation of the weak by the strong. Although not too openly advertised by most of Smith's famous followers, even if they knew of it, the most consistent theme running throughout Smith's book, besides that of liberty, is the need to uplift and support the aspiration of the workers and the poor. And these two central themes go hand in hand. It is the uplifting of the laborer that Smith's system of liberty was ultimately meant to accomplish. Therefore, whenever Smith specifically talks about liberty he also talks about justice. So, "liberty and justice for all," as quoted in the American Pledge of Allegiance, may very well be taken almost verbatim as Smith's motto in *The Wealth of Nations*.

Now, in order to achieve these aims, Smith had to somehow

disarm the opposition of their vested interests. The most powerful intellectual and moral defense that the aristocracy had for
retaining control of the economy was their paternalistic obliga-
tion to look after the welfare of the serfs and to guide the
economy and society along what they presumed was its proper
course. But, as we have already noted at that point in history
such justification had worn threadbare; it did not amount to
much more than a hypocritical excuse for self-indulgence and
extravagance. Smith points this out in very biting and passionate
terms and then sets out to make the case that the self-interest of
the aristocracy is no better, and probably worse, for society than
the self-interest of the commoners:

> It is the highest impertinence and presumption, therefore,
> in kings and ministers, to pretend to watch over the econ-
> omy of private people, and to restrain their expense, either
> by sumptuary laws, or by prohibiting the importation of
> foreign luxuries. They are themselves, always, and without
> exception, the greatest spendthrifts on the society. Let them
> look well after their own expence, and they may safely trust
> private people with theirs. If their own extravagance does
> not ruin the state, that of their subjects never will.[12]

Smith also had to counter the age-old paternalistic arrogance
of the elite: the argument that they were of different stock and
different blood, and thus by birth inherently wiser:

> The difference of natural talents in different men is, in
> reality, much less than we are aware of; and the very
> different genius which appears to distinguish men of differ-
> ent professions, when grown up to maturity, is not upon
> many occasions so much the cause, as the effect of the
> division of labor. The difference between the most dissimi-
> lar characters, between a philosopher and a common street
> porter, for example, seems to arise not so much from
> nature, as from habit, custom and education. When they
> came into the world, and for the first six or eight years of
> their existence, they were, perhaps, very much alike, and
> neither their parents nor playfellows could perceive any
> remarkable difference. About that age, or soon after, they
> come to be employed in different occupations. The differ-

ence of talents comes then to be taken notice of, and widens by degrees, till at last the vanity of the philosopher is willing to acknowledge scarce any resemblance.[13]

For his time this was again quite a radical statement, as it came down on the side of nurture and social circumstances, rather than genetic predisposition, in response to the question of what critical factors determine a person's potential. Turning to his favorite canine analogies, Smith goes on to say, "By nature a philosopher is not in genius and disposition half so different from a street porter, as a mastiff is from a greyhound, or a greyhound from a spaniel, or this last from a shepherd's dog." Smith, magnanimously here, uses his own profession of philosopher for the comparison, but the implication against the general equation of social status and superiority of birth is very clear.

Smith was attacking and undercutting the whole theoretical support system for the paternalistic structure of British society. But if the former "masters" were no longer the ones to guide and direct the economic affairs of England, then who or what was? It couldn't be the government, for the simple reason that the British government was the king, his ministers and lords, and the aristocracy that surrounded them—the very masters whose exploitive paternalism was what Smith wanted to get rid of. Parliament was merely their organ of social control. Indeed, government in Smith's day was conceived of very differently from our own. Even Smith himself did not have the right to vote for the members of Parliament; he did not own enough property. Neither did his illustrious friend David Hume. In fact, what we would now call the middle class, of which Smith was a member, did not obtain the right to vote until the Great Reform Bill of 1832. And this privilege was then only extended to the middle class; still excluded were the common working people—the vast majority of the population. This latter group finally won the right to vote in 1867, nearly a hundred years after the publication of *The Wealth of Nations*. In Smith's time the right to vote applied to no more than three or four percent of the adult male population. Seats in Parliament were routinely bought and sold; they were even advertised for sale in newspapers. However, it was considered a breach of privilege for those same newspapers to divulge the contents of parliamentary debates—for doing so the editor could be shipped to the Tower of London.[14]

Clearly, such a government operated as little more than an expression of the self-interests of the oligarchy. In order to argue against the suffocation of the English commoner at the hands of a small elite class, Smith also had to argue against their government. Therefore, admonitions against government and his attack on the ruling oligarchy were two sides of the same coin. We can now see, then, the meaning of the laissez-faire implications that are present in Smith's concept of liberty.

Smith's laissez faire message was not an absolute one, but something he was quite willing to set aside when he found that it conflicted with the public good. For example, in one little-known passage he speaks in favor of laws restricting the freedom of bankers. His justification for such regulation is illuminating:

> Such regulations may, no doubt, be considered as in some respect a violation of natural liberty. But these exertions of the natural liberty of a few individuals which might endanger the security of the whole society, are, and ought to be, restrained by the laws of all governments; of the most free, as well as the most despotical. The obligation of building . . . walls, in order to prevent the communication of fire, is a violation of natural liberty, exactly of the same kind with the regulation of the banking trade which are here proposed.[15]

Nevertheless, Smith could not conceive of government, or new government-created institutions, as agents of the new social order. Yet he was also not an anarchist. As radical as some of his ideas might have been for his day, he very much believed in order and propriety. Then what was left to make for social adhesion? As we have seen, between his first and second books Smith abandoned any reliance upon human benevolence or sympathy. Whereas these sentiments provided the central theme of *The*

Theory of Moral Sentiments, they are not even mentioned in *The Wealth of Nations*, except disparagingly. So, by elimination, Smith is brought to self-interest, which he now has to turn into a positive force. For this he brings in the "invisible hand"—an expression he had in fact first used in *The Theory of Moral Sentiments*, only there in reference to the benevolent hand of a just Providence. In *The Wealth of Nations* both benevolence and Providence are gone, and the hand hangs by itself as some sort of natural principle.

Smith saw that the self-interest of the ruling oligarchy had stifled the pursuit of livelihood of the rest of British society, but he interpreted the latter pursuit as being also motivated by self-interest. In order to remove the oppression of the oligarchy, he made an argument for the equal value of everyone's self-interest. This equality argument, which Smith expresses throughout *The Wealth of Nations*, comes out of Smith's innately democratic spirit. Now we are able to recognize the grand irony and paradox of Smith's book: his argument for self-interest is actually based on an argument *against* self-interest! Let us try to appreciate how this comes about.

Smith's advocacy of self-interest is an argument for the rights and welfare of the common person against the usurpation of those rights by the self-interest of the aristocracy. If nothing else, his thesis has to be taken as a case for the superior social value of one group's self-interests over those of another. But when we take this point and examine it in the light of our understanding of his mistake, we come to a further conclusion: self-interest without benevolence is ultimately destructive. Smith's mystification is that he believed his own self-interest arguments, without realizing that their only value would be to disarm the oppressive self-interest of the "masters." We are thus led to the paradox that Smith's arguments for self-interest are in fact really arguments against self-interest.

One of the reasons this paradox has been so widely missed is that Smith, and economists subsequently, have failed to distinguish between self-interest and the pursuit of livelihood, or enterprise. This failure, so ingrained in our culture, has come down to us as an essentially synonymous equivalence between two concepts which are in fact fundamentally different.

Smith, by an intellectual sleight of hand, but no doubt unwittingly, collapsed two very different principles into one. If we say "I get my dinner through my own self-interest" there is nothing wrong with this statement per se, as long as we understand self-interest as the natural pursuit of one's livelihood. *But*, Smith says something quite different in his butcher-baker statement. There he says, "I get my dinner out of *your* self-interest." Economists, following Smith, have taken these two different kinds of statement as equivalent. My self is nothing different than your self. My self-interest is identical to your self-interest. But this is nonsense. Of course people's self-interests may differ—otherwise the term *self*-interest would have no meaning. So, we can see that I won't get my proper dinner unless *your* self-interest takes into account *my* self-interest. And that is what benevolence and sympathy are all about. Without some measure of benevolence one of us—the weaker of the two—gets exploited (robbed). It is only when we talk about someone pursuing their own self-interest in an abstract way, outside of a specific social context of exchange, that the issue of benevolence does not enter the picture. Then we can talk about self-interest and livelihood as meaning the same thing. But this is precisely what Smith doesn't do in his butcher-baker statement—a statement describing exchange between two *different* persons.

We know that human behavior has a panoply of motives, which range from love to hate. People do things for a multitude of reasons, and unless they are pure saints or pure sinners a complex variety of motives is behind each of their social acts. What Smith did unwittingly was to rule out this variety and arbitrarily state that the only social (i.e., economic) motive is self-interest.

According to his biographer, Smith himself had claimed that *The Theory of Moral Sentiments* was the better of his two books.[16] In the final years of his life he decided to undertake what amounted to a major revision of it—with a third of it newly written and a new part 6 added. This new revision came out in 1790, the year of his death. Historian Lawrence Dickey has compared Smith's first version in 1759 to his 1790 revision and has shown, surprisingly, that the essential thrust of the final revision was to expand the earlier warning against the morally dubious effects of the pursuit of wealth. Dickey writes that despite Smith's "1759 warning about emulating the rich, 'the greater part of men' had chosen to do so by 1790. . . . Toward the end of the 1780's, Smith was becoming increasingly alarmed by what [has been] called 'the depleting moral legacy' of commercial society."[17] But, as history has shown us, if Smith wanted to save the moral legacy he saw eroding in the decade or so following the publication of *The Wealth of Nations*, he put his final efforts into the wrong book.

There is a second interesting feature of this revision that we should note. From it Smith removed the name of the French writer La Rochefoucauld, the author of the sly and morally cynical *Maximes*. In the 1759 edition Smith had associated the work of La Rochefoucauld with that of Bernard de Mandeville (who had written a rather scandalous book in England), referring to both of them as proponents of "licentiousness." On Smith's trip to France after the 1759 publication of *The Theory of Moral Sentiments* he had come to know the La Rochefoucauld family, and over the following years they importuned him that it was unjust to link the name of their famous ancestor with that of the notorious Mandeville. Eventually Smith agreed and removed La Rochefoucauld's name, leaving Mandeville alone to stand as a foremost representative of doctrines that were morally corrupt.[18] The irony here is that it was, as we shall see, the writings of this very same Mandeville that influenced Smith to take the self-interest position he did in *The Wealth of Nations*.

Historically, Adam Smith's mistake became a portal. The forces of the lower half of the continuum of motives are always seeking expression. This is only human nature—or one side of human nature. However, there is another side to human nature, and that is the top side, or the higher motives. It is from this source and direction that human beings derive their dignity and their nobility, and the ability to act with virtue. It is this part of human nature that serves to restrain the destructive propensities of the lower part. With his doctrine of self-interest in *The Wealth of Nations* Adam Smith provided a portal in the walls of respectable thought for the forces of the lower motives to come pouring through, now justified totally within themselves and seen as good.

6

NOISE IN THE WORLD

One of the Latin root meanings of the word *virtue* is "strength," relating it to the word *virile*. Strength, true strength, enables the higher self to overrule the lower. Plato uses the term *passion* to apply only to the lower end of the continuum of motives, calling that which is at the upper end *Reason*. The task, as Plato expresses it, is for Reason to restrain the passions. In this case Reason is not just something intellectual, without connection to feeling, but it is the thinking side of what we know of as love. For Plato then, Reason and love are intrinsically bound up with one another. Likewise, the passions are the self-centered emotions which use the brain as a calculating mechanism to rationalize, to plan and plot, in order to obtain the objects of desire.

When reason, or love, cannot restrain the passions, immorality and injury to others ensue. Smith has a perfect and classical rendition of this in *The Theory of Moral Sentiments*:

> All the members of human society stand in need of each other's assistance, and are likewise exposed to mutual injuries. Where the necessary assistance is reciprocally afforded from love, from gratitude, from friendship, and esteem, the society flourishes and is happy. All the different members of it are bound together by the agreeable bands of love and affection. . . . Society, however, cannot subsist among those who are at all times ready to hurt and injure one another. The moment that injury begins, the moment that mutual resentment and animosity takes place, all the bands of it are broken asunder.[1]

By the time of the publication of *The Wealth of Nations* a fateful change had occurred—one that allowed the forces of the lower self to gain respectability, shielded as they were from the bright illumination of truth by the walls of the doctrine that Smith now proposed. Smith had advised government to put up "fire walls" to protect society from the destructive self-interest of a few—the bankers in that case. But we have come to see that Smith's own self-interest doctrine ironically served to remove all moral fire walls, not only between government and the people, but between people and their environment, and between person and person. This is not the first time in history that a respected and accepted doctrine contained an implicit counsel for corruption, but it is probably the most significant and far-reaching occurrence of this that we know of. Indeed, we could say that Smith's doctrine has imprinted its peculiar stamp upon the mentality and morality of the modern world.

We are in a good position to observe through the lens of self-interest how this moral breach of the modern world developed with Smith's doctrine as the portal. We will see how the weight of self-interest bore down on Smith, the moral philosopher, and made an opening through him, ever so subtle and slight, but just enough so that selfishness could become sanctioned in the name of science and economics. Knowing what we know about Smith, in this we find great tragedy.

The existence of selfishness and deceit go back to the mythical beginnings of our culture, to Adam and Eve. But what we want to see is how these human tendencies made their impact on modern thought, with economics as their passageway into social acceptability. We fortunately don't have to go back to the expulsion from the Garden of Eden to do this; but the realm of religion gives us the right guide as to where to look.

There may have been many proponents of selfishness before Adam Smith, but the power of his doctrine lay in its respectability and acceptability. After all, *The Wealth of Nations* is not only a great work, but, as we have already seen, in many important respects it is also a *good* work. Traditionally, though, the most respectable members of society are not its philosophers, nor its academics, but its religious figures, and it is to the Church that we must look for the beginning of the moral breach of the modern world.

There is no greater impetus to immorality than when the foremost expositors of morality, the religious authorities, themselves betray the morality they speak of. It is in hypocrisy that the great opening to immorality appears, and there are no more damaging hypocrisies than the hypocrisies of religion. When Christianity betrayed its own values, it lost its hold upon society. Then the golden age of the High Middle Ages (approximately 1000–1300) gave way to the secular "moralities" of social science and economics—and the birth of the modern world with all its wealth and "illth."

The seed of this betrayal was planted well before the High Middle Ages, we could perhaps date it very precisely to the year 751. It was in that year, in France, that the son of Charles Martel sought a council with Pope Zacharias. Members of the Martel family had become major powers in the French kingdom, and Charles's son, called Pepin the Short, had the title of Mayor of the Palace. The Frankish king at the time was Childeric III, who was a rather weak figure. Pepin had aspirations for even greater state power. So he approached the Pope, God's regent on earth, with a question about power, and particularly about who should wield it. The Pope is reported to have answered Pepin that "power in the State belonged to him who was *actually* possessed of it." Pepin got the message, and he had Childeric banished to a monastery, which somehow was fitting. Shortly thereafter, Pepin himself was crowned *Rex Dei Gratia*, "King by the Grace of God." With this act of investiture the words *Dei Gratia* entered the kingly coronation service for the first time; it took almost one thousand years to get them out again. In return for its advice and good graces certain parcels of captured land were donated to the Church by the Frankish kingdom.[2]

This was the beginning of the founding of the papal state, and, according to the *New Columbia Encyclopedia*, with this the pope became "a powerful lay Prince as well as an ecclesiastical ruler." The encyclopedia goes on to say:

> This intermingling was a determining condition in the struggle between Church and State that was a main theme in the history of the West in the Middle Ages. Strong lay Princes attempted to direct the Church just as the Pope tried to establish secular as well as spiritual supremacy over the rulers. [Peppin's son, in turn, was Charlemagne, who was crowned King by Pope Leo III, and he reinstigated the Kingdom of the Holy Roman Empire.] From there the Papacy reached a high point of corruption in the 10th Century when the Holy See was cynically bought and sold.[3]

We can see here how a nexus of power and money based on self-interest began to be established. A battle for religious dominance between France and Rome slowly ensued until the Great Schism of 1378–1417, when rival popes simultaneously claimed the papacy in Rome and Avignon.

The papal court made Rome a brilliant Renaissance capital. However, the *New Columbia Encyclopedia* goes on to note that "the Renaissance popes were little distinguished from other princes in the extravagance and immorality of the courts." This state of affairs provided the impetus for the Protestant Reformation, and in 1517 Martin Luther, a Catholic priest, nailed his ninety-five Theses of reform to the church door in Wittenberg, Germany:

> Luther's action was not as yet a revolt against the Church but a movement for reform within. It was, however, much more than an objection to the money-grabbing and secular policies of the clergy. Luther had already become convinced that in certain matters of doctrine the purity of the ancient church had been perverted by self-seeking popes and clergy.[4]

In Renaissance Italy, Niccolo Machiavelli, powerful advisor to princes, asserted that the state is not an instrument for achieving the Good as defined by Aristotle or Christian theology. Instead, he claimed, it is a *force*, neutral or amoral, and like any force or power it can be used for the purposes of its possessor or ruler. Machiavelli sought to describe the "way it is," rather than the way it ought to be, and he counseled that a wise prince would do the same:

> It appears to me more proper to go to the real truth of the matter than to its imagination. . . . For how we live is so far removed from how we ought to live, that he who abandons what is done for what ought to be done, will rather learn to bring about his own ruin than his preservation. A man who wishes to make a profession of goodness in everything must necessarily come to grief among so many who are not good. Therefore it is necessary for a prince, who wishes to maintain himself, to learn how not to be good, and to use this knowledge and not use it, according to the necessity of the case. . . . For if one considers well, it will be found that some things which seem virtues would, if followed, lead to one's ruin, and some others which appear vices result in one's greater security and wellbeing.[5]

Here we see the early appearance of transvaluation, preceding Adam Smith by over two hundred years. In his explicitness Machiavelli is certainly controversial in a way that Smith is not, but, despite his controversial status, Machiavelli is credited by some historians with having "emancipated" the state from religion.[6] He is also considered to be the founder of modern political science, just as Smith is the founder of economics. Similarly, Machiavelli, like Smith, is appreciated as a scientist. It is perhaps of greater significance in terms of our attempt to understand the role of self-interest in the modern mind that many twentieth-century commentators on Machiavelli hold that he was "the first modern man."[7]

What Machiavelli was for Italy, Thomas Hobbes was for England. As a matter of fact, in 1642 Thomas Browne predicted such an appearance: "Every country hath its Machiavel." Like Machiavelli, Hobbes was considered a scientist, and he spent some of the early years of his life in the company of Descartes, Gassendi, and others; he even made a respectful pilgrimage to Galileo. Demonstrating the influence of Galileo's thought,

Hobbes's philosophy sees the person as only "a body," and particularly, "a body in motion." In chapter 12 of his most well-known work, *Leviathan*, he speaks of the self-interest of the Church in a way that we should find most telling: "For who is there that does not see to whose benefit it is . . . that a king, as Childeric of France, may be deposed by a pope, as Pope Zachary, for no cause, and his kingdom given to one of his subjects."[8]

In *Leviathan*'s famous chapter 13, Hobbes states that when men exist in a natural condition, "without a common power to keep them all in awe," they resort to a state of "war of all against all," and in this condition the life of man is "solitary, poor, nasty, brutish, and short."[9]

The answer for Hobbes lies in the absolute power of the state, grounded not in divine justification but in a "contract" with its citizenry. In this contract the people surrender their natural liberty and the unlimited pursuit of their desires to the sovereign in return for social control and peace. We can see here a late expression of the traditional feudal arrangement, now expressed as *contract* rather than as *divine sanction*.

For Hobbes, the state that sheds the Christian framework needs to be absolute, while the status and dignity of the individual does not. Then what is the value and worth of a man? Hobbes asks rhetorically. His answer: "The value and worth of a man is, as of all other things, his price—that is to say, so much as would be given for the price of his power—and therefore is not absolute but a thing dependent on the need and judgement of another."[10] Here we find the forerunner of Smith's later conception that labor is a commodity, to be bought and sold on the open market like any other commodity. As we shall see, Thomas Malthus and David Ricardo were to make much of this.

In a time of great civil wars, the breaking up of the institutional unity of Christianity, and the princely lust for power, the Machiavelli-Hobbesian conception had widespread appeal as an accurate description of the nature of mankind and society. This was certainly no less so in France than in Renaissance Italy and England. And in France this conception was to achieve even more far-reaching philosophical impact. The French story, like that of Machiavelli in Italy and Hobbes in England, revolves around the question of authority and power. It begins in the later 1600s, when the French nobility and the parliamentary body attempted to limit the power of the king. Acting in concert with the nobles were large segments of the French Protestant population—the Huguenots—who were also fighting to obtain religious tolerance from the Catholic monarchy. A series of wars known as the Fronde ensued. The word *fronde* came from a children's game played with slingshots; the slingshots were used to hurl stones at the windows of the palace of Cardinal Mazarin, minister to King Louis XIV. After some early victories, or at least truces, the forces of the Fronde eventually collapsed. The *Encyclopaedia Britannica* explains the effect:

> By revealing the selfish interests of the nobility and the Parliament and their inability to offer effective leadership, the Fronde lost for these groups a role as a counterbalance to the king. It was the last serious challenge to the supremacy of the monarchy until the revolution of 1789.[11]

The failure of the Fronde, as contrasted with the success of the dissidents against the Crown in England, may explain why France had to go through its bloody revolution while England did not.

In the wake of the Fronde's collapse there was widespread disillusionment and pessimism among the French intellectuals, many of whom were against the absolutism and intolerance of the king. They became increasingly interested in the writings of Cornelis Jansen, a Catholic theologian, whose major work was published four years after his death, in 1642. Jansen pointed to the depravity of man under original sin and taught an extreme form of predestination, in which every person's fate is predetermined by God's grace alone, quite independent of one's good actions. Jansenism, as this new religious philosophy came to be called, thus implied a sharp separation between this earthly life and the spiritual world, with each having very little bearing on the other. It spoke of the weakness of reason, the strength of the passions, and particularly the power of pride and vanity. It was very effective in unmasking supposedly virtuous action and finding the real motivation for such action in self-love. It saw vanity everywhere. It is quite interesting and important to recognize that these beliefs, though coming out of a tradition of religious faith, were almost totally consistent with the movement in France of scepticism toward religious belief, as exemplified by such figures as Montaigne and La Rochefoucauld. So Jansenism, originally formulated to support faith through a position of extreme antiworldliness, became compatible with religious scepticism, the latter differing from the former mainly by refusing to make a leap of faith.[12]

These two trends—Jansenism and religious scepticism—came together in French philosopher and teacher Pierre Bayle. In Bayle's *Historical and Critical Dictionary*, religious ideas, particularly those of Christian rationality, are subjected to a withering attack from the standpoint of a sceptical psychological account of people's motives. Bayles's thinking was frequently compared to that of Hobbes, particularly in its materialism and its emphasis on the predominance of the ego in human affairs. Although Bayle denied he was an atheist, his work is seen as one of the early entries in the line of thought that was to eventually culminate in the materialism and atheism of the Franch encyclopedists in the 1750s.

Bayle was forced to flee France, not so much for his ideas, but because he was a Protestant. He settled in Rotterdam, where he obtained a teaching appointment and became an important influence on a young Dutch student, Bernard de Mandeville. Mandeville later emigrated to England, where he did so well in his attempt to master the new tongue that he published in English a text of doggerel verse which was first called "The Grumbling Hive" and later, in 1714, *The Fable of the Bees*. The text was a huge success, and, like Bayle's work, it was also very controversial. In it Mandeville presents the thinly veiled story of a beehive as a model for English society and England itself. In the hive, the supplying of each member's lusts and vanities makes the society thrive:

> Vast numbers thronged the fruitful hive;
> Yet those vast numbers made 'em thrive;
> Millions endeavouring to supply
> Each other's lust and vanity.
> . . . .
> Thus every part was full of vice,
> Yet the whole mass a paradise.[13]

In the poem the moralists complain about all this sinfulness; finally heaven, moved by their complaints, turns "all the knaves honest" and brings the supposed benefits of virtue upon them. But these benefits turn out to be dubious since the presence of virtue removes the motivation and the means by which all their luxuries and comforts came to be. As result, the economy of the hive runs down and its stock of wealth diminishes. In his conclusion to the poem Mandeville calls on the moralists to stop complaining:

> Then leave compaints; fools only strive
> to make a Great an honest hive.
> To enjoy the world's conveniences,
> Be famed in war, yet live in Ease,
> without great vices, is a vain
> Utopia seated in the Brain.[14]

Mandeville, like the Jansenists, held that since virtue does not lie in this world, it can't be virtue that keeps society together— although Mandeville might have doubted that virtue lay anywhere. The social cement must be something else, and this something else is made up of pride, vanity, and self-love. From these comes the ego's need to secure esteem for itself, and this is what enables the individual to accommodate to others. Historian Thomas Horne notes, "It is this aspect of Jansenism—its refusal to see virtue as the cement holding society together—which constitutes its contribution to social thought, and which is most important to the consideration of the tradition out of which Mandeville emerged."[15] Mandeville summarized his point of

view in a short pithy phrase which became the epigraph to his
whole poem: "Private vice makes public virtue."

We can get a further flavor of Mandeville's thinking by looking
at the position he took in relation to some of the social issues of
his day. He opposed the "charity schools" that were set up to
educate the children of the poor:

> The economic well-being of the nation depends on the
> presence of a large number of men who are content to
> labor hard all day long. Because men are naturally lazy
> they will not work unless forced by necessity to do so. The
> education of the poor threatens to rob the nation of their
> productivity. . . . Every hour those poor people spend at
> their books is so much time lost to the society. Going to
> school in comparison to working is idleness.[16]

Mandeville believed that the basis of English wealth lay in
there being "a multitude of laborious poor." Thus labor would
be cheap, and thus England would "infallibly out-sell [her]
neighbours." Therefore, he advises "a wise legislature [to] culti-
vate the breed of them with all imaginable care." We can see in
these beliefs that Mandeville essentially forecasts the major principles of political economics.

Mandeville had quite a number of critics, particularly among
the moralists and among those in the spiritually inspired reform
traditions in British society (such as the Clapham Evangelicals,
discussed earlier). In 1724 John Dennis expressed pointedly the
outrage that Mandeville's work engendered among the English
moralists and reformers: "There have indeed been several cham-
pions" in the past, he said, for infidelity, folly, and the thousand
whimsies and errors that the human being is subject to, "but a
champion for vice and luxury, a serious, a cool, a deliberate
champion, that is a creature entirely new, and has never been
heard of before in any nation, or in any age of the world."[17]
Another of Mandeville's critics is Francis Hutcheson, Smith's
teacher at Glasgow, whom Smith succeeded in the chair of moral
philosophy.

Hutcheson is known in history as a champion of the Enlightenment conception of liberty and a proponent of the idea that the human being has an inherent "moral sense." In his *Theory of Moral Sentiments*, Smith attempts to show that his idea of the impartial spectator is both a different concept than Hutcheson's moral sense and a superior explanation of morality. Whether he succeeds in this attempt is questionable, and the differentiation of his theory from the admittedly close theory of Hutcheson is one of the least convincing parts of Smith's book.

Hutcheson, like Smith in his first book, was also a severe critic of Mandeville, and he didn't waver in this regard. He also had little trouble keeping apart his espousal of liberty from Mandeville's espousal of self-interest.

Hutcheson put forth an altogether different conception of nature than that imagined by Hobbes, Mandeville, and their "state of nature" tradition. According to Hutcheson, "the state of nature is that of peace and good will, of innocence and beneficence, and not of violence, war and rapine."[18] In describing the natural state Hutcheson uses the image of the child in the family, rather than that of animals in the jungle, as was the case in the Hobbesian tradition. Since the word *nature* comes from the Latin word for *birth* (*nature* as in *nativity*), there is certainly strong semantic justification for this sense of what is natural.

This difference in starting points for the conception of nature and what is natural was exactly what Mandeville noted when he wrote critiques of the English social philosopher Lord Shaftsbury. Shaftsbury had also proposed that the family was the origin of a natural affection for others and the basis for society; society has its first manifestation in the family and then spreads out to include relatives, the extended family, neighbors, and then society in general. Mandeville argued against this in his 1723 essay "Search into the Nature of Society."[19] He said that the first step toward society was taken in response to the threat posed by wild animals, and thus the need for security, as Hobbes also claimed, was the basis of society.

We can see that these two alternative conceptions very neatly split into a love and fear dichotomy. For Shaftsbury, and then for

Hutcheson, the basis of society is love, as first manifested by the child in the family, while for Hobbes and then Mandeville the basis is fear, as expressed in the need for protection against both wild animals and other people (the "wild animal" in human nature).

Arguing against Mandeville's economics, Hutcheson took the position that wealth need not be associated with vice, and that virtue and commercial activity may go hand in hand. This book, *Adam Smith's Mistake*, states the case even more strongly: virtue, of at least some kind, is actually necessary for the successful functioning of commercial society.

Hutcheson was aware that for liberty to lead to the public good it could not be interpreted as license, and that there must be checks on its excess: "We are never to put in the balance with the liberty or safety of a people, the gratifying the vain ambition, luxury, or avarice of a few. It may therefore often be just to prevent by agrarian law such vast wealth coming into a few hands, that a cabal of them might endanger the state."[20] In this statement, Hutcheson seems to have anticipated, by some 150 years, John Sherman's senate speech on behalf of antitrust.

Hutcheson is quite humorous in his attempts to account for what he sees as the extremity and countermorality of Mandeville's thought. He speculates that Mandeville "has probably been struck with some old fanatic sermon upon self-denial in his youth, and can never get it out of his head since."[21] He guessed that Mandeville had been fighting that fanatic sermon ever thereafter. And perhaps to speculate in Mandeville's favor, he had also been fighting in his own perverse way the hypocrisy he had found there.

Smith's first book, *The Theory of Moral Sentiments*, is in the great tradition of moral philosophy and certainly would be at great odds with Mandeville's Jansenist thesis that all or most of what we know of as morality is only self-interest in disguise. Smith's own theory of moral sentiments states that man can be moral, and indeed is moral, because he has the capacity to view the actions of others as well as of himself from the perspective of an "impartial spectator," rather than merely from the vantage point of his own interest. Smith also refers to this capacity as an "equitable judge," and he locates its place as "within the breast," clearly associating it with the heart.[22] This capacity to view oneself and others from a position that is fair and impartial is what makes for morality, and it is what makes a person capable of rising above self-interest. Smith comes very close to describing a polar self in the following explanation: "I divide myself, as it were, into two persons; and that I, the examiner and judge, represent a different character from that other I, the person whose conduct is examined into and judged of."[23]

Throughout his book Smith consistently denies the self-love thesis proposed by Mandeville and others. He could hardly be any more explicit about it than this: "Sympathy, however, cannot in any sense, be regarded as a selfish principle."[24] Contemporary economists and commentators on Smith, however, often misunderstand and misstate Smith's theory of moral sentiments, interpreting it as a self-interest conception of morality. So, for example, we find one economics textbook referring to *The Theory of Moral Sentiments* this way:

> Using ideas developed in his lectures at Glasgow, he wrote that two instincts—the ability to feel sympathy and the desire to be praised—had been given to man in order to increase his self-love. According to Smith, man controlled his own actions, and felt sympathy for others, not out of any inherent love of mankind, but rather to satisfy the need to be wanted and cared for. The end result was that, in trying to gratify himself, man unwittingly benefited society.[25]

Smith *could* have written such a book just after *The Wealth of Nations*, but he certainly didn't write it before then. And as Lawrence Dickey indicated when comparing the first edition of *The Theory of Moral Sentiments* to the last edition, Smith in the final years of his life had evidently come to recognize that "the virtuousness of prudent and frugal [economic] men could no longer be taken for granted."[26]

Smith deals with Mandeville near the end of his book, when he discusses "licentious systems." Here Smith says that all traditional systems of morality rest on the belief that there is a real and essential distinction between vice and virtue—the dual self that we have just referred to. This distinction "encourages the best and most laudable habits of the human mind." A licentious system, such as that of Dr. Mandeville, says Smith, asserts that such a distinction is false, "a mere cheat and imposition upon mankind." In it an individual need not attempt restraint and control of the lower passions because they are not really lower after all. In that way Mandeville's system gives "license." Smith regards Mandeville's ideas as "wholly pernicious," and "in almost every respect erroneous." In dispensing with Mandeville, however, Smith does acknowledge the following: "But how destructive soever this system may appear, it could never have imposed upon so great a number of persons nor have occasioned so general an alarm among those who are the friends of better principles had it not in some respect bordered on the truth." But for Smith this truth, at least in his first book, is just a bit of "sophistry" by which Mandeville "establishes his favourite conclusion that private vices are public benefits." So Smith is unperturbed: "Such is the system of Dr. Mandeville, which once made so much noise in the world."[27]

The phrase, "noise in the world" is characteristic and a favorite of Smith. It refers both to the prevalence of Mandeville's concepts in the social thought of the day and to Smith's repugnance toward these ideas when he was writing *The Theory of Moral Sentiments*, particularly the last revision. Such concepts are the "noise" of a morally confused society. Smith also uses this expression when he discusses Hobbes. He begins by saying that "according to Mr. Hobbes and many of his followers, man is driven to take refuge in society, not by any natural love which he bears to his own kind, but because without the assistance of others, he is incapable of subsisting with ease or safety." One of Hobbes's "followers" whom Smith specifically has in mind, is, of course, Mandeville. Smith concludes his discussion of Hobbes this way: "That whole account of human nature, however, which deduces all sentiments and affections from self-love, which has made so much noise in the world . . . seems to me to have arisen from some confused misapprehension of the system of sympathy."[28]

But this "noise in the world" was eventually to influence Smith himself. In the Modern Library edition of *The Wealth of Nations*, editor Edwin Cannan, notes the following in regard to the change in Smith between the two books: "We can scarcely fail to suspect that it was Mandeville who first made him realize that 'it is not from the benevolence of the butcher, the brewer or the baker that we expect our dinner, but from their regard to their own interest.' "[29] Cannan is an economist and, of course, sees the influence of Mandeville on Smith as a "realization" rather than a mistake. Cannan goes on to say that Smith put the doggerel verse of Mandeville "into prose and to this added something from the Hutcheson love of liberty when he propounded what is really the text of the polemical portion of *The Wealth of Nations*."

When Smith wrote *The Wealth of Nations* he did not follow in the footsteps of his mentor, Hutcheson, in his conception of what is "natural." Hutcheson had equated the natural state with the climate of love that surrounds the human infant. Hutcheson had perceived self-interest in his setting to be unnatural; a transition from love to self-interest in human relations must therefore be from the natural to the less natural. For Hutcheson, not only is benevolence natural, but it is one of those natural qualities which uniquely defines the human species, just as flight uniquely defines birds. All animals eat, but only birds fly. We don't say that it is only in eating that birds are natural; they are natural in their flying as well, but they are uniquely birds in the use of their wings. Similarly, we humans are self-interested like all species. This self-interest manifests in the instinct for survival. But we are uniquely human in our capacity for moral sentiments.

Smith, however, begins *The Wealth of Nations* by comparing humans to animals. And whereas Hutcheson saw benevolence as a unique and defining quality of the human species, Smith concludes that humans are unique in their capacity to "truck, barter, and exchange." From this odd idea of the uniquely human he then proceeds to derive the basis for the division of labor. This idea is "odd" because it runs counter to most of the findings of anthropological research, which, on the contrary, show that in the case of traditional and native peoples, trading exists only on the margin of their social activity.[30] In fact, it was precisely the economic revolution of which Smith was both a chronicler and an advocate that moved this peripheral activity to the center of society. In so doing it created a society that was intrinsically different, for better or worse, than any that had existed before.

In his conception of the division of labor, Smith once again ignored what Hutcheson had to offer, opting instead for Mandeville's version. Hutcheson had also referred to a specialization of labor, but he saw it as coming not out of a trading instinct, but out of a human capacity for social organization. He saw trading as only the means by which human beings' unique capacity for rationality and social organization is implemented: "One grows expert in tillage, another in pasture and breeding cattle, a third in masonry, a fourth in the chase, a fifth in iron-works, a sixth in the arts of the loom, and so on throughout the rest. Thus all are supplied by means of barter with the works of complete artists."[31] Without social organization "scarce any one could be dextrous and skillful in any one sort of labour." Hutcheson concludes:

> Again, some works of the highest use to multitudes can be effectually executed by the joint labours of many, which the separate labours of the same number could never have executed. The joint force of many can repel dangers arising from savage beasts or bands of robbers which might have been fatal to many individuals were they separately to encounter them. The joint labours of twenty men will cultivate forests or drain marshes, for farms to each one, and provide houses for habitation and inclosures for their flocks, much sooner than the separate labours of the same number. By concert and alternate relief they can keep a

perpetual watch, which without concert they could not accomplish.

As we know, in *The Wealth of Nations* Smith describes this phenomenon as "the division of labour." Up until that time this phrase was not a familiar one. In *The Fable of the Bees*, however, Mandeville talks of men "learning to divide and subdivide their labor" and refers to the same notion in the index to his book as "labor, the usefulness of dividing and subdividing it."[32] It is from here, Edwin Cannan believes, that Smith probably derived his concept of the "division of labor."

In following Mandeville in this regard, Smith was led into a contradiction that was a perfect forecast of one of the major human problems of the industrial age. As is well known, Smith began his whole account of how wealth is created, and thus a nation benefited, with the lauded principle of the division of labor. However, in a later place in the book he had this dolorous observation about the effects on the worker of this same division of labor:

> The man whose whole life is spent in performing a few simple operations . . . generally becomes as stupid and ignorant as it is possible for a human being to become. The torpor of his mind renders him, not only incapable of relishing or bearing a part in any rational conversation, but of conceiving any generous, noble, or tender sentiments, and consequently of forming any just judgment concerning many even of the ordinary duties of private life. Of the great and extensive interests of the country he is altogether incapable of judging.[33]

In the Smith of *The Wealth of Nations* we can see, then, a conflict between two very different influences—Hutcheson and Mandeville. Smith brings forth both of these voices in his own attempt at synthesis in his book. But the tragedy is that in history's judgment it is the Mandeville voice that is Smith's greater contribution. And so, for example, the atomization of work has been accepted into the modern world as a highly beneficial principle.

Yet, in *The Theory of Moral Sentiments*, Smith himself labels Mandeville's voice as a "noise." So there is a profound and sad irony in the legacy Smith has bequeathed us. Smith had listened to Mandeville's noise in the world and indeed has himself become a contributor to it, whether in the principle of the division of labor or in the more central theme of self-interest. The significance of this is stated by another Smith scholar, Louis Dumont:

> It is widely admitted that the central theme of Adam Smith, the idea that self-love works for the common good, comes from Mandeville. . . . We are thus sent back from Adam Smith to Mandeville for the origin of the key assumption of *The Wealth of Nations*, and this is more than a minute point of literary history, for, as we are going to see, the problem of the relation between economics and morality was acutely—indeed, explosively—posed by Mandeville at the beginning of the century.[34]

7

TALES OF ENTERPRISE AND AVARICE

The implications of Adam Smith's mistake and the moral breach it allowed in both social thought and economic practice are perhaps best illustrated through a few anecdotes.

There is a marvelous little tale that serves to convey the difference between the medieval and modern mind, particularly as it concerns matters economic.[1] Sometime during the late and waning days of the Middle Ages, two merchants and a monk were traveling together. The monk was just returning from a pilgrimage to Rome. As was the style then, before the days of media and headphones, people talked to each other while traveling; they would tell of where they had been and where they were going. The merchants in question, being men of the world, had much to tell, and they entertained both themselves and the monk with stories of wares they had bought and sold, and their various exploits. The monk, feeling somewhat badly that he didn't have much to offer in the way of stories, thought to show the two congenial merchants the silver chalice he had purchased in Rome to bring back to his cathedral. So he withdrew this lovely vessel from his chamois sack and showed it to them.

He was pleased when they were duly impressed, as he had been, with its simple elegance and beauty. Being merchants, they quickly wondered what it had cost him and, accustomed to being bold in such matters, they asked him the price. When the monk told them, they were amazed: he had paid far less for it than it was worth. Laughingly, they gave the monk a knowing poke in the ribs and congratulated this unworldly soul for driving a far better bargain than they could have. They were surprised, however, when the monk did not seem to take pleasure or satisfaction in their congratulations. Instead, he became rather morose and took to silently pondering. The mood of levity being thus dimmed, the merchants soon asked the monk what was wrong. The monk said, "This is terrible, no good. I must now turn around and proceed back to Rome to try to find the seller and give him a fair price." The merchants, at the very least, must have rolled their eyes.

The modern economist, of course, would side with the merchants. But not only that. The economist would also make the case that what the monk wanted to do would actually be socially damaging and even immoral. By wanting to pay more for the vessel than he needed to, the monk was going against "market efficiency." According to the economist, the market alone is the best determiner of fairness, and any attempt to moderate the market by such external considerations as fairness or justice only interferes with its perfect ability to allocate resources. Economists spend a lot of time, with a lot of mathematics, to show that this is the case.

Nevertheless, the monk's story calls forth a very fundamental question for us: Should we try to be fair in our business dealings, or should we try to get away with as much as we can, even while we are careful to stay within the law? Which attitude would make for a better society? If it is the former, then we have been misled by economic teaching for a long time.

At least as early as the thirteenth century, in the time of Thomas Aquinas, the matter of business enterprise was a topic of attention. Since all philosophers in those days were also theologians, they were naturally interested in the distinction between enterprise and avarice. Aquinas himself came to the conclusion that the "trader" was exonerated if he sought gain "not as an end, but as the wages of his labor."[2] Thus, for Aquinas, even though trading was not a widespread vocation and was perhaps regarded with a certain dubiousness, it was still seen as a legitimate and useful social function, and as such merited just recompense. But it merited no more than that. In other words, enterprising activity was seen as one vocation, like any other. It was not enterprise itself that was a sin, but money-seeking. The modern mind has trouble understanding this distinction, because it does not know why anyone would get involved in enterprise for any reason but to make money.

The term *avarice* has largely been replaced today by the word *greed*. And greed still arises periodically as an issue of serious social concern. In particular, this issue has arisen at the conclusion of the 1980s, as we have seen. There were the huge fees that investment bankers have drawn from promoting and facilitating such megadeals as the twenty-billion-dollar battle to buy RJR Nabisco; various high-money-stakes scandals, such as billionaire hotel magnates Leona and Harry Helmsley's trial for tax evasion; and the insider trading and junk bond scandals involving fabulously wealthy Wall Street traders and arbitragers. A *New York Times* article called the general reaction to this panoply of events "a growing backlash against greed."[3]

Dennis Levine, one of the major insider traders who was indicted and arrested, tells how as a college student he had listened attentively as his favorite business professor at Bernard Baruch College literally preached the sermon "Greed is a nice religion"—a perfect reversal of medieval philosophy. The professor had explained why this is the case: "If you are really greedy, you are going to keep your shoes polished, you won't run around on your wife or get drunk. You will do whatever it takes to maximize your lifetime income, and that doesn't leave time for messing up."[4] Well, it seems that Mr. Levine's greed allowed him plenty of time for "messing up."

Although society in general may be concerned about greed, not even the word, let alone the moral concern, exists in the vocabulary of economic theory. In economics, greed is essentially a nonword. Since financial self-interest is good, and the more of that good the better, the idea of *too much* economic self-interest has no meaning in economics.

Now let us turn to another instance from our own time—the

case of a young civil engineer with an interest in good bridge design. He gets a chance in the firm he works for to bid for his first municipal bridge. His firm and he win the bid, and he begins building the bridge. Toward the last quarter or so of the project, the engineer realizes that he has bid too low and that his company is not going to make any money on the project. He is fearful that they could even lose money. The engineer is chagrined, even though the bridge he is building is obviously very well designed and beautiful.

A senior engineer in the firm tells him: "You've made a textbook mistake. The business of business is to make money. You've forgotten that principle, and in your eagerness to get this project you underestimated the costs. It should never have been your job to estimate the costs. You should have just done the design, and someone who was not committed to the project should have been primarily responsible for estimating the costs."

Indeed, the senior engineer's point about separating the task of designing the bridge from that of estimating the costs is a good one. But it is actually a "textbook mistake"—and finds its way into this book as such—for another reason. Aquinas would say that the *senior* engineer has made a deadly mistake, and he would hope that the young engineer wouldn't pick up his view. The business of business is not to make money. The business of business is service. However, if a business doesn't make enough money it won't exist, and thus won't be able to provide its service. There are two values involved, and they need to be kept in the right order. One is service, and the second is making money. If the second value dominates, then the first value vanishes, so that in time the second value won't exist either. We see a good example of this in the increasing propensity of American businesses to emphasize immediate and short-term profits at the expense of long-term considerations, such as investment. This shortsightedness is damaging American industry in its competition with Japanese and other foreign industry, who have not, at least as yet, allowed the motive of money-making to drive them to a similar short-run orientation. The economically minded may want to solve this by trying to convince the Japanese to also go for the immediate bottom line. This would be similar to trying, as we have done, to convince them to increase their military expenditures, despite their post–World War II commitment to pacifisim. The general principle here is that of the proper ordering of values. This is also to say that not all values are economic values, and this is the case in or out of the business world.

Let us look at another example of this same general principle, but in quite a different context. A father tells his junior-high son that the purpose of playing basketball is to have fun. The team coach, however, emphasizes that he believes in the "Lombardi philosophy": winning isn't the important thing, it's the only thing. He justifies such an aggressive attitude at junior high school level by saying that such a philosophy develops the best qualities in players.

The boy is confused. What his father says seems quite different from what the coach says. Now why do I believe his father is right? Having fun does not stand in opposition to winning. In fact, it is fun to win, and nobody likes to lose. However, if winning becomes everything, then not only does the game not become fun, but even winning itself loses its joy. And then what's the point?

From an economic perspective we can see that all remunerative activities can be defined as business or industry activities. An example of the latter is the medical or health industry. Is it fair, then, to single out *business* per se as somehow grubby and morally inferior to other lines of work? If we respect business then the answer must be no. And if we don't respect business the economic argument makes no difference.

Let us take a closer look at the health industry. Should the doctor's purpose be to cure patients or to make money? Now, if she is a good doctor, we might expect she'll be making money. But this money will be a *consequence* of her good work as a doctor, and not its object. Let us now say that this doctor becomes increasingly interested in money. What we are talking about is a shift in motivation. As her attention and interests focus increasingly on making money they focus less and less on medicine. Too many patients have experienced the detrimental effects on their medical care of this kind of shift, at the level of both the individual doctor and the health care system as a whole.

Economics would want to say that there is no difference between the two motives, that the pursuit of wealth in a competitive economy must lead to effective delivery of goods and services. This is a generalized version of the business school professor's thesis that greed is a good religion. The extension of this thesis in the case of the health industry would be that greed is good medicine. We should already know by what we have seen that this equation is false.

To further understand the fallacy of equating service or task performance motives and money-making motives, we can note the negative effects of extrinsic motivation upon creativity in the performance of tasks. This has been demonstrated in numerous studies involving both children and adults. In one such study, two research groups of children played with magic markers and paper on two separate occasions a week or two apart. The children in one of the groups were told during the first session that they would receive an award for their drawings, which they did. At the second session, this group spent significantly less time playing with their markers than the other group, which was not given awards. In a similar study, two groups of college students made collages. The first group was told in advance that there would be monetary rewards for good performance.[5] When the artistic performance of the two groups of students was judged in blind ratings by artists, the first group was consistently found to be less creative than the second. In yet another study, a group of students of creative writing was told to think for five minutes about the extrinsic reasons for writing, such as impressing teachers, making money, and getting into a good graduate school. When their work was judged blindly by twelve independent poets, it was found to be significantly worse than the work they had done before this instruction. Psychologist Teresa Amabile describes this striking finding: "People who had been writing creatively for years, who had long standing interests in creative writing, suddenly found their creativity blocked after spending barely five minutes thinking about the extrinsic reasons for doing what they do."[5]

We said that making money ought to be only a by-product of one's vocation or profession. However, as human beings we are generally somewhere in the middle of the continuum of motives. We naturally exist in a tension, sometimes mild and sometimes acute, between the two ends of the continuum. We may try to exercise our highest values and motives, but there most often is that tug in the other direction as well. The doctor sees her patient and tries to give that patient decent time and attention, but one eye, so to speak, keeps glancing at the clock and beyond to the growing bank account—another patient, another fifty dollars. This is the inner battle of ethics in the vocational sphere. It is the classic conflict of interest which is ever present in human affairs. The outcome of this conflict—what kinds of compromises are struck between the two poles of motivation—determines the moral quality of a society, as well as its economic quality. Economics, besides not recognizing greed, also does not recognize a conflict of interests. There is only one self, and thus there is only one interest, and that is self-interest.

One of the most serious consequences of elevating money-making to the dominant, if not only, goal of society is the degradation and destruction of the environment. Critical economists have sometimes referred to this as the "problem of future generations." Short-run profit maximization excludes considerations of what future interests might be. This can be illustrated in what I will call "The Tale of the Technological Father."

A father who has been taught to fish by his father takes his son out fishing in order to pass on this lore (and lure) of the generations. But this father conceives of himself as a truly modern father and believes that everything taught to children should prepare them for success in later life. This father also works for IBM.

So not only does he teach his son how to fish, but he introduces him to the wonders of the sonar fish depth detector, which improves one's catch by twenty percent per unit/time. The son is duly impressed and appreciates how smart his father is. They catch a lot of fish and eat well. When this son grows up to become a parent he passes on the same principles to his son, and in addition to the sonar detector he also introduces him to something called the underwater guided dart. That boy catches even more fish than his father did as a boy, and not only do they eat well, but they have enough fish left over to sell at a faraway place where IBM has not yet set up a branch office (which unfortunately depresses the local fish market for a time).

But many years later the son is upset. It seems that the government has now put a ban on the use of sonar detectors and underwater guided darts, so that he is not able to pass on the principles that his father passed on to him. This is a real taking away of his freedom. With nothing more than his simple rod and reel, he and his son don't even catch enough fish to eat well. This makes him very mad. So he thinks about moving his whole family to that faraway place where there is no government regulation, and where IBM has just opened a branch office.

Is the moral of the story that more mothers and daughters should enter into the sport of fishing?

Let us now return to our medieval monk. Although his motives were admirable, we could say that he did not necessarily need to go back to the seller and give him a fair price. But we say this not because of the principle of market efficiency—the reason the economist would give. We may surmise that it was not through his being able to drive a hard bargain that the monk was able to purchase the chalice so inexpensively. More probably it was because he had bought it from another unworldly soul like himself, within the context of the Church. The person who sold it to our monk was no more looking for top dollar, or florin, than was the monk himself. So the seller was not being cheated by getting what the monk paid him. We can further surmise that this chalice had always been used within religious confines and had never been part of the open market for luxury goods. Had it entered this market, it is highly unlikely that it would have ever been available for use in the service of the simple folk of the community parish. Instead of its use in the sacrament for the masses, it would have found its place as a showpiece in some rich nobleman's palazzo.

Not that there is necessarily anything wrong with a palazzo. But in a world of both palazzos and peasants' huts, in a wide-open and unprotected market, in an environment of values measured in economical terms alone, the huts have considerable difficulty competing with the palazzos for needed goods (which is why the economist likes to speak about *wants* and not *needs*.)

Another vignette, recounted by Lewis Hyde, further illustrates this. Once, in the Amish country of rural Pennsylvania, Hyde witnessed what he says was the most unusual auction he had ever seen:

> A length of rope stretched around the farm yard full of household goods. A little sign explained that it was a private auction, in which only members of the Amish community were allowed to bid. Though goods changed hands, none left the community. And none could be inflated in value. If sold on the open market, an old Amish quilt might be too valuable for a young Amish couple to sleep under, but inside that simple fence it would always hold its value on a winter night.[6]

If the Amish sold not only their quilts to the highest bidder, but also their land, they would momentarily gain in financial wealth, but that would be the end of the Amish. If we do not understand that there are values that cannot be adequately measured by an amount of money we lose the wisdom of that length of rope.

We must be aware that all of the things that are valuable to us, that we need and cherish, are not necessarily economic values, that is, goods that can be adequately or even appropriately measured by the highest market price. One way to put this is to say that there is a greater economy, of which the money economy is only a part. This greater economy includes goods such as trust, love and human community, as well as those such as greenery and nature, peace and quiet. If we do not properly manage the boundaries of our market economy, so that it does not intrude on these other goods, we may find that we have unwittingly sold off and undermined the very things we need most.

The function of that piece of rope in the Amish auction is fulfilled in the larger society through regulation and zoning. Regulation and zoning need to be under the control of the political process, and not the economic process. The will of the community must be able to put itself above the market. Put succinctly, one person/one vote needs to placed above one dollar/one vote. Otherwise, if government mirrors only the market, then it is not able to fulfill its necessary and legitimate function of erecting that piece of rope; then the market economy swamps the greater economy, and all communities vanish.

The point is not that we should go back to the Middle Ages or that we should all become Amish. The point is to recognize that, in the great economic transformation that has brought us to the present, there has been not only gain, but also loss. It is the task of postmodern society to keep the gains and overcome the losses. What was lost has made the modern world soulless and, within the ample shadows of its abundance, foolish and cruel.

So our final tale needs to suggest the direction in which we need to look for answers. It is called "The Tale of the Long Spoons," and I have adapted it from the original version, which comes from the ancient East.[7] One implementation of its lesson will be discussed in chapter 10.

A woman was given permission to see both heaven and hell while she was still alive. Naturally, she elected to put hell first on her itinerary. To her immense surprise, she found hell to be a huge gathering of people at a feast, stretching as far as she could see. There were tables and tables laden with every imaginable delicacy, and people were seated at them. But the people's voices were raised in a cacophony of lamentation and woe. Her brain quickly went into action to try to figure this out. She came to the conclusion that this was hell because continual eating, and the endless provision of edible delicacies, must become eternally boring, and all the denizens of this region must suffer in the never-ending lesson of the futility of material desires. But she was wrong.

As her eyes adjusted to the candle-lit scene, she observed something she hadn't seen at first. The eating utensils were so long that, try as they might, the people were not able to bring the food to their mouths. And whenever they put down the utensils and tried to take the food in their hands, which these people were not averse to doing, it vanished right in front of them. Ah, so now she knew why this was hell. All that abundance did them no good. With a sense of deep sadness, but hopefully with relief in sight, she headed for heaven. What would this be?

To her surprise she found exactly the same scene: rows of dinner tables filled with culinary delights, and the same long-handled spoons. And the people here never even attempted to eat with their fingers. However, she noticed the absence of wails and lamentations. Instead, the people were laughing and rejoicing, and having a fine old time. Here they were feeding each other.

8

GIFTS OF SCIENCE

Science is one of the finest achievements of humankind. And yet when used as the means of constructing an image of the human being there is hardly anything more debasing. The reason for this is that science by its very nature, at least as classically conceived, can not help but be deterministic and mechanistic. While philosophers may quibble about whether determinism is the same thing as mechanism, history shows little doubt that the billiard-ball model of science as conceived by Newton, and the great clockwork universe as conceived by Laplace, have remained as the mainsprings of science's vision.

So when science casts the person in its own image it inevitably creates a thing, subject to forces of push and pull. It doesn't matter whether these forces are perceived as purely mechanical or whether they are translated into forces of instinct, emotions, desires or needs. The point is that the person in this model is ultimately an object that is pushed or pulled, not an agent with choice and free will who makes real decisions. In the process of creating this image a strange thing happens. Science, which is a creative product of human beings, ends up painting a picture of the human being as a product of blind, impersonal forces. The creation becomes the creator. This phenomenon and the great horror associated with it moved Mary Shelley to write *Frankenstein*. In this story, the scientist, Dr. Frankenstein, creates a mechanical being in his own image who then becomes independent of his maker and threatens his existence. *The Sorcerer's Apprentice* is another literary example of this theme, this time with a somewhat different cast of personae.

The horror of Frankenstein is not so much that he takes over, but that he is not human. He lacks the essential ingredients of humanity: free will and heart. Therefore he lacks the ability to reason (and not just calculate), to feel, to love, and to have compassion—in other words, he lacks the capacity for morality. The mechanical world of science really has no way and no room to conceive of this fundamental quality, which defines humanity. And this is not meant as a criticism of science (God forbid)—as we just said, science's particular power also lies in its deterministic imagery—but it is a criticism of the misapplication of science. This misapplication has occurred grandly in the social sciences and certainly, with great destructive consequences, in economics.

Being enamored of Newton and the picture he created of a mechanical and perfectly harmonious planetary universe, Adam Smith, along with numerous other thinkers of the time, tried to apply the same kind of conception to the universe of people. In order to make that comparison as much as possible an identity— rather than just a useful analogy—these thinkers looked within the human context for an ordering force that would be equivalent to the force of gravity in the context of the heavenly bodies. Smith and others thought they had found that force in self-interest. Self-interest was for society what gravity was for the heavens.

This conception we have seen in a very early form in Thomas Hobbes's talk of people as mere physical entities, or "bodies in motion," and it was taken up later by materialist philosophers such as Helvetius, who wrote around 1760 that "as the physical world is ruled by the laws of movement, so is the moral universe ruled by the laws of interest."[1] (It is an interesting sidelight for us to note in Helvetius's statement the fundamental contradiction of self-interest: if the moral universe is ruled by interest, then there can be no moral universe.)

After Smith, the political economists believed that their work was the discovery and formulation of the laws of a science, exactly as was taking place in physics. For example, Nassau

Senior, who was the principal author of the revision of the Poor Laws in 1836, said that the pursuit of wealth and advantage functioned in economic theory like "gravity in physics," and that this was the "ultimate fact beyond which the reader cannot go and of which almost every other proposition is merely an illustration."[2]

Down to the present day, this identification of the world of people with the world of physics has blunted and distorted Smith's otherwise deeply felt humanism. For although human beings have bodies, they are not bodies like those studied by physics. In physics the person studies an object; in the social sciences the person studies a person. It is subject-to-subject, rather than subject-to-object.

These errors of overidentifying with the world of physics and conceiving of humanity as an extraneous and alien latecomer within nature led Smith to raise self-interest to the level of the paramount principle of social relations. They also contributed considerably to the humanistically fatal errors of seeing labor as a commodity—an object produced in an economy like any other object—and seeing the bearing and raising of children as "production"—as responding to the laws of supply and demand. These conceptions then opened the way for Thomas Malthus to advance his barbaric repeal of the laws of social protection.

When the conception that labor is a commodity is taken out of the spellbinding context of a supposed science of economics and held up to the clear light of common sense, it can be seen for the grotesque moral distortion that it is. To talk about labor is really to talk about the person, because labor is nothing other than the person in action, or the person at work. So labor *is* the person. So to say that labor is a commodity is to say that the person is a commodity—a commodity to be bought and sold on the open market. The first exposition of this point of view, as we already saw, can be found in Hobbes, and its seemingly scientific spirit commended itself to Smith.

In economics, production is considered a function of three factors (inputs): land (resources), capital (money and tools), and labor. All three are subordinate to production, the overall goal. Therefore, in this *production function*, production is higher in principle than land, capital, or labor, which all serve production. However, of these three factors, land and capital are things, whereas labor is people. So in this concept of production, people are put on the same level as things, and in that way *become* things. Apart from its general principle of self-interest, this is economics' most dehumanizing idea. Instead of the economy being for people, it implies that people are for the economy. Here we find the roots of the characteristic modern experience that we are all cogs in a machine. We anxiously feel that our lives are not in our own control and that we are caught up in some vast, impersonal process which is bigger than us and which carries us implacably forward to some destiny that is neither desired nor desirable. This is a particularly modern experience. Whatever insecurities the person in feudal society had, this was not one of them.

That Smith's ideas lent themselves to this commoditization of the person is again sadly ironic, for his main aim in *The Wealth of Nations* would seem to be just the opposite. His thralldom in relation to the physical sciences unwittingly obscures his intent to advance the rights and dignity of the workers. It is this intent, as well as his description of what economists came to call the *labor theory of value*, that drew the interest of Karl Marx and Friedrich Engels to his work.

The labor theory of value proposes that all value produced in the economy comes from labor and that, furthermore, the role of the landlord, and perhaps also of the merchant or entrepreneur (the capitalist), in producing value is at least dubious. These latter classes in the economy are those who by dint of their ownership have the opportunity, as Smith says, "to reap where they never sowed." It is in this sense that Marx and Engels are historically viewed as economists in the classical tradition that goes back to Smith. Socialists have tried to argue that their position is the proper interpretation of Smith, as opposed to the capitalist direction derived from his work by Thomas Malthus, David Ricardo, and those who followed in their footsteps.[3]

Ironies abound in the relationship of economic theory to modern society. Marx and Engels ultimately foundered on the same rocks that led Smith aground: an overzealous adherence to a scientific and, especially, materialistic conception of the person. Indeed it can be said that this penchant was the intellectual plague of the "Age of Enlightenment." Marx and Engels, in their own thralldom to science, came to believe that the earlier critics of industrial society, such as the English religious and humanitarian reformers, were foolishly caught up in the concepts of "bourgeois idealism." They derisively labeled the approach of these critics as utopian. Engels, in his famous essay "Socialism: Utopian or Scientific," spells out the difference between this utopianism and his and Marx's own concept of "scientific socialism": "The Utopians' mode of thought has for a long time governed the socialist ideas of the nineteenth century, and still governs some of them. . . . To all these Socialism is the expression of absolute truth, reason and justice, and has only to be discovered to conquer the world by virtue of its own power." But scientific socialism is different: "From this point of view the final causes of all social changes and political revolutions are to be sought, not in men's brains, not in men's better insights into eternal truth and justice, but in changes in the modes of production and exchange." These changes have led to conflict—"not a conflict engendered in the minds of man, like that between original sin and divine justice. It exists, in fact, objectively, outside us, independently of the will and actions even of the men that have brought it on. Modern Socialism is nothing but the reflex, in thought, of this conflict in fact. . . ." The socialist advance, then, has nothing to do with thought and ideals, but is a result of purely objective, material, economic conditions: "Like every other social advance, it becomes practicable, not by men understanding that the existence of classes is in contradiction to justice, equality, etc., not by the mere willingness to abolish these classes, but by virtue of certain new economic conditions."[4]

This scientifically inspired philosophy is really very strange, and it is a deep self-contradiction. By saying that ideas, thought, and reason have nothing to do with social change it does no less than to rule out philosophy itself. For that reason it would seem to be a waste of time for Marx and Engels to bother writing at all. If people choose to ignore this point and go ahead and read Marx and Engels anyway, and if they furthermore become inspired by what they read to try to do something about social conditions, then that very attempt contradicts the theory that Marx and Engels are proclaiming. They are saying that will doesn't matter, intent doesn't matter, and personal freedom is only an illusion. This is a perfect expression of scientific causality as applied to society. But the self-contradiction cannot be sustained: "Man cannot live by bread alone." So the scientifically inspired social philosophy tries to work itself out of its own box: "Active social forces work exactly like natural forces: blindly, destructively, so long as we do not understand and reckon with them."[5] But how is this understanding and reckoning possible, when it has already been described as only a reflex in response to economic conditions?

These anti-utopians, Marx and Engels, go on to say that when socialism has arrived, humanity's intrinsic mode of being will be fundamentally different: "Man's own social organization, hitherto confronting him as a necessary imposed by Nature and history, now becomes the result of his own free action. The extraneous objective forces that have hitherto governed history, pass under the control of man himself. Only from that time will man himself, more and more consciously, make his own history—only from that time will the social causes set in motion by him have, in the main and in a constantly growing measure, the results intended by him. It is the ascent from the kingdom of necessity to the kingdom of freedom."[6]

This proposition is fatally flawed. We are told here by Engels that human values, principles, ideals, and all communication (which by implication must include the very telling of this) have had nothing to do with social improvement. Social change only occurs through the inevitable mechanism of the scientific laws of history, much as a frozen block of arctic ice melts in the summer under the impersonal forces of thermodynamics, with little need of philosophy, literature, poetry, or Carnot's writings on heat transfer.

With such a nonhuman conception of "natural forces," Marx and Engels saw little need to try to describe a better society. This new world would all come about automatically and inevitably, and there was little useful place for thinking about it. As we have already indicated, the best refutation of this scientific thralldom is Marx and Engels's own writings. Certainly the changes that occurred in their wake in the name of socialism or communism did so largely under the banner of their writings and theories, in complete contradiction to their concept of the impersonal way in which a new society would come about. But since they had very little to say about how this society should look, it was left to Lenin and Stalin to fill in the details. And this they did.

In rejecting ideals, and in effect the human spirit itself, Marx and Engels naturally rejected religion and any form or expression of spirituality. Many Marxists think that Marx rejected spirituality because of the alliance, in his day, of the Church with the ruling power of the aristocracy, which resulted in the corruption of religion. But whatever the roots of Marx's antispirituality, his writings on religion make it clear that it was the very concept of spirituality, corrupt or not corrupt, that he rejected. Marx and Engels's scientism and materialism ruled out the existence and reality of spiritual values. According to Alexander Solzhenitsyn, the underlying driving force of Marxism is its atheism.[7]

So we find that the best humanistic intuitions of Smith, as well as of Marx and Engels, were blunted and diverted by their susceptibility to Enlightenment scientism, with destructive and disastrous consequences. It is probably well here to recall the oft-said but still apt adage: In capitalism man exploits man, but in socialism it is the reverse.

The exaltation and debasement that have been science's dual offering to humanity are also well illustrated in Charles Darwin's theory of evolution. As an explanation of the adaptation, change, and development in species Darwin's theory is one of the landmark achievements of human thought. Yet, as a foundation for a picture of the human being, it has had an even more demeaning effect upon humanity's special dignity than economics. No other product of social science can touch it in this regard. Out of the theory of evolution has come the belief, propagated by many of its adherents, that human beings are fundamentally not different from animals. Such a view might have been used to raise the status of animals, but this has hardly been the case, as evidenced by the animal cruelty that has been a regular and unquestioned feature of scientific laboratories until very recently. Instead, the overwhelming effect of this equation has been to lower the status of the human. Seen as only an animal—at best one with a bigger brain—the human was characterized by Darwin's theory as a creature of instinct, emotion, and the will to survive. Rationality, morality, love, and poetry are considered only the rarefied cover for what is really going on, which Hobbes described long ago as nature's war of "all against all."

Darwin's *Origin of Species* was published in 1859. Engels read it at once, and he wrote to Marx: "Indeed Darwin—whom I am reading at this very moment—is truly famous. One aspect of teleology had not so far been destroyed, but this has now occurred." A year later Marx read Darwin, and he then wrote back to Engels, "Even though it is developed in the clumsy English fashion, this is the book which contains the historico-natural basis for our views." A month later he wrote to the socialist Ferdinand Lassalle, and repeated Engels's comment about the book: "In spite of all its shortcomings, it has for the first time dealt a death blow to the 'teleology' of natural science."

This happiness at Darwin's overthrow of teleology is to be expected. Teleology is the idea, extending back to Aristotle, that there is a purpose or design in nature and creation, and it is closely akin to the belief that there is a Creator. Nothing could be more congenial to Marx and Engels as staunch materialists

and atheists than the supposed demonstration that science at last
had toppled these false idols of human sentiment.

For a long time it was even believed that Marx had written to
Darwin, asking him if he could dedicate the English translation
of volume 1 of *Das Kapital* to him. The evidence was a letter
from Darwin, presumably written to Marx, politely declining
the offer: "Although I am a keen advocate of freedom of opinion
in all questions, it seems to me (rightly or wrongly) that direct
arguments against Christianity and Theism hardly have any effect
on the public; and that freedom of thought will best be promoted
by that gradual enlightening of human understanding which
follows the progress of science."[8] It eventually was discovered
that this letter was not written to Marx, but to Marx's son-in-
law and translator, Richard Aveling, about a book on Darwin's
theory that Aveling was writing.

Capitalist economics, however, has an even more intimate
connection with Darwin. The fact is that Darwin got the flash of
inspiration for his concept of natural selection in 1838, while
reading Malthus's *Essay on Population.*[9] He knew that it was
possible to produce hardier varieties of plants and animals by
selective breeding, but he was searching for a way in which
nature could do it without the guiding direction of a breeder, or
selective intelligence—in other words, without teleology. He had
reached a dead end in this quest when he was struck by Malthus's
account of the struggle for existence; in that struggle, he felt, he
had found the basis of the answer. But the connection doesn't
stop there. Herbert Spencer, another Englishman and one of the
founders of modern sociology, was a staunch adherent of political economy and radical laissez-faire, and out of that formulated
his scientific sociology. His first book appeared in 1850, some
nine years before Darwin's. In it he claimed that social progress
had occurred as a result of competition, between individuals and
between races. When Darwin's *Origin of Species* appeared,
Spencer immediately saw its affinity to his own work, in their
common reliance on the Malthusian interpretation of Smith. He
brought both together in a grand synthesis of sociology and

biology which came to be known as *social Darwinism*. Further-more, in one of his later books, Spencer used the term *survival of the fittest* to describe the process of evolutionary progress, and it was from that book that Darwin himself got the term, to use for the first time in the fifth edition of his *Origin of Species*.[10]

In the view of social Darwinists, as articulated by Spencer, social progress had resulted from "a continuous over-running of the less powerful or less adapted by the more powerful and more adapted, a driving of inferior varieties into undesirable habitats, and, occasionally, an extermination of inferior varieties."[11] The parallels with the teachings of political economy were obvious. The poor generally represented an "inferior variety." By being driven into undesirable and non-life-supporting environments, they would naturally tend to die off, and thus the species of *Homo sapiens* would strengthen, evolve, and progress. Social welfare legislation was bad because it interfered with this natural process and thus retarded social evolution.

Spencer, Darwin himself, and other Darwinists were uneasy with some of the brutal, and what we would later come to call fascistic, social implications of their way of thinking, and they tended to back off from the full and consistent advocacy of these policies. A less troubled advocate was William Graham Sumner, an American economist and Episcopalian minister. Sumner, a convert to the new field of scientific sociology, was, like Malthus, able to back up his doctrines of political economy with the justifications of religion. As economist E. Ray Canterbery puts it, Sumner "ingeniously put Newton, God, and the science of biology all on the side of classical economics."[12] His sociology equated the hard-working, thrifty, and ultimately rich individual of the Protestant ethic with the "fittest" in the struggle for survival. Sumner's literary output peaked in about 1900, at the time when the new American industrialists were rising to monop-olistic power. Among his essays were such titles as "The Concen-tration of Wealth: Its Economic Justification" and "The Forgot-ten Man." In case you wonder, the latter title referred to the man who worked hard, produced, saved, invested, and paid taxes, and yet who bore the burden of supporting social services and the high costs imposed by labor unions. During the New Deal, Franklin Roosevelt ironically reversed Sumner's phrase, using the term *forgotten man* to describe the poor and downtrodden, who would benefit from his policies.

Sumner's teaching was picked up by other ministers, such as Henry Ward Beecher, later implicated in the Crédit Mobilier scandal; Noah Porter, a Congregational clergyman and the head of Yale University; and the Reverend John McVicker of Columbia University, who noted earlier that "science and religion eventually teach the same lesson, is a necessary consequence of the unity of truth, but it is seldom that this union is so early and satisfactorily displayed as in the researches of Political Economy."[13] Here is quite a conceptual achievement. Darwin's theory, which was intended as disproof of the tenets of spiritual faith, now comes in as support for such faith when seen through the filter of the beneficial and uplifting effects of competition.

The most prominent layman in the New York Episcopal Church was probably J. P. Morgan. Half of the seventy-five multimillionaires in New York at the time were communicants of this church. John D. Rockefeller and his brothers were prominent Baptists. Rockefeller taught a Sunday school class in which he explained the economic system in the following way:

> The growth of a large business is merely a survival of the fittest. . . . The American Beauty rose can be produced in the splendor and fragrance which brings cheer to its beholder only by sacrificing the early buds which grow up around it. This is not an evil tendency in business. It is merely the working-out of a law of nature and a law of God.[14]

The remarkable achievement in America of social Darwinism—the bringing together of religious faith and the theory of evolution—was not something that Darwin himself received any comfort from. As someone who had originally gone to Cambridge University to study for the ministry, he remained a man deeply committed to humanitarian principles and morality. He tried to reconcile his theory of a naturalistic, blind, impersonal process of "brute" force with a belief in morality. And yet the logic of his theory at times led him to write passages that, in the words of historian John Greene, "out-Spencered Spencer." Following is one such passage:

> With savages, the weak in body or mind are soon eliminated; and those that survive commonly exhibited a vigorous state of health. We civilized men, on the other hand, do our utmost to check the process of elimination; we build asylums for the imbecile, the maimed, and the sick; we institute poor-laws; and our medical men exert their utmost skill to save the life of every one to the last moment. . . . Thus the weak members of civilised societies propagate their kind. No one who has attended to the breeding of domestic animals will doubt that this must be highly injurious to the race of man. It is surprising how soon a want of care, or care wrongly directed [in animals] leads to the degeneration of a domestic race, but excepting in the case of man himself, hardly any one is so ignorant as to allow his worst animals to breed.[15]

Although it is not evident in the above quote, Darwin recognized the absence of morality in these conclusions from his theory. He thus sought a way out through the conception that morality had developed in the human species because it had survival value, which is sometimes called a *utilitarian* theory of morality:

> A tribe including many members who . . . were always ready to aid one another, and to sacrifice themselves for the common good, would be victorious over most other tribes; and this would be natural selection. At all times throughout the world tribes have supplanted other tribes; and as morality is one important element in their success, the standard of morality and the number of well-endowed men will thus everywhere tend to rise and increase.[16]

The contradiction between these two passages should be obvious. Moral sentiments are moral precisely because they are not destructive of others—not "dog eat dog"—and thus directly oppose the survival-of-the-fittest principle that supposedly brought them into existence. Darwin tried to say that the force of competition yields its opposite, which is somehow continuous with competition. He was troubled by these problems and tried to reassure himself and other adherents of his theory. He writes: "Looking to future generations there is no cause to fear that the social instinct will grow weaker, and we may expect that virtuous habits will grow stronger, becoming more fixed by inheritance. In this case the struggle between our higher and lower impulses will be less severe, and virtue will be triumphant." But this is strange talk for the mechanistic scientist. Higher and lower impulses, indeed. By what criterion?

As he got older, Darwin appeared to become even more troubled by the social and moral conundrums his theory had created. He wrote to a correspondent that he had an inner conviction that the universe was not the result of chance. "But then," he adds, "with me the horrid doubt always arises whether the convictions of man's mind, which has been developed from the mind of lower animals, are of any value or at all trustworthy. Would any one trust in the convictions of a monkey's mind, if there are any convictions in such a mind?"[17]

With these words, Darwin perfectly expresses the paradoxical dilemma of the modern mind, which lauds itself in the reach of its own scientific intellect, and yet, out of a need for consistency, must discredit its ability to know or believe anything. What can an intellect with no telos know? In his autobiography, Darwin candidly and poignantly describes for us the mind of one who has become the purely scientific:

> Up to the age 30, or beyond it, poetry of many kinds, such as the works of Milton, Gray, Byron, Wordsworth, Coleridge, and Shelley, gave me great pleasure and even as a schoolboy I took intense delight in Shakespeare, especially in the historical plays. I have also said that pictures formerly gave me considerable, and music, very great delight. But now for many years I cannot endure to read a line of poetry: I have tried lately to read Shakespeare, and found it

so intolerably dull that it nauseated me. I have also lost any taste for pictures or music. . . .

This curious and lamentable loss of the higher aesthetic tastes is all the odder, as books on history, biographies and travels (independently of any scientific facts which they may contain), and essays on all sorts of subjects interest me as much as they ever did. My mind seems to have become a kind of machine for grinding general laws out of large collections of facts, but why this should have caused the atrophy of that part of the brain alone, on which the higher tastes depend, I cannot conceive, . . . for loss of these tastes is a loss of happiness, and may possibly be injurious to the intellect, and more probably to the moral character, by enfeebling the emotional part of our nature.[18]

Can there be a greater testimony to the fact that the gifts of science do not come free? And, ironically, this is also an economics point: nothing comes free. In this book I am trying to show the importance of applying this point to economics itself. Economics as a conceptual system has imposed great costs on us, both morally and environmentally. The great critic of economic thinking Thomas Carlyle titled one of his famous books *Sartor Resartus*, "the tailor reclothes himself." We must reclothe ourselves in a new economic ethic if we are to wear garments that do not bind and distort the true human shape.

9

THE ETERNAL SOPHIST

In chapter 1 we said that we would return to the definition of self-interest. It may seem curious that we do this now, since we have already been talking about self-interest for the length of this book, with the assumption that we knew what we were talking about. Nevertheless, economists of this century have been debating just what *self-interest* really means.

For the first hundred years or so following the publication of *The Wealth of Nations*, economists had few qualms about seeing self-interest as the near economic equivalent of self-centeredness or selfishness. In 1844 John Stuart Mill approvingly described the image of the self-interested person as one "abstracted of every other human passion or motive, except . . . aversion to labor, and desire of present enjoyment of costly indulgences."[1] In 1885 Alfred Marshall, the "neoclassical" successor to Mill, coined the term *Homo Economicus*, or Economic Man, to name this being. Many economists today still have no trouble with this image. For example: "Rule number one for the social analyst is to take people as they are. They are—among other characteristics—acquisitive and grubby, interested in their own well-being, preferring more rather than less of what they desire. They have been like that since the fiasco in the Garden of Eden."[2] So now our story is extended back to Adam and Eve.

Earlier I mentioned that William Stanley Jevons, founder of the neoclassical formulation of economics, defined economics as the study of "the mechanics of utility and self-interest." *Utility* means usefulness, but here economists are talking only about usefulness as seen by the individual, with no concern for actual or objective usefulness. It is probably the case that the economist would say there is no such thing as objective usefulness. So, for example, if an individual wants to poison someone, poison will be a commodity with a high degree of utility for them. Leon Walras, the economist who founded equilibrium theory, confirms this view: "From other points of view the question of whether a drug is wanted by a doctor to cure a patient, or by a murderer to kill his family, is a very serious matter, but from our point of view, it is totally irrelevant. So far as we are concerned, the drug is useful in both cases, and may be even more so in the latter case than in the former."[3]

This focus on the individual as a self-contained world, with no judgment about objective or public usefulness being attempted or even seen as possible, is evident in economists' claim that you can't compare the relative value of the utilities that different persons seek. This is explained in the following example from the 1974 economics textbook *Basic Economic Concepts*:

> If $200 is taken away from an industrial tycoon and given to a poor sharecropper, the tycoon may decide not to paint his yacht a new color this year, while the sharecropper may decide he can afford to add meat to his diet for one meal a day. If we looked at these alternatives from the perspective of a single individual, we would say that the additional utility, or satisfaction, from gaining the meat would be far greater than the loss of utility from doing without the paint job, so that total utility would be higher. However, we cannot prove that the sharecropper increases his utility by more than the tycoon decreases his, because these are two distinct individuals with differing capacities for deriving pleasure from worldly goods. (A hedonistic tycoon may get more satisfaction from the paint job than an ascetic sharecropper would get from the meat.)[4]

The great Jevons himself harkened back to the work of a relatively obscure German economic writer, Hermann Gossen, for a depiction of Economic Man that Jevons said was "even more general and thorough than I was able to scheme out."[5] He thus brought Gossen's name into the history of economics as someone who had anticipated the neoclassical concept of utility (actually, *marginal* utility). A few excerpts from Gossen's book, *The Laws of Human Relations*, first published in 1854, should help to dispel any doubts about what economists have traditionally intended when they talked about self-interest, although they might not have always expressed it in as messianic a way as Gossen did.

Gossen believed that by following self-interest we were following God's will, and any moral control over self-interest would block God's purpose: "It would frustrate totally or in part the purpose of the Creator were we to attempt to neutralize this force in total or in part, as is the intention of some moral codes promulgated by men." He then goes on, with his own unique sense of moral indignation, to ask: "How can a creature be so arrogant as to want to frustrate totally or partly the purpose of his Creator?" So, just as Thomas Malthus had claimed, most humanitarian legislation to help others will actually make them worse off. It is the task of economics to demonstrate the social reformers and moralists wrong. These poor misguided moralists seemed to believe that egoism was a negative force, and "they held that egoism would destroy human society were it allowed to work unchecked." Economics was the science of "Lebensgenuss," or life pleasure, which is indeed rendered perfect by the Creator, and thus there is no way we can improve on it. Gossen observes that "we have learned to recognize the [true] force whose strength we have occasion to admire daily and in innumerable instances, namely the *egoism* of the human race." Again, in calling for a social attitude of a rather complete laissez-faire, Gossen concludes by asking the reader to contemplate in what "beautiful a fashion did the Creator know how to remove the obstacle that egoism seems to oppose to the welfare of society and to bring about through this egoism exactly the opposite: *He made egoism the sole and irresistible force by which humanity may progress in the arts and science for both its material and intellectual welfare*"[6] (italics added).

Gossen here extends Adam Smith's invisible hand doctrine to what may be its outer limit, but in so doing he is not really saying anything very different from Bernard de Mandeville. We can see that this theme of justifying selfishness or egoism has been the leitmotif of basic economic thought. It's good that we learn to recognize it, because the human urge to transvalue selfishness springs eternal, and we should expect to keep finding it in new contemporary expressions. We believe that Ayn Rand is one such instance: in her writings and philosophy we find as outspoken an advocate of selfishness or egoism as Hermann Gossen himself. As we might expect, transvaluation comes with an attempt to redefine, reinterpret, and in general bend the meaning of common words, so that it is typically accompanied by obscurity and deep confusion. Aristotle, ages ago in his writings on ethics, described this phenomenon and pinpointed it with a word—sophistry. The essential motivating force behind sophistry is the wish to transvalue egoism. Recognizing this, we realize that the theory of economics *as based on self-interest* is ultimately not other than a very elaborate and learned modern expression of sophistry.

This leads us to an answer for our question of why it is necessary, at this point, to define what we mean by self-interest. As it turns out, some economists have become uncomfortable with the implications of the selfishness that seems to lie at the core of their doctrine. Critics of self-interest from within the profession have included Jean C. L. Sismondi, at times John Stuart Mill, Thorsten Veblen, and John Maynard Keynes. The big blow to the confidence of economists in the virtue of self-interest was the Great Depression. We have already quoted the president of the United States at the time, Franklin D. Roosevelt, as saying in his 1937 inaugural address that "we have always known that heedless self-interest was bad morals; we now know that it is bad economics."

Put in an embarrassing position during the early years of the Great Depression by the very palpable failure of their traditional laissez-faire advice, economists scrambled to redefine and, at least in a few instances, to rethink their beliefs. A prime candidate for redefinition was, of course, self-interest. In the early 1930s the prestigious British economist Lionel Robbins announced that self-interest did not mean selfishness, and never had. Just as Jevons had harkened back to Gossen's work as a forerunner to his own, Robbins announced that the true principle of self-interest had been laid out at least sixty years earlier in the work of his fellow English economist, the little-known Phillip Wicksteed. Robbins claimed that, as a result of what Wicksteed wrote, particularly in his book *The Common Sense of Political Economy*, anyone who believed that economics was founded on a principle of selfishness "showed a failure to understand the last sixty years of economic science. . . . Before Wicksteed wrote, it was still possible for intelligent men to give countenance to the belief that the whole structure of economics depends on the assumption of the world of economic men, each accentuated by egocentric or hedonistic motives. For anyone who had read *Common Sense*, the expression of such a view is no longer consistent with intellectual honesty. Wicksteed shattered this misconception once and for all."[7]

Let us see how Wicksteed "shattered" this misconception. Wicksteed proposed that although people do seek their own interests, these interests could be anything, even social concerns such as philanthropy or human and civil rights, as well as the usual economic private gain. Economics need not presume what an individual's personal interests and goals are. Different people have different interests; some may be selfish, others not. All economics is saying is that people pursue their own ends, and they do so in as efficient and as calculated a way as possible. Economics is really about the means, about how people go about achieving their ends, and not about what those ends are.

Wicksteed coined an interesting term to describe this conception. He called it *nontuism*. *Tu* is the French familiar word for "you." We do not have a good equivalent for *tu* in the English language, but the word *thou* comes the closest. Wicksteed said that what we need for economic theory to work is not selfishness, but merely to assume the principle of nontuism in economic exchange. This means that the economic actor should go about his or her exchanges without concern for the interests or needs of another. This is comparable to the task of an agent for a charity, who is obligated to drive as hard a bargain as possible in negotiating the financial interests of that charity. The agent's responsibility is to get the best deal possible. Similarly, one could coldly maximize one's wealth in business dealings with the goal of making a large contribution to an unselfish end, such as one's family or a favorite cause. In the business world, this is known as the role of the fiduciary, such as one's stockbroker or banker. We wouldn't want them to be less than aggressive in pursuing our charitable interests, and that doesn't mean that we are being selfish, does it? For Wicksteed, then, economics was merely saying that although people behaved like fiduciaries in their exchanges, that didn't mean that the purposes motivating these exchange were necessarily selfish.

Robbins presents Wicksteed's interpretation of self-interest as follows:

> So far as we are concerned, our economic subjects can be pure egoists, pure altruists, pure ascetics, pure sensualists or—what is more likely—mixed bundles of all these impulses. . . . All this means is that my relation to the dealer does not enter into my hierarchy of ends. For me (who may be acting for myself or my friends or some civic or charitable authority) they are regarded merely as means.[8]

This attempt to disconnect self-interest from selfishness, and to thus turn it into a morally neutral concept, doesn't work. One way to see this is to realize that egoistic and unethical behavior comes about precisely when other people are treated as means rather than as ends in themselves. The popular term for expressing this is "using people." Robbins and Wicksteed are trying to tell us that one can have ethical and noble ends, such as giving to charity, and yet treat the person with whom one is dealing without any regard to that person's own welfare or well-being. This, of course, is a contradiction, and it is a perfect description of moral hypocrisy. It is not that people do not act that way. They can and all too often do. But this is hardly a defense of nontuism as morally neutral.

This contradiction can be further brought out in the following way. Let us say that a particular individual is an altruist, that is, someone who is devoted to the well-being of other people. The nontuistic principle would suggest that the altruist should engage in her economic dealings in a nonaltruistic way in order to be able to then seek their altruistic ends. This is clearly a paradox; the principle of nontuism collapses here. If we define self-interest as being concerned about the interests of another, as economics tries to do in an example such as this, then in what sense are we still talking about self and other? In this case self-interest and benevolence become one and cannot be differentiated. Thus, Adam Smith's original premise in putting forth the concept of self-love or self-interest is made completely irrelevant. If my self-love means love for others, then these terms and their distinctions lose their meaning.

In making a case for what Wicksteed called nontuism, Robbins inadvertently makes a case for the dual polarity of the self and the necessary choice the individual faces in deciding between one end of the vector of motives and the other; in other words, he makes a case for moral, or ethical, choice. Robbins quite rightly says that the economic actor may be a mixture of various motives, such as egoism and altruism, or sensuality and asceticism. But then Robbins, and other economists who followed his lead in adopting this principle, want to claim that we can still take this economic actor as maximizing his utility or net advantage across these different motives. But the problem is that these motives are mutually exclusive, or incompatible. You can't be going in both directions at the same time. When you fulfill one you defeat the other. An altruist is an altruist precisely because he is not an egoist; an ascetic becomes an ascetic by renouncing sensualism. Therefore, purposes or motives such as these cannot be treated as a mixture of independent items, like so many goods in a shopping cart whose total value or utility can be added together. When these economists recognize correctly that most people are a mixture of motives, they do not realize that they are also making a fatal argument against their cherished concept of utility maximization and for the necessity of moral choice.

There is still one more telling blow against this attempt at face-saving. And it is perhaps a more effective blow than is the recognition of the above logical contradictions, simply because it is an instance of economics shooting itself in its own foot. Here we are referring to what economists call the "problem of the free rider."

Free riding is the term economists use to describe the situation where someone participating in a joint, group, or public activity derives benefit from the activity without contributing his or her fair share of the effort or costs. Perhaps the most obvious example of free riding is the literal case of someone jumping on a bus without paying the fare. The cost to the regular fare payers will, of course, have to ultimately include the lost revenue from free riding, and thus others pay the cost of the free rider. Instances of this don't have to involve only money, but can refer to other costs as well. So, let us say that four people are carrying a heavy piece of furniture. One person pretends to be carrying his end, but in fact he is only faking it. This too is free riding. We can see then that *free riding* is fundamentally synonymous with *cheating*.

The telling point is this. Economics textbooks tell us, when they define self-interest, that it does not mean selfishness, and that to believe it does is to be ignorant as to what economics is all about. Yet the same textbooks, usually at a later point, tell us that it is expected in economic theory that the individual will free-ride. In other words, economics conceives of people as inherently free riders. For example, in chapter 1 we referred to the textbook *The Economic Way of Thinking* and quoted the author's description of self-interest. Right after the previously quoted passage, the author goes on to give the following clarification:

But don't misunderstand. Economic theory does not assume that people are selfish, or materialistic, or short-sighted, or irresponsible, or interested exclusively in money. None of these is implied by the statement that people try to secure for themselves the largest possible net advantage. Everything depends on what, in fact, people find in their own interest. As we know, some derive enormous satisfaction from helping people. A few, unfortunately, seem to derive satisfaction from actually hurting others.[9]

We can see here the author's exact restatement of the Wicksteed-Robbins nontuistic interpretation of self-interest. Here, on page 4 of this textbook, we are informed that self-interest has essentially no content whatsoever. We are warned not to misunderstand self-interest as a form of selfishness. As a matter of fact, we are told that perhaps most people are well-meaning, and presumably honest, and only a few want to hurt others (which, in the language of economics, would mean to impose unwarranted costs on them). But on page 277 of the same book the problem of the free rider is described: "When people can obtain a good whether they pay for it or not, they have less incentive to pay. They're tempted to become *free-riders: people who accept benefits without paying their share of the costs of providing those benefits.*" This author still tries to salvage self-interest and to contain the damage done by the free-rider assumption. Therefore, he goes on: "In stressing the significance of the free-rider concept, the economist is insisting only that people have *limited* concepts of self-interest, that they do not by and large entertain the inner feelings of others, especially more distant others, with as much vividness and force as they experience benefits and costs that impinge on them more directly." The problem is that, while this may be a perfectly accurate description of people, it does not leave self-interest as a morally neutral concept. It does admit that self-interest has to mean some form of self-centeredness if it is to mean anything. The cat is really out of the bag seven pages later when the free-rider theme is discussed in regard to elected officials. Here the author plainly tells us: "Economic theory assumes that people act in their own interest, not that they act in the public interest."[10]

In the free-rider concept the interest of the self is clearly differentiated from the interests of others or the public, and the self is said to come first. Not that it ordinarily or often does not. But let us remind ourselves that economics, following Smith, promotes just this very self-interest; it says that it is a good thing, and that it is beneficial for society that this is the case.

Other economic writers are even more explicit about the free-rider principle than the writer just discussed. Some even use the word *rational* to describe the free-rider tendency. Nobel Prize laureate James Buchanan says, "Regardless of how the individual estimates the behavior of others, he must always rationally choose the free-rider alternative." In a similar vein, another Nobel Prize laureate, George Stigler, acknowledges in his acceptance speech that "any preoccupation with fairness and justice is uncongenial to a science in which these concepts have no established meaning."[11] So, despite the wavering and waffling and attempts at redefinition, the free-rider assumption of economics shows us that self-interest means what it has always meant, if the word is to have any meaning at all. The *self* is me, and it's not you. Self-interest is my interest; it's not your interest.

It may be helpful here to point out that there are circumstances in which self-interest *is* morally neutral. This is when one is acting by oneself and there are no other people involved, as in the case of Robinson Crusoe. In going about his island and undertaking his various activities—building his house, picking fruit, catching fish, and so forth—we can say that Crusoe is acting "economically," in the sense that he expends effort (costs) to gain benefits. In this economic activity we can also say, if we want to, that he acts out of self-interest. But the word has no moral meaning because there are no other people involved. Crusoe acts out his survival instincts or will to live, and at best we can say that he is either prudent or not in his choice of actions. But benevolence does not and cannot enter into the picture. All this changes when Friday arrives on the scene.

We bring this up because it sheds light on why economists so often specifically use the image of Robinson Crusoe when they discuss the economic actor. For example, Milton Friedman describes his model of the economic system as follows:

> In its simplest form, such a society consists of a number of independent households—a collection of Robinson Crusoes, as it were. Each household uses the resources it controls to produce goods and services that it exchanges for goods and services produced by other households, on terms mutually acceptable to the two parties to the bargain.[12]

But a society which is a collection of "independent Robinson Crusoes" is no society at all—or a pseudo-society. No one needs anyone else, and no one's actions are seen to affect anyone else, except by free exchange. In any real society, interpersonal effects and dependencies are precisely what define it as a society. In a society of Robinson Crusoes it is hard to see why anyone would exchange at all, since they already own resources and are defined as perfectly self-sufficient. As a matter of fact, it is only in such a society that if there somehow were exchange, it would truly be free, since there would be no necessity for, and no compulsion to, exchange. Friedman gets advantage by proposing this model, for in it no one can affect another except by that person's choice, and no one can impose unwanted costs on another. Thus, for example, there can be no such thing as pollution, since everyone is defined as self-contained. Similarly, the free-rider situation is virtually impossible. By conceiving of society as independent Robinson Crusoes, Friedman is able to avoid dealing with the moral and human dimensions of the unmoderated pursuit of self-interest.

For Friedman, all the problems of a market economy stem from government interference. In regard to the Great Depression, he writes: "The fact is that the Great Depression, like most other periods of severe unemployment, was produced by government mismanagement rather than by any inherent instability of the private economy." As for the problem of monopolies, he has little concern: "The most important fact about enterprise monopoly is its relative unimportance from the point of view of the economy as a whole." In fact, if monopolies are a problem, it too is because of government. Friedman assures us that monopolies "are generally unstable and of brief duration unless they can call government to their assistance."[13]

Friedman's world, while admirably simple, obscures rather than reveals. The resources are owned by households rather than corporations. Each is a little, self-sufficient economic unit, and there are no employers and employees. And if Robinson Crusoe is too limiting an image then a close cousin will probably do quite as well: Swiss Family Robinson.

A final attempt to defend self-interest against the charge that it is selfishness is the concept of *enlightened self-interest*. This is a popular and appealing idea in many quarters today, especially among thinkers who are more liberal than Friedman. The claim is made that the kind of self-interest that economics really advocates is not the grubby, selfish, narrow kind, but a more enlightened variety. Not an economist, but the psychologist Robert Parloff, quoted in chapter 1, would seem to be intending enlightened self-interest when, in his presidential address to the American Psychological Association, he refers to self-interest as a way to understand even such phenomena as "people extending helping hands to others."

Such a conception of enlightened self-interest is the perennial attempt to make a silk purse out of a sow's ear. Albert Schweitzer traces this tendency in Western thought back to Socrates' attempt to understand ethics as the application of rationality to pleasure, so that the good was the "rationally pleasurable," instead of the merely pleasurable.[14] Jeremy Bentham, in the latter part of the eighteenth century, laid the foundation for utilitarianism by conceiving of the individual as a "felicity calculator" who computed the *amount* of pleasure or pain in each choice of actions and made the choice that promised the maximum pleasure or minimum pain. In a phrase that was to become a hallmark of utilitarian thought, Bentham wrote: "Nature has placed mankind

under the governance of two sovereign masters, pain and pleasure. It is for them alone to point out what we ought to do, as
well as to determine what we should do."[15]

What Bentham is saying here is that "pleasures" do not differ
between themselves in type or kind, but only in their amount,
that is, in their strength or intensity. Therefore, the difference
between the pleasure of eating a piece of chocolate and the
satisfaction, say, of resisting the temptation to cheat, is not one
of two different *kinds* of pleasure, but only one of *degree*. For
the new social scientists, the importance of this doctrine was that
it generally allowed them to sidestep the classic, eternal human
issues of morality, ethics, and justice by treating these problems
as if they were only a matter of quantity. The need to discrimi-
nate between the good and the pleasurable or between truth and
mere personal expediency was increasingly seen as only a difference between two amounts of pleasure. Taking a cue from the
apparent lessons of science, the utilitarian economist concluded
that what is good is what is pleasurable, and what is bad is what
is painful. Therefore, all the philosophical questions of good and
bad, right and wrong, could be reduced to the matter of the
amount of pleasure or pain.

We can note in Bentham's very influential formulation another
instance where the idea of quantity pushes out and replaces that
of quality. Since the difference between vice and virtue is really a
difference in quality or kind, and not a difference in the amount
of something (such as pleasure or happiness), the idea of enlightened self-interest, like all other such attempts to sanitize self-
intent, fails. Once again using our depiction of the higher and
lower self as two poles of a vector, we can show why this is the
case. We will briefly present the discussion using this metaphor
and then do the same thing in more general terms.

A vector is not an *arithmetic* scale starting from zero and
going to a higher number, such as we find on a ruler, but it is
rather a *geometric* concept showing location in a space, in this
case in a moral space. So, north is not just more of south, any
more than south is less of north. Therefore, as has been pointed

out several times previously, you can't go north and south at the same time (although in the State of Maine, on some roads that seems to be possible). You have to choose one direction or the other. If there is a zero point on such a vector it is at the middle, halfway between north and south. By choosing the southern direction you are at the same time subtracting from the northern direction; you are not just adding an amount of some single quantity of which you would add a larger amount if you instead went north. For Bentham and the utilitarian economists, the moral act was simply that which brought a greater amount of pleasure than the merely pleasurable act. Thus they saw the issue in arithmetic rather than geometric terms.

This fallacy can also be brought out through a simple logic. If there is enlightened self-interest, then there must, by implication, be unenlightened self-interest—which is, of course, what led to the idea of enlightened self-interest in the first place. So, if we have two self-interests we are presented with the necessity of choosing between the two. We see, then, that the concept of enlightened self-interest leads to *the cancellation of self-interest* as the sole principle determining economic action, or human action in general. We wind up back with the necessity of moral choice, between unenlightenment and enlightenment.

Some traditional Smithian economists have themselves recognized this problem, either explicitly or intuitively. In order to maintain the "purity" of the economic way of thinking they have properly ruled out such revisionist and heretical notions as enlightened self-interest as alternatives to plain old self-interest. For these economists enlightened self-interest *is* self-interest, and there is no difference between the two. So, for example, William Field, in his textbook *Basic Economics*, labels one of his sidebars "In defense of greed." In it he tells students: "One human characteristic which consistently gets a bad press is greed. We are all urged by religious and social leaders to resist the temptation to be greedy and instead be altruistic—self-sacrificing in service to our fellow man. While there is certainly nothing wrong with altruistic behavior, the question we want to address here is whether there is anything wrong with enlightened self-interest (a much nicer phrase meaning basically the same thing as greed)." He goes on to let the student know that "the market makes socially productive use of selfishness." The author is good enough to allow that *well-meaning* altruism is not morally bad, and fortunately he tells his economics students exactly that in the following statement, but he concludes by also letting them know that it is useless: "Self-interest is probably a better guide than altruism for all individuals to follow if each is to benefit from the actions of others. Well-meaning altruism is in no sense morally bad behavior but is both unrealistic and an ineffective guide to action in relationships with someone not a close friend or a relative."[16]

Ayn Rand, however, is much more certain that altruism *is* morally bad, and in fact she sees it purely and simply as the cause of society's ills. In Ayn Rand we have, along with Hermann Gossen, an ultimate case of moral transvaluation. In her book *The Virtue of Selfishness*, Ayn Rand sets forth her philosophy of moral principles, which she calls *Objectivism*. This she defines as the "philosophy that holds man's life, the life proper to a rational being, as the standard of moral values—and regards altruism as incompatible with man's nature, with the creative requirements of his survival, and with a free society."[17] Rand connects this philosophy with capitalism, but a capitalism that presumably has never been tried. This is expressed in her book of essays, *Capitalism: The Unknown Ideal*. In this book we are told simply and starkly that "the foundations of capitalism are being battered by a flood of altruism, which is the cause of the modern world's collapse."[18] Lest the reader think that Rand is merely an extremist whose only influence is to disturb more moderate adherents of self-interest such as Robert Parloff, it should be noted that Alan Greenspan, who was appointed chairman of the Federal Reserve Board in 1987, is a noted Rand disciple, and he has contributed three essays of his own to her above-noted book on capitalism. One such essay is a critique of antitrust. In it he writes: "To interpret the railroad history of the nineteenth century as 'proof' of the failure of a free market, is a disastrous error. The same error—which persists to this day—was the nineteenth century's fear of the 'trusts.' "[19] In these remarks Greenspan echoes the sentiments of Milton Friedman, quoted earlier, who regards monopoly and its dangers as a chimera of an anxious imagination. In other essays Greenspan criticizes virtually *all* governmental regulation, including minimum food and drug standards, security and exchange regulation, and, yes, the establishment of the Federal Reserve System. The master herself, Ayn Rand, refers to Greenspan's contribution in this regard:

> To borrow an invaluable metaphor from Alan Greenspan: if, under laissez faire, the banking system and the principles controlling the availability of funds act as a fuse that prevents a blowout in the economy—then the government, through the Federal Reserve System, *put a penny in the fuse-box.* The result was the explosion known as the Crash of 1929.[20]

We would have to assume that, in the intervening twenty or so years since Greenspan advocated these principles, further experience and reflection have led him to change his mind in regard to the agency which he currently leads and for which he provides policy. Or is it a case, as it recently seemed to be in regard to the "protection" of the environment by another agency, that he sees it as his justifiable purpose, in accordance with his radical laissez faire beliefs, to destroy and eliminate the governmental regulatory function he has been appointed to manage. Fortunately, descriptions of Greenspan carefully and agonizingly dealing with the delicate matters of Federal Reserve policy would indicate that the former is more likely the case.[21]

We noted in chapter 1, in discussing Parloff's speech about self-interest, that another psychologist wrote in to tell the president of the American Psychological Association that his discomfort with the self-interest advocacy of Ayn Rand was quite unwarranted, and that her teachings were, in fact, "profoundly moral." We should be able to see at this point that the profundity of such teachings lies, apart from the rich subtlety of their justificatory arguments, in the depths of their transvalued confusion.

10

FATHER ARIZMENDI COMES TO MONDRAGON

What does an economy look like in which the person, or the worker, is not treated as a commodity?

To attempt to answer this question let us return again to the historical origin of what eventually culminated in Adam Smith's mistake. When Pepin the Short asked Pope Zacharias for advice back in 751, instead of advising power and dominance, Zacharias should have counseled Pepin to seek mutuality and cooperation. In time Zacharias's mistake became Adam Smith's mistake, just as it is each of our mistakes whenever we opt for the dictates of our lower self over the still, small voice of the higher.

What Zacharias set in motion had dire ramifications when it reached the English king, Henry VIII, who reigned from 1509 to 1547 and preceded Elizabeth by about a half century. Henry is described as a willful individual and a supreme egotist. Despite Zacharias and some of the other morally weak popes, the Catholic Church had stood as a guardian and restraint against the grosser passions of rulers. But Henry, through the shrewd eyes of self-interest, knew that the Church had more than a few peccadillos of its own, and he exploited them. When the Church stood in the way of one of his two divorces, he moved to divest the clergy of their authority, and he then appointed himself head of the clergy. This served him well in carrying out his eventual six marriages—and the murder of two of his wives along the way. His other murders include that of the saintly Thomas More.

More had described the inequities and iniquities of the society in Henry's time. He had envisioned the possible alternatives of a new social order in his book *Utopia* and thus brought that word into our language for the first time.

King Henry also cast a covetous eye upon the vast Church estates, which had begun to resemble more and more the worldly fiefdoms of the nobility, rather than the charitable ideal of a monasterial estate dedicated to providing livelihood and welfare for those peasants not adequately accommodated in the manors and fiefs.[1] So in 1536 Henry, through a series of parliamentary acts, began taking away church lands in the name of the Crown, and he distributed some of these to the parliamentary nobility who gave him their support. The new, nonclerical landholders had little sense of responsibility toward the peasants, who for generations had used these lands as common fields for their own maintenance and sustenance. Richard Henry Tawney, the English economic historian, social critic, and one of the foremost scholars to write about this period, describes this in *Religion and the Rise of Capitalism*, written in the early 1900s:

> For a decade there was a mania of land speculation. Much of the property was bought by needy courtiers, at a ridiculously low figure. Much of it passed to sharp businessmen, who brought to bear on its management the methods learned in the financial schools of the City. Much was acquired by middlemen, who bought scattered parcels of land, held them for the rise, and disposed of them piecemeal when they got a good offer. . . . Rackrenting, evictions, and and the conversion of arable land to pasture were the natural result, for surveyors wrote up values at each transfer, and, unless the last purchaser squeezed his tenants, the transaction would not pay. Why, after all, should a landlord be more squeamish than the Crown?[2]

This historical process greatly accelerated a practice which had only been happening at a slow trickle earlier: enclosure.[3] Land that had been formerly subject to common rights was being seized by the aristocracy and enclosed with fences, ditches, hedges, or other barriers. Earlier statutes allowing enclosure

(1235, 1285) did so only on the condition that sufficient land be left available for the previous tenants. Pressure to increase this practice intensified when the growth of the wool trade made the lands more profitable when used for grazing sheep than when used for tenant farming. Whereas Christian feudal social obligations of the lord of the manor had held this in check, under Henry's material and other appetites these checks were being quickly broken down. When peasants of the Sussex manor of the monastery of Sion protested to the new owner about his seizure of their commons, he answered: "Do ye not know that the King's grace hath put down all the houses of monks, friars, and nuns? Therefore, now is the time come that we gentlemen will pull down the houses of such poor knaves as ye be."[4]

The English clergy who had any moral sense protested; among these was the outspoken John Latimer, who noted plainly that "the poor man hath title to the rich man's goods."[5] Enclosure constituted a robbery because the poor in feudal society also had their property rights, even though they were not as explicit as the property rights of the nobility. The nobles' right of land proprietorship included the peasants' right of land tenancy and livelihood. These implied land rights of the peasantry were torn assunder by enclosure, thus creating for the first time in English history the condition of pauperism, or poverty. It is in this sense that poverty can be seen as a modern condition. Thus, when Elizabeth completed her tour of England at the end of the sixteenth century and saw "paupers everywhere!" she may not have fully appreciated how her father, King Henry VIII, through his policy of estate confiscation, had contributed to that condition.

The Frenchman Pierre Joseph Proudhon, responding to similar historical conditions in his country, and disappointed by the failures of reform of the Revolution of 1789, wrote an essay in 1840 whose title asked the question "What Is Property?" His famous answer was that "property is theft." Proudhon's apparent radicalism attracted the interest of Marx and Engels for a while. But when they found that Proudhon's position was based on ethical principles rather than those of the "material laws of social motion," and that he condemned communism, they abandoned him in acrimonious dismissal and wrote a book against him: *The Poverty of Philosophy*. Similarly, on the right the advocates of privilege have painted Proudhon's message as standing against *personal* property, such as one's house, garden, or even toothbrush. They do not see that Proudhon's criticism was actually of the denial of the right to *have* personal property, namely the right to be economically productive and to survive. Living in a largely agrarian age, Proudhon focused on land and believed that ownership, rather than tenancy, of land was wrong, and that that was what made for poverty.

Proudhon's answer to the question "What is property?" can also be understood and rephrased as "*Poverty* is theft"; that is, there are poor because others have appropriated the basis of their livelihood. Charges often made today against the poor, such as that they are lazy and don't want to work, were not an issue for Proudhon. Since he largely conceived of livelihood as land, the notion of someone having their share of land but not working it to sustain themselves and family would have been absurd. A significant difference enters the picture when we talk about livelihood through jobs rather than land husbandry, and we will turn to this shortly.

Several recent scholars and researchers since Tawney have tried to make the point that an increase in population, rather than enclosure, was what largely accounted for the economic changes in the period of time that marked the transition from the feudal to the industrial economy. This is an obviously Malthusian approach, in that it attempts to see social changes as due to impersonal social "forces," such as population pressure, rather than to the ultimately free-will decisions of individuals. It was part of Tawney's genius to be able to depart from this abstract and presumably "scientific" approach and to investigate historical and social change as being fundamentally issues of human choice and responsibility, such as that of the landowners.

A commentator on Tawney, Lawrence Stone, while himself

believing that the enclosures history should be seen within a broader context of population change and other forces, nevertheless captures for us the essential and fundamental difference between a free-will or moral point of view and a mechanistic or traditionally scientific one when he describes Tawney in the following statement: "Tawney was above all a Christian moralist, a prophet, who tended to ascribe the evils of the world to the activities of wicked men rather than to the inexorable grip of circumstances or the defects of institutions."[6] Lest the significant point of this description be obscured, we should note that the critical issue is that Tawney is described as a moralist in the large sense, and not necessarily as a Christian moralist.

We can see then that in order to allow for the possibility of morality, we need to have room in our conceptualization for choice—that is, free choice, or free will. The destructive effect of science on morality, as we have previously seen in chapter 8, was that its causality and determinism really eliminated the idea of free choice or free will. What we further point out here is that if choice is not conceived of as being free, then it is really not choice at all. This becomes clear in the case of economics. Besides its definition as the science of self-interest, economics is also sometimes defined as the science of choice. But, as is the case with other words that economics uses, such as *rationality* and *efficiency*, the word *choice* in economics no longer means what it does in common usage. In economics *choice* means calculating one's utility or gain and then "choosing" the action that promises the greater amount of utility. We have seen the basis of this principle when we discussed Bentham in chapter 8.

The problem with this is that if choice is based on calculation, then it is not choice at all, but arithmetic. It is like "choosing" which is greater, two or nine. Calculation makes choice automatic, and thus removes choice. For choice to be real, that is, free, it has to be qualitative and not quantitative. In terms of human behavior real choice would have to be between ends, not means, and this kind of choice is exactly what economics doesn't allow in its ballpark.

As regards Proudhon's concern about the problem of poverty, the peasants who were forced off their land (either by "forces" or by the decision of the landlords) did not go easy into the new environment of the city workshop and factory. They did not experience this change as a liberation from feudalism, as some economic commentaries like to picture it. For the peasants it was an exchange of what was theirs and what was familiar for what was alien and harsh. Tawney himself describes this early condition of the peasants quite clearly: "Living, as they did, with the marks of villein tenure still upon them, the small cultivators of our period were fettered by the remnants of the legal rightlessness of the Middle Ages, without enjoying the practical security given by medieval custom, and felt the bitter breath of modern commercialism, undefended by the protection of the all-inclusive modern state which alone can make it tolerable."[7] This latter "protection" which Tawney refers to is, of course, the social security, unemployment insurance, and welfare provisions of the modern industrial state.

It has been hypothesized that the removal of the Poor Laws from the dispossessed peasantry was a necessary condition for making them submit to the rigors of city and factory life, to thus become wage labor for a new industrial society. Christopher Hill writes, "Wage labour and the Poor Laws rise together and complement one another."[8] The economic historian Karl Polanyi says that "nothing could have been more potent than the mutual incompatibility of institutions like the wage system and the 'right to live.' "[9] By this, Polanyi is referring to the belief that the conversion of the serfs into the members of a newly forming working class could never have occurred without the removal of the life supports of the manorial system. If they had had the choice, these peasants would never have opted for the mills and factories. All other means of survival had first to be removed.

Thus it was a matter of obviousness to the political economists of the 1800s that work—or more specifically *labor*, as it is still called in economic theory—is inherently painful and distasteful. No one would engage in it unless they were forced to do so by want and necessity. As Thomas Malthus states, the proper effect of want on the poor, which relief would have undermined, was "that of making the lower classes of people do more work."[10] David Ricardo, of course, was in strong accord with Malthus on this point. Jeremy Bentham, for his part, phrased it quite definitively: "Aversion is the emotion—the only emotion—which labour, taken by itself is qualified to produce. . . . In so far as labour is taken in its proper sense, love of labour is a contradiction in terms."[11]

It should be clear from these remarks, taken in their historical setting, that the position of the new factory workers was only the smallest degree higher than that of a slave. After all, a slave has to be provided with minimal sustenance if that slave is to live and continue as a productive worker. The wages paid to these laborers were barely higher than those provided to a slave, and, when compared to those of well-treated slaves, even less. When Ricardo developed Smith's concept of the "natural price" of labor, as arising out of the laws of supply and demand in a labor market, he theorized that the price ought to be the amount needed to assure the laborer's subsistence and ensure his reproduction. According to Ricardo, it is only when these natural laws are interfered with by relief for the poor or wage supports that the actual price paid for labor rises above the "natural" price.

The idea of laziness as an inherent trait of the laborer can now be better understood. This is traditionally the complaint of the master against the servant, or, in economic terms specifically, of the employer against the employee. The reader may recall that in the eighteenth century Smith commonly and naturally used the language of his time, referring to the employer as the "master." In law, the relationship between employer and employee has traditionally been referred to as "master-servant." We can see from this that the prototype of the "lazy" worker is the slave; in slave-keeping societies the common complaint, again of the master, is that their slaves are lazy and don't want to work. If one works for oneself, or owns the means of one's livelihood, as advocated by Proudhon's model, the issue of laziness doesn't arise. Of course, individuals do differ in their capacity and motivation for "work," but in the context of working for oneself the issue is one of lack of ambition, or values perhaps, rather than one of "laziness."

Smith himself was well aware of these issues. In *The Wealth of Nations* he argues against the opinion that high wages ("cheap years") encourage idleness. He says, "That a little more plenty than ordinary may render some workmen idle, cannot well be doubted; but that it should have this effect upon the greater part, or that men in general should work better when they are ill fed than when they are well fed, when they are disheartened than when they are in good spirits, when they are frequently sick than when they are generally in good health, seems not very probable." He observes the basis for the erroneous belief that scarcity, or "dearness," encourages workers: "Masters of all sorts . . . frequently make better bargains with their servants in dear than in cheap years, and find them more humble and dependent in the former than in the latter. They naturally, therefore, commend the former as more favorable to industry." But Smith then goes right to the heart of the matter, by talking about self-employment versus working for another: "Nothing can be more absurd, however, than to imagine that men in general should work less when they work for themselves, than when they work for other people. A poor independent workman will generally be more industrious than even a journeyman who works by the piece. The one enjoys the whole produce of his own industry; the other shares it with his master."[12]

The coercion, by threat of starvation, that transformed the feudal serf into the early industrial factory worker is at a far remove from the lot and life of today's employed worker. Even though economic theory still maintains the term *labor* to describe anyone working for a wage, whether he or she is a millionaire athlete, a TV star, a research scientist, or, indeed, a factory worker, common sense tells us that many of these jobs provide a lot more intrinsic satisfaction than just the wage compensation for the supposed pain or "disutility" of labor. A major source of fulfillment in life is in work—not in consumption, as economists and the advertising industry would have us believe.

The change that most distinguishes the early industrial world from that of today has been the introduction of the welfare provisions of the modern industrial state, such as social security, sickness and health benefits, minimum wage legislation, and unemployment insurance. Underlying these developments, and perhaps most significant of all, has been the overcoming of the traditional *anticombination* laws, resulting in the formation of labor unions. If anything has proved the socialists wrong in their dire predictions of the destructive effect of capitalism it has been this.

However, it should be remembered that, ironically, each of these provisions for the improvement of working life was generally opposed by economists at the time it was introduced. Such changes were seen as running against and undermining the laws of the free market, and they were only finally passed into law when the will of the political system was able to override the opposition of business interests. We can now see, as a result of our historical survey, that the essential function of the modern social and welfare provisions has been to restore to the wage labor system the security institutions of the Middle Ages— institutions which were torn away by the elimination of the Poor Laws and the creation of the industrial worker. Nevertheless, the security of the modern employee is still a precarious one, as the ups and downs of the business cycle—plant closings and relocations, mergers, and buy-outs—can all too suddenly and dramatically make clear. The modern worker is certainly immeasurably better off than his or her counterpart of the early industrial era. Nevertheless, the modern worker still exists, by the fact of his being an employee, in the condition of *precariousness*, particularly as we understand Proudhon's analysis of that term in regard to employment.

Proudhon explains: "Just as the commoner once held his land by the munificence and condescension of the lord, so today the working man holds his labor by the condescension and necessities of the master and proprietor: that is what is called possession by a precarious title."[13] Proudhon then elucidates that the word *precarious* comes from the Latin *precor*, which means "I pray"; the act of granting employment by the master expressly signified that he had answered the prayers of his men and allowed them permission to labor.

Proudhon's analysis should reveal to us that any job holder, no matter how adequately paid or how humane his working conditions, still exists precariously, as a commodity. The worker's present situation is not *intrinsically* different from how it has always been, ever since the beginning of the new system of wage employment that followed the dissolution of feudal serfdom. Given that this is so, we could say that working for a wage may not be an economic form that is ultimately consistent with full human dignity. In a modern, technological economy is there any answer to this?

If Pope Zacharias, along with some other popes, seem in our history to be the villians of this piece, that designation does not apply to the Catholic Church as a whole, and we are now about to look at some Catholic heroes. The ironies of history can also be sweet, and it may be the case that the Catholic Church, in seeking its own possibilities for renewal and redemption, can offer something to a worldwide society seeking the same.

A different order of papal statement than the advice of Zacharias to Pepin can be seen in the 1896 encyclical of Pope Leo XIII, *Rerum Novarum*, sometimes called, "The Condition of Labor." In it, Leo, who had become increasingly critical of the existing social order from the perspective of the original teachings of Jesus, expressed his belief that "a remedy must be found . . . for the misery and wretchedness which press so heavily at this moment on the large majority of the very poor." He continued with an indictment of laissez-faire market economics that was as bitterly critical as that of avowed socialists, although the pope himself also condemned socialism:

Working men have been given over, isolated and defenseless, to the callousness of employers and the greed of
unrestrained competition. The evil has been increased by
rapacious usury . . . still practiced by avaricious and grasp-
ing men. And to this must be added the custom of working
by contract, and the concentration of so many branches of
trade in the hands of a few individuals, so that a small
number of very rich men have been able to lay upon the
masses of the poor a yoke little better than slavery itself.[14]

The tradition of Leo XIII has been continued by subsequent
popes, the Catholic trade union movement, the Catholic peace
and social reform movement of Peter Maurin, Dorothy Day and
the *Catholic Worker*, the "liberation theology" movement in
Latin America, and other Catholic-based groups of social reform. This body of developing Catholic thought has come to be
known as *Catholic social doctrine*. As Pope John Paul states in
his recent encyclical *Sollicitudo Rei Socialis* ("On Social Concern"), "The characteristic principle of Christian social doctrine
[is that] the goods of the world are originally meant for all."[15]
Catholic social doctrine is consistently critical of both capitalism
and socialism, suggesting that they are both "structures of sin,"
while seemingly groping for a third way.

A student of Catholic social doctrine in the 1930s was the
young Basque priest Father Don Jose Maria Arizmendi-Arrieta.
When civil war broke out in Spain in 1936, Arizmendi—at the
time a Basque student priest loyal to the constitutional government—joined an army battalion against Franco's attempt to
overthrow the government. When the constitutional Spanish
government fell to Franco and the fascists, Arizmendi spent a
month in prison and barely escaped execution. Upon his release
he returned to studying for the priesthood, and at the seminary
library in the Basque town of Vitoria he pursued a strong interest
in social problems and social theory. When the time of his
ordination approached, he applied to be sent to the University of
Louvain in Belgium to pursue a degree in sociology. His request

was turned down; instead he was sent to a small and inconspic-uous Basque town, Mondragon, to serve as a parish priest.[16]

The name *Mondragon* derives from "tail of the dragon" and refers to the ragged shape of the mountain ridges that surround and isolate the town. Arizmendi arrived in Mondragon on Feb-ruary 5, 1941, succeeding a priest who had been executed by the Franco regime. The Mondragon that Father Arizmendi found upon his arrival was a defeated community—hopeless, de-pressed, and with widespread unemployment. Later on this time came to be called the "hunger period." Father Arizmendi told the people that work should not be seen as a punishment but as means of self-realization. There should be dignity in work. He also spoke of the need for cooperation and social solidarity. But he had a poor public speaking style, and his ideas were new and strange and hard to follow. He did not deliver sparkling oratori-cal sermons as the previous priest had done, and in general his debut in his new parish was a disappointment to the people. But they found him a very active priest, particularly with regard to his study circles. These discussion groups covered a wide range of topics, and seemed to be as much about sociology as they were about theology. They discussed conflicts between capital and labor, reform of private enterprise, and the participation of workers in management.

The major employer in Mondragon was a foundry and metal-working company, the Union Cerrajera. This traditional, con-servative company had successfully overcome efforts at unioni-zation and was continuing to keep a list of people who were not to be employed because they were potential troublemakers. The company ran a technical training school for their apprentices, and entrance into the school was restricted to the sons of employees. As was the custom, the new priest was invited to provide religious instruction as part of the apprenticeship pro-gram. Father Arizmendi took advantage of this opening to urge the company to expand its program by accepting boys who were not related to employees. The company refused.

Father Arizmendi then decided to try to interest local parents in making contributions toward starting an independent school. This effort proved to be successful, and about fifteen percent of the adult population of Mondragon responded with pledges of support. In 1943 the school opened, with twenty students. The enrollment eventually included girls—a first for Mondragon. What was notable about the school, however, besides its very existence, was the degree of democratic participation of the sponsors and supporters. There were four different membership groups: those who simply expressed an interest, those who made a certain minimal contribution, active members, and teachers. Each membership group elected ten representatives to a general assembly, which then elected a fourteen-member school board. This may seem overly elaborate for what appears to be a rather small operation—as if Father Arizmendi were playing at democracy the way children play house. However, time proved this not to be the case (perhaps in the same way that time proves playing house to be more than just playing).

The school expanded its program by adding a new grade level each time the students had completed the previous one, so that eventually it had all the grades through the American equivalent of high school. Its first graduating class went to work, of course, in the Union Cerrajera, but they were interested in continuing their education—something which no Mondragon student had ever done before. At first this seemed impossible because there was no university anywhere near Mondragon. Father Arizmendi looked into this, and eventually he was able to work out an arrangement with the University of Zaragoza, outside of the Basque country, where the students could matriculate by studying off-campus—something that was no doubt unusual back then. Out of this arrangement, eleven men of the first graduating class of the Mondragon school went on to receive degrees in technical engineering from the university.

Meanwhile, the students continuing their employment at the Union Cerrajera were finding the traditional and archaic labor/management environment stifling. After a number of unsuccessful attempts to introduce some measure of worker participation

in the plant, five of these new graduate employees—Luis Usa-
torre, Jesus Larranga, Alfonso Gorronogoitia, Jose Maria Or-
maechea, and Javier Ortubay—became interested in forming
their own company, along the lines that they had been discussing
over the years with their mentor, Father Arizmendi. Though they
had by this time a small amount of their own funds, they did not
have nearly enough capital to get a manufacturing business off
the ground. They discussed this problem with Father Arizmendi,
and he suggested they go to the community, as he had done to
start the school. These proponents of the new business venture
did not know what their new firm would produce, or where it
would be located, or anything else about it. Nevertheless, because of the respect they had as the first university-educated
children of blue-collar working parents, and also because of the
townspeople's faith in Father Arizmendi, the group was able to
raise about $360,000 in pledges—an enormous sum for that
community at the time (1955).

But that was only the first challenge. In Spain at that time,
citizens did not have the freedom to create their own companies.
This was a privilege jealously guarded by state authorities, who
had to issue permits, and who did so relatively rarely and with
great reluctance. The five new graduates presented the idea of
starting a foundry to the licensing officials, but the proposal was
buried in the government's files. A break came when they found
out that an existing firm in a nearby town had gone bankrupt
and was up for sale. The assets of the firm were of little value,
but the Mondragon group realized that by buying the firm they
would also gain the firm's license; to them that was a prize much
greater than any building or equipment that was up for sale.
They were able to do this, and they then moved that company to
Mondragon. They renamed the company Ulgor, an acronym
made up of the first letter of the last names of the five founders.
With Father Arizmendi they discussed the form that the company
should take, and they all agreed that it should be a cooperative.
Since the company was chartered to produce electrical and
mechanical products for home use, they took this direction with

their first product, which was a small kerosene heater and cooker of British design.

Father Arizmendi, having studied the history of cooperatives, knew that conventional wisdom said that, while consumer cooperatives might succeed, manufacturing or producer cooperatives were bound to run aground. The idea of a worker cooperative had always existed as a romantic ideal—one that various economists, including John Stuart Mill, the last of the great classical economists, had waxed enthusiastic over. In practice, though, these enterprises had invariably run into a curious dilemma. Either they were destined to remain as small, labor-intensive companies, with little economic significance and impact, or, if they were successful and grew, they were doomed as cooperatives by their own success.

This latter fate is illustrated by the case of one of the earliest and best-known experiments in producer cooperatives, the Rochdale Cooperative Manufacturing Society, which was begun in England around 1850. It began when, twenty-four weavers who were jobless organized a consumer cooperative grocery store, which proved to be successful. They then ventured into manufacturing and began a woolen mill. Again, their enterprise was successful, and in 1859 they decided they needed to raise additional capital to expand. They did the natural thing, which was to sell shares. They had little trouble doing so, and before long each share was quite valuable. However, as more and more of the original worker-owners sold out to outside investors, who could afford the shares, the company rather quickly began to resemble a conventional firm. Outside stockholders received the profits, and they employed workers in the company, who were paid a wage.

This same pattern had proved to be the fate of other cooperative ventures, for example a number of highly successful plywood companies on the American West Coast, such as the Olympia Veneer Company and Anacortes Plywood. As these companies became successful, new workers could no longer afford to buy shares and they had to come on as hired employees. The shares of these companies were eventually sold to the United States Plywood Corporation.[17]

Through studying the history of cooperatives, Father Arizmendi knew that the problem was share ownership. He felt that in principle it was wrong for someone to profit from the work of others, and also direct their work life, when they themselves did not work in the company with the workers. To have one group of people, the stockholders, deciding the fate of another group of people, the employees, was like having the citizens of one country making decisions for the citizens of another country. Therefore, the idea of stock shares had to be dropped, and investment in the firm had to be separated from rights of participation in the firm's governance. Father Arizmendi's solution, based on what came to be called the *individual capital account* (ICA), was an ingenious one.

In the Mondragon cooperative, each worker owner had a record with the company of his or her capital input into the company (a capital account, or ICA). All of the company's capital assets were covered by these accounts, so that the worker-owners, or members, constituted the total capital holders of the firm. The firm could seek outside capital, but only through loans or bonds, not through selling shares of stock in the company. Only members—those who actually worked in the company—could have capital accounts. Furthermore, and this is the most critical point, voting participation in the company's policies and direction occurred on a one person/one vote basis (one member/one vote), regardless of the amount in one's capital account. This is the full implementation of the principle of democracy in the context of work, in contrast to the stock ownership principle of voting, which is based on number of shares, or wealth. If we applied the latter principle to the political arena, it would be comparable to people voting in elections in proportion to what their income was: those who earned more would have a greater vote. In the Mondragon cooperative, labor employed capital, rather than capital employing labor.

The one person/one vote principle does not mean, however,

that everyone makes every decision, so that the company soon bogs down in a welter of inefficiency. The Mondragon cooperative was to have a board of directors and a general manager like any other large, efficient business organization. The difference was that the worker-owners elected their own board, which in turn appointed or hired a manager. This manager had a term of office or appointment just like any other executive, but the vote for renewal (through the board) was based on a one person/one vote of the company membership, not on any outside interests. In the early discussions of the Mondragon cooperative form, Father Arizmendi articulated this need for organizational discipline, and that the need did not have to be incompatible with the cooperative form:

> Human work must be subjected to discipline and its performance as a team effort requires order and thus authority. The members of this cooperative, once they have elected those most suitable for governance, must show spontaneous and rigorous respect for the order of those who hold positions of command within their internal structure.[18]

Thus, in the one stroke of internal democracy, and with no outside control, the worker's place in industry as a commodity ends. He or she is no longer an "input" into the productive system, serving the interests of outside stockholders, or a mere tool of the industrial process to be discarded or replaced when conditions warrant. The member of a Mondragon cooperative, by being a full owner with voting rights equivalent to any other member's, no matter how disparate their capital holdings in the firm, becomes master of his or her own fate and attains full human dignity. The paternalism of feudalism is abolished; the indifference of the wage labor system is abolished; and the fraternalism of human community comes into being.

A few other details of the system that the early Mondragon pioneers worked out need to be mentioned so that the reader can have a minimally sufficient idea of how it works and of how some of the long-standing problems of producer cooperative businesses have been solved. Each member receives a regular weekly paycheck, which is viewed as a measure of that member's contribution to the company's performance. This is not a wage, but an advance on profits. At year's end the remaining profits (or losses) get credited to each member's ICA, in proportion to his or her weekly paycheck. The buildup of capital in one's ICA is gradually paid out to each member in a certain schedule that balances the need for the internal retention of funds by the firm for its capital development and the return to members of their earned equity. Upon retirement or leaving the firm, the remainder of one's ICA is paid out over a several-year period (in order not to risk too-sudden decapitalization of the firm). Again, this is not retirement pay, but real equity which exists in addition to a retirement income program.

Now what about the question that all previous cooperative businesses stumbled over: how to add needed new workers without turning them into the hired hands of the existing owners, thus eventually reducing and devolving the firm back into a situation where capital employs labor? The answer has already been foreshadowed in the discussion of the ICA. The existing wealth of current owners presents no barriers to new members coming in, since they don't have to buy out anyone's shares of stock. All they have to do is make an investment in the firm, which can be any amount that the firm has chosen as the entering investment fee. This fee becomes capital for the firm, and it is also the start of the new member's own ICA; the fee gets recorded in his or her account. But what is to be done if an interested person wants to join, and would apparently be good for the firm (and thus accepted by the firm), but cannot afford the starting investment fee? The firm, in this case, makes a loan to the individual in the form of the requisite beginning balance in their ICA, and he or she can pay it back to the firm over time through deductions from the weekly paycheck. And what is to be done if the firm itself wants to take on new member(s) but cannot afford to loan them their entrance investment fee? In that case the firm can turn to the bank. What bank? Ah, we have gotten ahead of the rest of our story of how all this came to be.

In 1956, in the spirit of the new business form they had created and through their genuine business and technical skills, the small new company that was founded and designed by Father Arizmendi's former pupils did well. They began with 24 worker-owners, but by 1959 there were 170, making this a fairly large company for the district. They built several new factories and also established their own brand name, Fagor. Each of the new plants was set up as a separate cooperative, independent of Ulgor, the founding company, but naturally connected to each other through their common origin and form. These growing, successful firms, which were producing technological products, would need even more capital than they were able to generate internally to be able to thrive in the greater Spanish economy, beyond the local Basque areas. But where was this new capital to come from? Most private banks in Spain at the time would hardly lend large sums of investment capital to a worker cooperative. This time Father Arizmendi came up with an idea that was too much even for most of his followers and students: they should start a bank. One of them reports their reaction: "We told him, yesterday we were craftsmen, freemen, and engineers. Today we are trying to learn how to be managers and executives. Tomorrow you want us to become bankers. That is impossible."

But part of the moral of this story is that with vision, faith, persistence, and a little bit of cleverness nothing may be impossible. So in 1959 a small bank was chartered, the Caja Laboral Popular, "the bank of the people's labor." And now we can move ahead very fast with our story. The bank has since become one of the biggest success stories in Mondragon. Ten years after its founding it had 54 branches, and by 1986 the number was 171. In 1986 it had assets of over two billion dollars and an overall staff of 1,223, making it one of the two dozen largest banks in a now thriving Spanish economy. The large number of staff is very pleasing to the Mondragon group, since they have never forgotten that the main purpose of their enterprises is to create employment, with profit serving as the means to this end. Apart from supplying investment capital, the bank also of course makes loans to new member-owners so that they can join the growing firms.

Since the early 1950s over one hundred separate worker co-operative businesses have been created in Spain in almost every manner of industry: from steel manufacturing, to robotics, to plastics, to consumer appliances, to housing construction, to agribusiness. Of these, only three have failed—a record unmatched in any other industrial development. The comparable statistic in the United States is that only twenty percent of all business startups *survive*.

The total employment in all cooperatives is now around 20,000. Eroski, a new consumer cooperative supermarket that was set up in 1968, today has over 150,000 consumer members, a staff of about 1,400 and approximately 100 supermarkets spread all over the Basque region. Eroski now ranks as Spain's eighth largest consumer goods outlet. A social security cooperative set up in 1970 today provides its 50,000 associated members with comprehensive health and pension benefits. In 1977, a research and development cooperative, Ikerlan, was set up to provide the industrial cooperatives with state-of-the-art science and technology. In just a few short years it has gained a reputation as one of the leading industrial research institutes in Spain, and it has won increasing international attention. More recently, a cooperative business college was established to help develop and teach the special approach to management that is called for in the cooperative enterprise.

If Mondragon represents such an economic miracle, why isn't it better known? The answer is, mainly, Franco. Up until his death in 1975, Mondragon had no intention of keeping anything but a low profile. After his death the word began to leak out. But cooperative businesses that today are identified by the name Mondragon are not missionaries and have no interest in either trumpeting their message to the world or in having the world beat a path to their door. They are ordinary men and women engaged in the business of making a living, and they perhaps already have been overly intruded upon by the relatively few outsiders who have learned of them and have gone over to investigate.

It is promising to note that efforts similar to that of the Mondragon example are now getting underway in the United States and other countries, including China and the Soviet Union. There are several consulting groups in the United States, such as the Industrial Cooperative Association in Somerville, Massachusetts, and the National Center for Employee Ownership in Washington, D.C., that advise businesses, government, and communities on establishing the worker-owner form.

In mentioning Spain, the United States, China, and the Soviet Union in one economic breath, we may get the clue that the cooperative enterprise as originally developed in Mondragon may in fact be a new form that transcends the traditional capitalist and socialist forms. One good indication of this is that the cooperatives have often been condemned by each side as belonging to the other. The socialists think that the cooperative is capitalist because it is not owned and run by the state, and it can only exist in a market environment (i.e., where the individual firm makes most of its own decisions). The capitalists think it is socialist because it has abolished the division between labor and capital, and also because they cannot "buy" a piece of the action.

And what about Father Arizmendi? He died in 1976, within a year of Franco, but the passing of the dictator received more notice. Don Jose Maria spent the last years of his life living in the college tower in the center of the Mondragon complex, where he could look around him and, hopefully with satisfaction, survey the fruits of what he and the others had created. Although his role as a priest would not have prevented it, he never became a member of any of the cooperatives and never had a formal role in their structure. He remained as he had always been, a curate of simple tastes whose role and purpose was to serve as a teacher and advisor. He otherwise stayed out of the way—with one exception.

This one exception points out to us that it would be a mistake
to see Father Arizmendi as a saint. For one thing, he is not
technically a saint, because he has not yet been so canonized by
the Church. Another reason involved the creation of the cooperative bank, the Caja Laboral Popular. When Father Arizmendi
approached the Ulgor founders with the idea, they found it to be
so outrageous that they almost literally threw him out. So he
proceeded about the business of establishing the bank all on his
own. As a prerequisite for the establishment of such an institution, the Spanish government required that there be a preorgani-
zation business meeting with minutes. So Arizmendi presented a
document to the government in which it was recorded that the
members had approved a constitution and bylaws. The document
was also signed by two of the Ulgor founders. This meeting and
the resulting agreements had never, in fact, taken place; the
document was a complete creation of Father Arizmendi, including the signatures of the founders, which he forged. When the
fictitious "founders" found out about this little bit of deception
from the good father, they were mildly annoyed, if not amused,
but they didn't take it too seriously because they didn't think the
whole idea would amount to anything. In time they all came to
recognize that they had underestimated their own capabilities,
and the Caja has since become the central institution in developing and coordinating the cooperatives. Perhaps a more important
reason for not viewing Father Arizmendi as a saint is that, if we
do so, we separate him from the rest of us and believe that what
he achieved is something unique that cannot be achieved by other
human beings.

But as important as the newly emerging cooperative form may
be, in that it is apparently one corrective for Adam Smith's
mistake, it may still not be at the bottom line, so to speak, of
what that mistake is most fundamentally all about.

11

TEXTBOOKS OF THE TEMPLES

Since self-interest is about the self it goes to the core of the person, so that the problem of self-interest is a problem at the core of society. It is, therefore, much more than a problem in economics. It touches all areas of our lives, and it is always present as an issue when we are dealing with other people.

We have tried to show that a doctrine that promotes self-interest as the good is a doctrine that promotes selfishness. In social situations we are always faced with a choice between the lower and the higher: between a concern for ourselves regardless of others and a concern for others as well as ourselves. This choice is always present, although it is more acute and critical in some situations than others. Moral and spiritual development depends upon one's increasing awareness of the presence of this choice. A choice of the higher means a concern for others *as well as* oneself; it does not mean a concern for others regardless of oneself. Being altruistic does not necessarily mean that one sacrifices oneself for the sake of the other, but only that one is good-willed or benevolent toward the other, responding to them in a spirit of common interest or mutuality.

To the extent that we are no longer callous to this issue, a doctrine of self-interest that promotes itself as preferable to benevolence should strike us with a moral shock. A society such as the United States, which not only does not feel a shock at this but, even more, has come to accept it as correct, is a society that we can expect to be broadly marked by a lack of caring. In fact this lack shows itself in an array of forms, from the gross and violent to the subtle callousness of indifference.

First the gross. The United States, which more than any other modern industrialized society has an economy based on unrestrained self-interest, also has the widest gap between the rich and the poor and the most meager provision of social welfare supports.[1] This country also has an astounding amount of crime. The rate of criminal homicide in the United States is ten times as great as that found in the major cities of Western Europe, and the rate of armed robbery is twenty times as high. The prison population is currently at an all-time high, having more than doubled in the past ten years, and now represents a higher percentage of the total population than in any other country in the world except for two: South Africa and the Soviet Union.[2] The United States' drug problem, which at an estimated sixty billion dollars a year is in the same economic class as consumer electronics, automobiles, and steelmaking, should be seen as intimately connected to its surrounding economic environment. An anthropology student who has lived in the inner-city drug culture relates this: "Based on my experience, I believe the assertion of the culture-of-poverty theorists that the poor have been badly socialized and do not share mainstream values is wrong. On the contrary, ambitious, energetic, inner-city youths are attracted to the underground economy precisely because they believe in the rags-to-riches American dream. Like many in the mainstream, they are frantically trying to get their piece of the pie as fast as possible."[3]

Some of the subtle effects of the self-interest philosophy are revealed in the following little anecdote. An American couple took a motor trip to Canada in the early 1970s, to visit Nova Scotia. They began having trouble with their muffler in the United States, but decided to wait until they got to Canada to have it fixed. They made it into Canada, relieved that their vehicle was still intact, and pulled into a "Monsieur Muffler" in Nouveau Brunswick. They were happy to be rather quickly accommodated at this shop, and after about twenty minutes of work a

Textbooks of the Temples   193

new clamp has been put on the muffler pipe. That was all it took to fix the problem.

The couple waited for their bill, feeling relieved but with some concern that perhaps as tourists they would be given a rather hefty bill for what had turned out not to be a major repair. They were certainly familiar with the surprisingly large charges for small repairs that auto repair shops in the United States were often known to charge. Thus, they were disbelieving when the shopkeeper told them that there was no charge. "No charge?" they asked, thinking this must be some kind of trick. But no charge turned out to be the case. "Why no charge?" they now asked, needing an explanation for what to them was completely anomalous behavior on the part of the dealer. They were told, simply and pleasantly, that it wasn't a big job, and since they were on a visit they should go on and enjoy themselves. The Americans had trouble accepting this and felt constrained to offer money, but this was again turned down. They left the shop, not only in amazement, but with some sense of guilt that they should have paid something.

It is hard to say whether it was specifically that they were Americans, or just that they were members of modern Western consumer society that made this experience, as small as it was, so surprising to these visitors. Our tourists, perhaps primed by this first experience, then found the rest of their visit to this relatively poor but picturesque land marked by a quality of relations between themselves and others that was different, although certainly subtly so, from the relations they had been used to in the United States. This same difference was present in other shopkeepers, in waiters and waitresses, in people whom they stopped to ask for directions. Each person took just a little more time with them, was a little more attentive to their needs, and answered questions with just a bit more completeness, a bit more concern. This difference, though again subtle, was also certainly present in the public employees they encountered, such as the national park officials and guides, the police, and so forth: they took more care, seemingly, in what they did, and had more awareness of the other, the public.

Years later, in 1988, Canada had a general election whose central campaign issue was whether to increase free trade with the United States. Although the free-trade candidate won the election, a majority of the votes were split between two other candidates who opposed increased trade. Besides concerns that increased trade with the United States would have bad economic consequences for Canada, those against expanding trade appeared to be at least equally concerned about a projected detrimental effect on Canada's way of life. Canadians seem to take pride in their extensive network of social programs, which is comparable to that in Scandinavia. In Canada, as reported even in American newspapers, "Rates of violent crime are a fraction of those in the United States; urban slums are virtually unknown. Canadians also take pride in what they see as a higher level of environmental consciousness and a more efficient and equitable legal system."[4] So, perhaps, the experience of our American tourists, while certainly local and minor in scope, was a somewhat accurate reflection of the contrast between a society with the world's most extreme commitment to self-interest and a society that has learned to moderate that commitment.

The *New York Times* also noted 1988 as the year that could well be remembered as the time "when nastiness came into its own and became a commodity" in the United States. The *Times* notes some of the events leading to this conclusion: "Morton Downey, Jr. sneered at guests on his talk show and drew three million viewers a night. Geraldo Rivera's nose was broken, along with rating records, in a brawl on his own talk show when it presented a segment called 'Teen Hatemongers.' The harsh, scatological humor of performers like Eddie Murphy spawned a new phrase: attack comedy. And the presidential campaign was fueled by extraordinarily negative advertising and more than a few nasty one-liners."[5]

The everyday interactions between people, whether economic in nature or not, form the fabric of a society and define the quality of social life of that society. Furthermore, in the modern world it becomes increasingly impossible to draw any kind of clear distinction between what is economic and what is not, since the economic is so closely intertwined with all areas of our lives. The sociologist Christopher Lasch describes a culture in which the quality of caring has been diminished as a "culture of narcissism."[6] Lasch is more concerned with psychology in his analysis than economics but, as stated in the beginning of this book, I believe that psychology alone will not give us sufficient understanding of this problem. The present writer, who is a psychologist, is here making a case that the roots of our narcissism lie in thinking that is based in economics. No other academic discipline today understands that self-interest is the core of the ego as does economics. Furthermore, this narcissism should be seen ultimately as a moral disorder, rather than as a psychological one. The phenomenon of self-interest is so fundamental that it radiates outward from the core of the self and touches all aspects of society, from basic cultural values to economic behavior and onward to social policy.

Another psychologist, Martin Seligman, gets closer to the economic background of our cultural ills than Lasch does. Seligman is a noted expert in psychological depression, and he has contributed seminal research and theory in this area. In his analyses, Seligman looked at two extensive interview studies conducted by the Alcohol, Drug Abuse and Mental Health Administration of the United States government. One study found that people born after 1945 are ten times more likely to suffer depression than people born fifty years earlier. The other study found that there is a twentyfold increase in the likelihood of depression for those born after 1950 as compared to those born before 1910. It was also found that not only is depression becoming more common, but it is also occurring much earlier in life. This latter finding was initially puzzling since it is usually expected that the possibilities for depression increase as one gets older. The authors of the government studies, who had a biological and medical orientation, believed that the results showed an interaction between genes and the environment. Seligman seriously doubts this interpretation and instead notes other research that shows that non-Western cultures that are "pre-modern," that is, in which the economic point of view has not yet taken hold, show very little in the way of symptoms of depression as we know them: suicide, hopelessness, resignation, low self-esteem, alcoholism, and so forth. All these symptoms dramatically increase when modernization occurs and appear to be part of what are now well known as "diseases of civilization." Seligman's conclusion is that these changes occur as a result of changes in the self. In a trendy use of language, Seligman uses the term *California self* to refer to the self that is so prone to depression and defines it as representing an extreme "individualism." Its nature is that it has no basis of attachment to or belief in "something larger" than itself. Seligman describes the historical development of this self as "the waxing of the individual and the waning of the commons."[7]

The analysis of Robert Paul Mohan, a professor of philosophy, ethics, and theology at Catholic University in Washington, gets still closer, perhaps, to the economic roots of our contemporary social disorders, particularly in American society. In regard to the increasing nastiness in American life, as exemplified by the events described in the 1988 *New York Times* article, Mohan points out that the importance of something as apparently pedestrian as civility should not be underestimated. While we may take something like simple courtesy for granted—as we did clean air before there was pollution—we may find that it is in fact a precious social achievement which has been hard won over ages of human life and culture, and that once lost or squandered, it will be extremely costly to recover. Mohan's words correspond closely with our own discoveries: "I define civility as the outer ramparts of morality. I think civility has been replaced with the ethic of self-interest, accompanied with an inadvertent assumption that principles don't mean much. That has made us a rather rude, insensitive people."[8] This is counterpoint to the presumed glories of self-interest that were proclaimed by another professor,

Robert Parloff, to say nothing of Ayn Rand and her eminent and well-educated followers.

With the waning of the influence of religion in Western society, the university came to assume a prominent place in the formation and communication of ideas and beliefs. In time it came to supplant even the Church as the prime source of the modern world's values and truths, so that the university became the new temple—a temple of intellect to replace the old temple of the spirit. In this book we have taken a look at this new temple, and we have found what we believe to be a serious flaw in its preachments. If this new reigning institution can be symbolized by an apple—a common symbol for it—then the theory of self-interest in economics is a worm in the apple. In this sense, the discipline of economics is fundamentally different from every other discipline in the academic world, including the other social sciences. No other academic field, unless influenced by economics, teaches and promotes self-interest. All other fields, apart from temporary and local aberrations (which are indeed most likely due to the self-interest of its practitioners), essentially teach knowledge and truth. There is an underlying assumption in our society that if one enters into the temple of intellect, the acquisition of its wares will be of benefit to the individual and to society as a whole. To put it simply and directly, it is assumed that what is taught in this temple is good and not bad.

To illustrate this, let us look at criminology, another academic field which is also a social science. Criminology is the study of crime. Crime is of grave consequence for all members of society. Now, in studying crime, criminology is not value-neutral; it doesn't say that crime is neither good nor bad, that it just *is*, that we should study the behavior of criminals in the same way an entomologist might study the behavior of ants. Furthermore, it doesn't say that it is of no concern to us whether this thing we call crime increases or decreases. If, in fact, criminology was value-neutral toward its subject matter, we might imagine that it would have different schools of thought, some of which were procrime, and some of which were against it. Each could then occupy certain rooms of the temple. In one would be the criminal law school, consisting largely of police officers and judges, which would be devoted to the study of how to reduce crime. In another would be a second criminal school, consisting, say, of street burglars, the Mafia, a few white-collar embezzlers and inside traders, which would study how to expand its activities.

Our imagined scenario of a value-neutral criminology is indeed absurd, even comical, because it twists the true meaning of scientific objectivity. Criminology needs to be objective in studying crime in order to obtain the clearest and most accurate understanding of its nature, and this would be the true "naturalism" of the criminologist. But the criminologist is not neutral, nor a "naturalist," as to whether crime is good or bad. There he or she very much makes a value judgment. In fact, the very justification for the field of criminology lies in its identification of crime as undesirable. The same would apply in the harder sciences, especially in the study of ecology and the environment.

But economics takes quite a different stance, and once its intellectual mystifications are stripped away, that stance appears to be quite startling. It is as if, to stick with our metaphor, one were to open the door to a certain classroom in the temple and find a group of people who are wearing shirts and ties like everyone else in the temple—but something makes you look more closely, and you notice that they are making incendiary bombs.

Economics is not only naturalistic or neutral toward self-interest. If that were the case its teachings, while somewhat dubious, would not necessarily be objectionable. But economics *promotes* self-interest. Yes, the survival instinct or will to live, which is the basis of self-interest, is an inevitable force in society, as we have already had occasion to point out. It is a deeply instinctive force, present in all living species. As such it is a given. But it does not need to be boosted or given a forward push, any more than the flow of blood through the veins needs to be boosted.

Self-interest does not need a push; the impediments to its

natural and proper fulfillment need only to be removed. Those impediments, as we have seen in analyzing Adam Smith's work, are precisely the self-interest of others who are more powerful. In specifically economic terms, these others are the monopolists, whose own self-interest, running out of bounds, blocks the just fulfillment of the self-interest of the less powerful. In our analysis of Adam Smith's mistake we noted that in some parts of his work he makes it quite clear that self-interest must be tempered by justice. Justice, or fairness, is also natural, but it is also what makes the human species uniquely human. Justice is a principle that is on the side of the virtues and thus aligned with other virtues, such as mutuality, cooperation, honesty, integrity, and, yes, benevolence.

Once its elaborate justifications are removed, we find that economics, in teaching self-interest without teaching benevolence or justice, is in essence teaching *crime*—if we understand this word as a more direct expression of the latinate word *immorality*. This is an amazing discovery, and on the face of it so incredible that it is almost bound to be rejected. But a face is a surface, and in our analysis we have gone behind the face and beneath the surface to see what is the real meaning of naked self-interests. Our society is wracked by many ills, amidst its many achievements, and we should realize that the reason for these widespread ills has to be something very basic, which is as pervasive as the ills themselves. Furthermore, we should suspect that this something, in order to be such an effective malignant force, would need to disguise itself as something benign so that it could successfully invade the social body and do its destructive work—in much the same way that a virus can disguise itself as an agent of immunity in order to insinuate itself into the interior of the physical body.

If we are able to see then that naked self-interest is a malignant or malevolent force, it should also be quite clear that it can't at the same time be seen as the reason for our positive achievements. It is erroneous to assign the cause of both good and evil to the same principle. But those under the influence of economic teaching tend to do this all the time. If they don't fall into the Ayn Randian or Chicago school fallacy of seeing self-interest as totally good, they instead, more weakly, say that self-interest leads to both good and bad. But it can't do that. Good and bad are different. As a matter of fact, they are opposites. And the same principle by itself can't lead to opposites. Opposite effects can only come out of opposite principles. And we have seen in our study that within the framework of economics those opposites are benevolence and self-interest.

Thus, for self-interest to parade as a virtue rather than as a vice, it has to lie. It has to claim it is good when it is really bad. This is how immorality works all the time—through lying—just as a virus lies by hiding its true colors, its true purpose. Lying is hypocrisy and La Rochefoucauld expressed it as artfully as seems possible in the most famous of all his maxims: "Hypocrisy is the tribute that vice pays to virtue."

In addition to the word *bad* we have, from time to time, used the word *evil*. Such a word may seem even more out of place than the word *bad*; it seems too strong, too colored. But by using it we are able to appreciate another epigram which pithily, ages ago, expressed our thesis. Our thesis is nothing new: it is a moral truth, and moral truths are eternal; only the justifications and rationalizations that cover them over are new. We are referring to an epigram that is found in the New Testament, one of the textbooks of the first temple—the temple of the spirit. As we have seen, the teachings of that textbook have been obscured by the hypocrisy of some of the faculty of that temple, but we still may have an inkling that some of its teachings are indeed true. The epigram is in a letter from Paul to Timothy, and we all are familiar with it: "The love of money is the root of all evil."[9] As a result of our analysis we now can see that Adam Smith's textbook of the second temple—the temple of intellect—has been used as an elaborate system of mystification, sometimes going by the name of laissez-faire economics, to precisely deny this truth by turning it into its opposite. This is the discovery of

Adam Smith's mistake, and by this discovery we isolate a most fundamental and pervasive social virus.

One of the early economic critics of radical laissez-faire economics, the Frenchman Antoin Buvet, bitterly satirized the phrase *laissez-faire*, which had been coined in his own tongue, as *"laissez-faire la misère, laissez-faire la mort"*: "Do not interfere with misery, do not interfere with death." He saw that laissez-faire, taken in its unmoderated nakedness, was a counsel of moral indifference.

But for the pure economist, laissez-faire is nothing but the purest logic. Since we are all motivated by only self-interest, a move to restrict one's self-interest is itself only self-interest, so that such moves can only mean the loss of liberty. For the pure economic thinker, such restrictions can never mean the gain of liberty. In 1986 James Buchanan was awarded a Nobel Prize in economics for having formulated this very view, as what he calls his *public choice* theory of government. In his Nobel acceptance speech, Buchanan said that any difference in results between the market and politics is only a difference between the structures of these two institutional settings "rather than any switch in the motive of persons as they move between institutional roles." Furthermore, "Politics is a structure of complex exchange among individuals, a structure within which persons seek to secure collectively their own privately defined objectives that cannot be efficiently secured through simply market exchanges. In the absence of individual interest, there is no interest."[10]

Perhaps the most penetrating critique of this economic way of thinking, and one that applies to much of the theorizing about the person that takes place within the mechanistic and nonmoral framework of science, is that it is another instance of the classic liar's paradox.[11] This is the paradox of someone asserting that all people are liars. Since this statement must also apply to the person who utters it, it is a fundamental contradiction, or an absurdity. Economics, instead of saying that all people are liars, says that people are always motivated by self-interest. If, as Buchanan states, individuals do not shift away from self-interest motives when they move from the market to politics, and indeed they have no capacity for doing so, does this also apply to persons as they move from the market to academia? That is, does it apply to the economic thinker himself as a theorist? If so, then following his logic, we ought to conclude that his argument has no relation to what is true; he only writes whatever he believes will advance his own self-interest. In this the economic profession appears to have done very well.

Buchanan is generally seen as part of the pure self-interest wing of economics, which is most closely associated with the University of Chicago, and we have met up with this school frequently in our analysis. It is the belief of this school that the theory of self-interest should not be confined to economics, but, since it is the fundamental way people do act and should act, it ought to underlie all of the social sciences, and perhaps the humanities as well. This stance has been termed as academic *economic imperialism*, and not all who use this term do so critically—economic thinkers of this wing proudly advocate it.[12] It has been absorbed into law by the very "advocates" themselves, and it is present in all those in the legal profession who are influenced by the Chicago school of economics, including Supreme Court Judge Anthony Scalia and rejected nominee Robert Bork. Chicago Circuit Court Judge Richard Posner, himself mentioned as a future Supreme Court nominee, codified this way of thinking for the legal profession in his influential book *The Economics of Justice*. It is this system of beliefs that gives these individuals their odd, counterintuitive, and often countersocial, way of thinking and reasoning. Here is Judge Posner's recommendation in regard to what he considers "excessive" government regulation of child adoptions: "The baby shortage and black market are the result of legal restrictions that prevent the market from operating as freely in the sale of babies as of other goods. This suggests as a possible reform simply eliminating the restrictions."[13]

For these economists the birth of children is "production," as we would expect from the commodity conception. In their

Chicago school economics textbook, Richard McKenzie and Gordon Tullock describe a relationship where sex is involved, such as marriage, as a calculated, rational exchange, similar to prostitution. The only difference is that in prostitution the payment is "monetary" and in "ordinary" sexual relationships the payment is "non-monetary." Therefore, from the standpoint of the economic way of thinking, "it follows that the quantity of sex demanded is an inverse function of price. . . . The reason for this relationship is simply that the rational individual will consume sex up to the point that the marginal benefits equal the marginal costs. . . . If the price of sex rises relative to other goods, the consumer will 'rationally' choose to consume more of other goods and less sex. (Ice cream, as well as many other goods, can substitute for sex if the relative price requires it.)"[14]

We already have seen that this same way of thinking has also been applied in spades to the environment. Indeed, it is our belief that the promotion of economics driven by self-interest has been the mainspring of pollution and environmental degradation. This again follows from the principle of the free rider, where it is economically "rational" for the individual to externalize "costs" on to the environment. Economics both promotes self-interest and admits that the logic of self-interest is to free-ride. We have been free riding on the environment for generations now, and the day of the returning bill is fast upon us. To paraphrase one critical environmental economist, Herman Daly, they who put all their faith in the invisible hand, will eventually get kicked by the visible foot.[15]

The worm in the apple threatens to bring rot to the whole apple, and then we will have neither the temple of the spirit nor the temple of intellect as socially beneficial sources of moral guidance and strength. The temple of the intellect replaced in preeminence the temple of the spirit because of a fatal flaw in the latter: the flaw of hypocrisy. Now we have seen an inherent flaw in the temple of the intellect, and it is contained within the doctrine of economics. The failures of this temple are coordinate with the peculiar ills of modern society, which might be generally characterized as immense insecurity in the midst of immense material abundance. These ills may be even further generalized as poverty amidst plenty, if we take these words in their broadest meaning. This is a situation that should not endure, and probably cannot endure.

In this book we have tried to show that the doctrine of self-interest has been the primary culprit in this state of affairs. In order to correct it, in all of its pervasive manifestations, we must find guiding principles that are above and beyond self-interest— the principles of the higher self. The offering of those principles was part of the original purpose of the temple of the spirit. In an ironic historical turning, it may be that the two temples, while no doubt continuing to stand separate, will infuse each other with what the other is in need of. Spirit will lend heart to intellect, in a new integration.

We see this process of integration in the lives of the reformers, some of whom we have touched upon in our study. It may be from lives such as these, where heart and intellect are indeed integrated, that the wellspring of social regeneration lies. Another great reformer of our time, Mahatma Gandhi, used an integration of two Sanskrit words to describe this wellspring. He called it *satyagraha*, from *satya* ("truth") and *graha* ("force"), so that *satyagraha* is truthforce.

The composer Philip Glass wrote an opera about Gandhi called *Satyagraha*. In each of the acts of the opera, Gandhi's struggles are watched over by a relevant satyagraha figure. In act 1 it is Count Leo Tolstoy; in act 2, Rabindranath Tagore; in act 3, Reverend Martin Luther King. As the opera ends, Gandhi, under the watchful eye of Reverend King, looks out into the night as his companions sleep. A future satyagraha "army" appears for fifteen seconds in the night sky as a collection of stars, and then fades out. Gandhi sings these lines from the *Bhagavad Gita*, another textbook of the first temple, which refer to Light and Truth incarnating once again within the midst of humanity:

For whenever
the law of righteousness
withers away
and lawlessness arises:
then I generate
myself on earth.

I come into being
age after age
and take a visible shape
and move a man with men
for the protection of good,
thrusting the evil back:
and setting virtue
on her seat again.[16]

NOTES

Introduction: The Age of the Economist

1. Burke's phrase appears in his *Reflections on the French Revolution* (1790), as quoted in Daniel Fusfeld, *The Age of the Economist*, 3rd ed. (Glenview, Ill.: Scott, Foresman and Co., 1977), p. 39.

2. John M. Keynes, *The General Theory of Employment, Interest and Money* (1936), p. 383.

3. Francis Fukuyama, the state department official, published an article entitled "The End of History" in the Summer 1989 issue of the *National Interest*. See also the *New York Times Magazine* article by James Atlas, 22 October 1989.

4. References documenting the involvement of economics in academia in general have been gathered from Steven R. Rhoads, *The Economist's View of the World* (Cambridge: At the University Press, 1985), Introduction.

5. Ibid.

6. John Bunker, Benjamin Barnes, and Frederick Mosteller, *Costs, Risks, and Benefits of Surgery* (New York: Oxford University Press, 1977), esp. p. xiii.

7. Mark A. Lutz and Kenneth Lux, *Humanistic Economics: The New Challenge* (New York: Intermediate Technology Development Group [Bootstrap], 1988).

8. Robert L. Heilbroner, *The Worldly Philosophers* (New York: Simon and Schuster, Touchstone Books, 1980).

9. Richard H. Tawney, *Religion and the Rise of Capitalism* (New York: Harcourt, Brace & Co., Mentor Books, 1955), first published in 1926; and Karl Polanyi, *The Great Transformation* (Boston: Beacon Press, 1957), first published in 1944.

10. Paul L. Wachtel, *The Poverty of Affluence: A Psychological Portrait of the American Way of Life* (Philadelphia: New Society Publishers, 1989).

11. Werner Sichel and Peter Eckstein, *Basic Economic Concepts* (Chicago: Rand McNally, 1974), pp. 128–29.

12. William R. Allen, *Midnight Economist: Broadcast Essays III* (Los Angeles: International Institute for Economic Research, 1982), p. 23.

13. Campbell McConnell, *Economics*, 8th ed. (New York: McGraw-Hill, 1981), pp. 22–23.

14. Adam Smith, *An Inquiry into the Nature and Causes of the Wealth of Nations*, ed. Edwin Cannan (New York: Modern Library, 1937), first published in 1776.

15. Heilbroner, *The Worldly Philosophers*, pp. 38–39.

16. In Max Lerner's introduction to Smith, *The Wealth of Nations*, p. vi.

17. *New York Times*, 12 October 1986, sec. 3.

Chapter 1. The Journey of Adam Smith

1. Much of the biographical material on Adam Smith comes from the classic biography by John Rae: *The Life of Adam Smith* (New York: Reprints of Economic Classics, A. M. Kelley, 1965), first published in 1895.

2. Smith's description of Newton's work is in E. Ray Canterbery, *The Making of Economics*, 2nd ed. (Belmont, Calif.: Wadsworth, 1980), p. 35.

3. The ninety-percent estimate comes from Gerrit P. Judd, ed., *Readings in the History of Civilization* (London: The Macmillan Co., 1966), p. 71.

4. The "double chains" quote is by historian Eric Hobsbawm, source unknown.

5. The Huizinger quote is from Judd, *The History of Civilization*, p. 115.

6. In Canterbery, *The Making of Economics*, p. 44.

7. Cumberland's work is described in Milton L. Myers, *The Soul of Modern Economic Man: Ideas of Self-Interest, Thomas Hobbes to Adam Smith* (Chicago: University of Chicago Press, 1983).

8. Jacob Viner, *The Role of Providence in the Social Order* (Princeton: Princeton University Press, 1972), p. 68.

9. Adam Smith, *The Theory of Moral Sentiments* (Indianapolis: Liberty Classics, 1976), pt. 1, sect. 1, chap. 1, p. 47; first published in 1759.

10. Ibid., pt. 1, sect. 1, chap. 5, p. 71.

11. Ibid., pt. 1, sect. 3, chap. 3, p. 126.

12. Smith, *The Wealth of Nations*, ed. Edwin Cannan (New York: Modern Library, 1937), book 1, chap. 1, p. 4.

13. Ibid., book 1, chap. 8, p. 79.

14. See, for example, Canterbery, *The Making of Economics*, p. 63; N. Rosenberg and L.E. Birdzell, Jr., *How The West Grew Rich* (New York: Basic Books, 1986).

15. Smith, *The Wealth of Nations*, book 1, chap. 2, p. 14.

16. Ibid., book 3, chap. 2, p. 423.

17. William Stanley Jevons, *The Theory of Political Economy* (New York: Reprints of Economic Classics, A.M. Kelley, 1965), p. 101.

18. Paul Heyne, *The Economic Way of Thinking*, 4th ed. (Chicago: Science Research Associates, 1983), p. 4.

19. Campbell McConnell, *Economics*, 8th ed. (New York: McGraw Hill, 1981), pp. 41, 35.

20. Robert Parloff, "Self-Interest and Personal Responsibility Redux," *American Psychologist* 42 (January 1987): 3–11.

21. Edwin A. Locke, "The Virtue of Selfishness," *American Psychologist* 43 (June 1988): 481.

Chapter 2. A Christmas Carol

1. References to Charles James Fox appear in Brian Inglis, *Men of Conscience* (New York: Macmillan, 1971), pp. 50–54; and in John Rae, *The Life of Adam Smith* (New York: Reprints of Economic Classics, 1965), p. 289. In addition to Inglis, my primary references for this period of English history are: Raymond G. Cowherd, *Political Economists and the English Poor Laws* (Athens, Ohio University Press, 1977); Rajani J. Kanth, *Political Economy and Laissez-Faire* (Totowa, N.J.: Rowman & Littlefield, 1986); Pauline Gregg, *Black Death to Industrial Revolution: A Social and Economic History of England* (New York: Barnes & Noble, 1974); and Karl Polanyi, *The Great Transformation*, (Boston: Beacon Press, 1957).

2. Reginald Copeland, *Wilberforce: A Narrative* (Oxford: Clarendon Press, 1923), p. 35.

3. Ibid., p. 234.

4. Adam Smith, *The Wealth of Nations*, ed. Edwin Cannan (New York: Modern Library, 1937), book 1, chap. 5, p. 33.

5. Inglis, *Men of Conscience*, pp. 51–52.

6. Biographical material on Malthus comes primarily from Everett J. Burtt, Jr., *Social Perspectives in the History of Economic Theory*

(New York: St. Martin's Press, 1972); Phillip Appleman, ed., *An Essay on the Principle of Population* (New York: Norton Critical Edition, 1976); and Robert L. Heilbroner, *The Worldly Philosophers* (New York: Simon and Schuster, Touchstone Books, 1980).

7. Thomas R. Malthus, *An Essay on the Principle of Population*, in Leonard D. Abbott, ed., *Masterworks of Economics*, vol. 1, (New York: McGraw-Hill, 1973), p. 260.

8. Ibid., p. 259.

9. Appleman, *Essay*, p. 2.

10. Malthus, *Essay*, p. 187.

11. Ibid., pp. 187–93.

12. The statement that appears in the second edition of Malthus's *Essay*, as well as the statement from the later version, are quoted in Kanth, *Laissez-Faire*, p. 49.

13. Malthus's three reform proposals are quoted in Appleman, *Essay*, p. xxii.

14. Quoted in Cowherd, *Political Economists*, p. 55.

15. Malthus, *Essay*, p. 192.

16. Whitebread's statement and Malthus's reply are both quoted in Cowherd, *Political Economists*, p. 29.

17. In Inglis, *Men of Conscience*, p. 74.

18. Ibid., p. 70. Evidence that Malthus also distorted many of his crucial population "facts" is presented in Salim Rashid, "Malthus's 'Essay on Population': The Facts of 'Super-Growth' and the Rhetoric of Scientific Persuasion," *Journal of the History of the Behavioral Sciences* 23 (January 1987): 22–36.

19. Inglis, *Men of Conscience*, p. 90.

20. Cowherd, *Political Economists*, p. 45.

21. Malthus, *Essay*, p. 235.

22. Ibid., pp. 232–33.

23. Ibid.

24. Kanth, *Laissez-Faire*, p. 88.

25. Ibid., p. 131.

26. Ibid., p. 51.

27. Cowherd, *Political Economists*, pp. 267–68.

28. Ibid., p. 234.

29. Lester Brown, *In the Human Interest* (New York: W.W. Norton, 1974), pp. 113–14.

30. Ibid.

31. Lafayette G. Harter, Jr., *Economic Responses to a Changing World* (Glenview, Ill.: Scott, Foresman and Co., 1972), p. 72.

32. Leonard Silk, *Contemporary Economics: Principles and Issues* (1975), p. 530.

33. Appleman, *Essay*, p. xxii.

34. Kanth, *Laissez-Faire*, p. 78.

35. Inglis, *Men of Conscience*, p. 167.

36. Ibid.

37. Charles Dickens, *A Christmas Carol* (Boston: Atlantic Monthly Press, 1920), first published in 1843. The following excerpts are from pp. 12–13, 33, 96–97, 118–20.

38. J. L. Hammond and Barbara Hammond, *The Age of the Chartists 1832–1854* (New York: A.M. Kelley, 1967), p. 275; first published in 1930.

39. Ibid., p. 274.

40. Ibid., p. 289.

41. Ibid., p. 340.

42. E. Ray Canterbery, *The Making of Economics*, 2nd ed. (Belmont, Calif.: Wadsworth, 1980), pp. 68–70.

43. Hammond and Hammond, *Age of the Chartists*, p. 358.

44. Heilbroner, *The Worldly Philosophers*, p. 138. The biographical account of Marx and Engels comes from this and a number of other sources, including two by Robert C. Tucker: *Philosophy and Myth in Karl Marx*, 2nd ed. (Cambridge: At the University Press, 1972); and *Marx-Engels Reader* (New York: W.W. Norton, 1972).

Chapter 3. The Gilded Age

1. The major sources for this chapter are: Robert L. Heilbroner, *The Worldly Philosophers* (New York: Simon and Schuster, Touchstone Books, 1980); E. Ray Canterbery, *The Making of Economics*, 2nd ed. (Belmont, Calif.: Wadsworth, 1980); Andrew S. Berky and James P. Shenton, eds., *The Historian's History of the United States* (New York: Capricorn Books, 1966); Henry C. Dethloff and Joseph C. Pusateri, eds., *American Business History: Case Studies* (Arlington Heights, Ill.: Harlan Davidson, 1987); Mathew Josephson, *The Robber Barons* (New York: Harcourt, Brace & Co., 1934); Samuel E. Morison, *The Oxford History of the American People* (New York: Oxford University Press, 1965); Glenn Porter, *The Rise of Big Business, 1860–1910* (Arlington Heights, Ill.:

Harlan Davidson, 1973); Edwin C. Rozwenc and A. Wesley Roehm, *The Entrepreneur in the Gilded Age* (Lexington, Mass.: D.C. Heath and Co., 1965).

2. This demarcation in American economic history is noted in John D. Clark, *The Federal Trust Policy* (Baltimore: The Johns Hopkins Press, 1931), p. 3.

3. Josephson, *Robber Barons*, p. 76.

4. Dethloff and Pusateri, *American Business History*, pp. 184–85.

5. Ibid.

6. The figures for the land involved in the railroad acts are from ibid., p. 201, and from Josephson, *Robber Barons*, pp. 78–79.

7. Josephson, *Robber Barons*, p. 80.

8. Ibid., p. 98.

9. Dethloff and Pusateri, *American Business History*, p. 193.

10. Ibid., p. 199.

11. Ibid. and Mathew Josephson, *The Politicos* (New York: Harcourt, Brace & Co., 1938), p. 182.

12. Josephson, *Robber Barons*, pp. 62–76.

13. Walt Whitman, "Democratic Vistas" in *The Portable Walt Whitman* (New York: Viking, 1974), p. 325; first published in 1871.

14. Josephson, *Robber Barons*, pp. 62–76.

15. Ibid.

16. The depression of 1873 is described in Berky and Shenton, *The Historian's History*, pp. 834 and 955; and in Bryant M. French, *Mark Twain and the Gilded Age: The Book That Named an Era* (Dallas: Southern Methodist University Press, 1965).

17. This account of the 1876 centennial, including Lowell's ode, is from Morison, *Oxford History*, p. 732.

18. Berky and Shenton, *The Historian's History*, p. 885.

19. Porter, *Big Business*, p. 63.

20. In addition to the above sources, the account of the development of Standard Oil is also taken from David Horowitz and Peter Collier, *The Rockefellers: An American Dynasty* (New York: Holt, Rinehart & Winston, 1976). The statement from the New York State investigation is quoted in Rozwenc and Roehm, *The Entrepreneur*, p. 41; the accuracy of the indictment is attested to in Porter, *Big Business*, p. 68.

21. This attitude toward competition is referred to in Porter, *Big*

Business, p. 55; and in Berky and Shenton, *The Historian's History*, p. 919.

22. Josephson, *Robber Barons*, p. 119.

23. The weak congressional inquiry is reported in Rozwenc and Roehm, *The Entrepreneur*, p. 42.

24. Ibid., pp. 39–43; and Berky and Shenton, *The Historian's History*, p. 919.

25. Josephson, *Robber Barons*, p. 382.

26. Rozwenc and Roehm, *The Entrepreneur*, p. 44.

27. Sherman's Senate speech is excerpted in ibid., pp. 55–60.

28. Berky and Shenton, *The Historian's History*, p. 928.

29. Heilbroner, *The Worldly Philosophers*, pp. 213–14.

30. Pierpont Morgan's remark was recently quoted on the cover of the June 27–July 10, 1989 issue of *Financial World*—an issue devoted to business ethics. Also on the cover, and in contrast to this remark, was a policy statement of Johnson & Johnson: "We are responsible to the communities in which we live and work and to the world community as well."

31. The Standard Oil dividend is given in Morison, *Oxford History*, p. 818; and in Dethloff and Pusateri, *American Business History*, p. 226.

32. Edward Berman, *Labor and the Sherman Act* (New York: Harper, 1930), p. 3.

33. Morison, *Oxford History*, pp. 762–63; Berky and Shenton, *The Historian's History*, p. 929; Josephson, *Robber Barons*, p. 368.

34. In Berky and Shenton, *The Historian's History*, p. 929.

35. Porter, *Big Business*, p. 78.

36. Berky and Shenton, *The Historian's History*, p. 1057.

37. "Recovering from the Era of Shocks," *New York Times*, 8 January 1984, sec. 3.

38. Ann Crittenden, "The Age of 'Me-First' Management," *New York Times*, 19 August 1984, sec. 3; Walter Adams and James W. Brock, *The Bigness Complex* (New York: Pantheon Books, 1987).

39. The role of the Chicago Mercantile Exchange in the stock market crash is described in William Glaberson, "How Risk Rattled the Street," *New York Times*, 1 November 1987, sec. 3. A two-year investigation of the Chicago Exchange beginning in 1987 turned up widespread brokerage and trading fraud, as described in "The

Scandal in Chicago: Of Fraud, Markets and the Future," *New York Times*, 22 January 1989, sec. 3.

40. *New York Times*, 30 March 1986, sec. 3.

41. *Newsweek*, 21 May 1990.

42. Louis Uchitelle, "Futures Trading: Does Chicago Run Wall Street?," *New York Times*, 22 April 1990, sec. 6.

43. Anise C. Wallace, "A Growing Backlash Against Greed," *New York Times*, 13 November 1988, sec. 1; "The '80's: Decade of Excess," *USA Today*, 27 November 1989; Haynes Johnson, "Are We Now Ending Our Era of Greed?," *Portland Press Herald*, 29 October 1989 (this column also appeared in the *Washington Post*).

44. Canterbery, *The Making of Economics*, p. 120.

45. Roosevelt's address appears in E. Will and H. Vatter, eds., 2nd ed., *Poverty in Affluence* (New York: Harcourt, Brace and World, 1970), pp. 7–8.

Chapter 4. The Mistake

1. Smith, *The Wealth of Nations*, ed. Edwin Cannan (New York: Modern Library, 1937), book 1, chap. 2, p. 14.

2. Smith, *The Theory of Moral Sentiments* (Indianapolis: Liberty Classics, 1976), pt. 1, sec. 1, chap. 1, p. 47.

3. Smith, *The Wealth of Nations*, book 3, chap. 2, p. 423.

4. Ibid., book 1, chap. 11, p. 250.

5. Paul Heyne, *The Economic Way of Thinking*, 4th ed. (Chicago: Science Research Associates, 1983), pp. 22, 245.

6. Ibid., p. 245.

7. Ibid., p. 251.

8. "The Heat Is On: Calculating the Consequences of a Warmer Planet," *New York Times*, 26 June 1988, sec. 4.

9. Joan Robinson, *Economic Philosophy* (New York: Anchor Books, 1964), p. 54.

10. Smith, *The Theory of Moral Sentiments*, pt. 2, sec. 2.

11. Albert O. Hirschman, *The Passions and the Interests* (Princeton: Princeton University Press, 1977).

12. Cheng-ming in Fung Yu-Lan, *A History of Ancient China*, vol. 1, (Princeton: Princeton University Press, 1952).

Chapter 5. Reap Where They Never Sowed

1. John Rae, *The Life of Adam Smith* (New York: Reprints of Economic Classics, 1965), pp. 205–6.
2. Thomas R. Horton, *"What Works for Me": 16 CEO's Talk About Their Careers and Commitments* (New York: Random House Business Division, 1986).
3. "A Visionary's Spartan Life," *New York Times*, 17 February 1985, sec. 3.
4. Douglas McGregor, *The Human Side of Enterprise* (New York: McGraw-Hill, 1960).
5. John Kenneth Galbraith, *The New Industrial State*, 4th ed. (Boston: Houghton Mifflin, 1985).
6. Nathan Rosenberg, "Adam Smith and Laissez-Faire Revisited," in Gerald P. O'Driscoll, Jr., ed., *Adam Smith and Modern Political Economy: Bicentennial Essays on "The Wealth of Nations"* (Ames: Iowa State University Press, 1979), pp. 19–34.
7. Smith, *The Wealth of Nations*, ed. Edwin Cannan (New York: Modern Library, 1937), book 5, chap. 3, pp. 890–91.
8. Ibid., book 1, chap. 6, pp. 47–49.
9. Ibid., book 1, chap. 8, p. 66.
10. Ibid., book 1, chap. 10, part 3, p. 142.
11. Ibid., book 3, chap. 8, p. 626.
12. Ibid., book 2, chap. 3, p. 329.
13. Ibid., book 1, chap. 2, p. 15.
14. Rosenberg, "Laissez-Faire Revisited," pp. 19–34.
15. Smith, *The Wealth of Nations*, book 2, chap. 2, p. 308.
16. Rae, *Adam Smith*, p. 436.
17. Lawrence Dickey, "Historicizing the 'Adam Smith Problem': Conceptual, Historiographical, and Textual Issues," *Journal of Modern History* 58 (September 1986): 579–609.
18. Rae, *Adam Smith*, p. 427.

Chapter 6. Noise in the World

1. Smith, *The Theory of Moral Sentiments* (Indianapolis: Liberty Classics, 1976), pt. 2, sec. 2, chap. 3, pp. 166–67.
2. Hendrik Willem Van Loon, *The Story of Mankind*, rev. ed. (New York: Washington Square Press, 1972), pp. 133–34.
3. *New Columbia Encyclopedia* (1975), s.v. "papacy."

4. Ibid., s.v. "Reformation."

5. Niccolo Machiavelli, *The Prince,* intro. Christian Gauss (New York: New American Library, 1952), p. 84; first published in 1532.

6. That Machiavelli's emancipated the state from religion is noted in Richard H. Tawney, *Religion and the Rise of Capitalism* (New York: Harcourt, Brace & Co., Mentor Books, 1955), p. 14.

7. Machiavelli as a scientist and the first modern man is the assessment of Christian Gauss in his introduction to *The Prince,* pp. 16, 24.

8. Thomas Hobbes, *Leviathan,* intro. Herbert W. Schneider (Indianapolis: Bobbs-Merrill, 1958), p. 104; first published in 1651.

9. Ibid., pp. 106–7.

10. Ibid., p. 79.

11. *Encyclopaedia Britannica,* 15th ed., s.v. "The Fronde."

12. Much of the material on Jansenism and its relation to Mandeville is drawn from Thomas A. Horne, *The Social Thought of Bernard Mandeville: Virtue and Commerce in Early Eighteenth Century England* (New York: Columbia University Press, 1978).

13. Bernard de Mandeville, *The Fable of the Bees,* vol. 1 (London: Oxford University Press, 1966), pp. 18–24.

14. Ibid., p. 36.

15. Horne, *Bernard Mandeville,* p. 23.

16. Ibid., pp. 67–68.

17. John Dennis, Introduction to Phillip Harth, ed., *The Fable of the Bees* (New York: Penguin Books, 1970), p. 15.

18. Horne, *Bernard Mandeville,* p. 87.

19. Ibid., p. 42.

20. Ibid., p. 87.

21. Ibid., p. 89.

22. Smith, *The Theory of Moral Sentiments,* pt. 2, sec. 2, chap. 2, pp. 161–2., pt. 3, chap. 1, pp. 203–9., and throughout the book.

23. Ibid., pt. 3, chap. 1, pp. 206–7.

24. Ibid., pt. 7, sec. 3, chap. 1, p. 501.

25. Leonard Silk, *Contemporary Economics,* 2nd ed. (New York: McGraw-Hill, 1975), p. 16.

26. Lawrence Dickey, p. 609.

27. Smith, *The Theory of Moral Sentiments,* pt. 7, sec. 2, chap. 4.

28. Ibid.

29. In Smith, *The Wealth of Nations,* p. liv.

30. See, for example, Karl Polanyi, *The Great Transformation* (Boston: Beacon Press, 1957), chap. 4.

31. Canaan in Smith, *The Wealth of Nations*, pp. xliv–xiv.

32. Ibid., p. 3 n.

33. Smith, *The Wealth of Nations*, book 5, chap. 1, pt. 3, art. 2, pp. 734–35.

34. Louis Dumont, *From Mandeville to Marx: The Genesis and Triumph of Economic Ideology* (Chicago and London: University of Chicago press, 1977), p. 61.

Chapter 7. Tales of Enterprise and Avarice

1. The story of the monk appears in Fusfeld, *Age of the Economist*, 3rd ed. (Glenview, Ill.: Scott, Foresman and Co., 1977), p. 10.

2. Richard H. Tawney, *Religion and the Rise of Capitalism* (New York: Harcourt, Brace & Co., Mentor Books, 1955), p. 35.

3. For a psychological account of greed in the 1980s, see Ann Landi, "When Having Everything Isn't Enough," *Psychology Today*, April 1989, pp. 27–30.

4. Patricia O'Toole, "Greed Is a Nice Religion," *New York Times Book Review*, 25 October 1987.

5. Alfie Kohn, "Art for Art's Sake," *Psychology Today*, September 1987, pp. 52–57. For a full account of the significance of these findings, particularly for the social sciences, see Barry Schwartz, *The Battle for Human Nature* (New York: W.W. Norton), chap. 8.

6. Lewis Hyde, "Laying Waste to the Future," *New York Times Book Review*, 27 September 1987.

7. I have adapted my version from that told by economist Don Cole in "A Tale of the Long Spoons," *Human Economy Newsletter* 7, no. 3 (September 1987).

Chapter 8. Gifts of Science

1. Albert O. Hirschman, *The Passions and the Interests* (Princeton: Princeton University Press, 1977), p. 43.

2. The relationship between classical economic thought and physics is explained in Israel Kirzner, *The Economic Point of View* (Kansas City: Sheed and Ward, 1960).

3. For accounts of how the works of Marx and Engels fit into the history of economics, see Robert L. Heilbroner, *The Worldly Philosophers* (New York: Simon and Schuster, 1980), chap. 6; Everett J. Burtt, Jr., *Social Perspectives in the History of Economic Theory*

(New York: St. Martin's Press, 1972); and E.K. Hunt, *History of Economic Thought: A Critical Perspective.* (Belmont, Calif.: Wadsworth, 1979), chaps. 9, 10.

4. Friedrich Engels, *Socialism: Utopian and Scientific* (1875), trans. Edward Aveling (1892), in *The Essential Left* (New York: Barnes & Noble, 161), pp. 117, 126.

5. Ibid., p. 140.

6. Ibid., p. 144.

7. Alexander Solzhenitsyn, *Letter to the Soviet Leaders* (New York: Harper & Row, 1974), p. 59.

8. The Marx and Darwin letters appear in Enrique M. Urena, "Marx and Darwin," *History of Political Economy* 9, no. 4 (winter 1977): 548–59; and the Edward Aveling connection is explained in Ralph Colp, Jr., "The Myth of the Darwin-Marx Letter," *History of Political Economy* 14, no. 4 (winter 1982): 461–82.

9. E. Ray Canterbery, *The Making of Economics*, 2nd ed. (Belmont, Calif.: Wadsworth, 1980), p. 74.

10. John C. Greene, *Darwin and the Modern World View* (New York: New American Library, 1963), chap. 3; first published in 1961.

11. Ibid., p. 85.

12. Canterbery, *The Making of Economics*, pp. 96–101.

13. Ibid., p. 120.

14. Ibid., p. 98.

15. John Greene, *Darwin and the Modern World View*, pp. 87–89.

16. Ibid.

17. Ibid.

18. Charles Darwin, *The Autobiography of Charles Darwin* (New York: Harcourt, Brace & Co., 1958), pp. 138–39.

Chapter 9. The Eternal Sophist

1. John Stuart Mill, *Essays on Some Unsettled Questions of Political Economy*, in D. Hausman, ed., *The Philosophy of Economics* (New York: Cambridge University Press, 1984), p. 57.

2. William R. Allen, *Midnight Economist: Broadcast Essays III* (Los Angeles: International Institute for Economic Research, 1982), p. 23.

3. Leon Walras, *Elements of Pure Economics* (New York: A.M. Kelley, 1977), p. 65.

4. Werner Sichel and Peter Eckstein, Basic Economic Concepts (Chicago: Rand McNally, 1974), p. 403.

5. William Stanley Jevons, *The Theory of Political Economy* (New York: Reprints of Economic Classics, A.M. Kelley, 1965), p. xxxv.

6. Hermann H. Gossen, *The Laws of Human Relations* (Cambridge: MIT Press, 1938). Quotations are from Mark A. Lutz and Kenneth Lux, *Humanistic Economics: The New Challenge* (New York: Intermediate Technology Development Group [Bootstrap], 1988), pp. 44–46.

7. Lionel Robbins, Introduction, Philip H. Wicksteed, *The Common Sense of Political Economy* (London: George Routledge & Sons, 1933), p. xxi.

8. Lionel Robbins, *The Nature and Significance of Economic Science* (London: Macmillan, 1984), pp. 95, 97; first published in 1932.

9. Paul Heyne, *The Economic Way of Thinking*, 4th ed. (Chicago: Science Research Associates, 1983), pp. 4–5.

10. Ibid., p. 284.

11. James Buchanan and George Stigler are quoted in Lutz and Lux, *Humanistic Economics*, pp. 100, 105. See also: James Buchanan, "The Demand and Supply for Public Goods," J. Margolis and H. Guitten, eds., *Public Economics* (International Economic Association Conference Proceedings, 1969); George Stigler, "Economics, the Imperial Science," *Scandinavian Journal of Economics* 86, no. 3 (1984): 304.

12. Milton Friedman, *Capitalism and Freedom* (Chicago: University of Chicago Press, 1962), p. 13.

13. Ibid., pp. 38, 121, 131.

14. Albert Schweitzer, *The Philosophy of Civilization* (Gainsville: University of Florida Presses, 1981), pp. 115–17; first published in 1949.

15. Jeremy Bentham, *An Introduction to the Principles of Morals and Legislation* chap. 1, pt. 1, quoted in G. Miller, *Psychology: The Science of Mental Life* (New York: Harper & Row, 1962), pp. 230–31.

16. William G. Field, *Basic Economics* (Boston: Allyn and Bacon, Special Topic 13B, 1983).

17. Ayn Rand, *The Virtue of Selfishness: A New Concept of Egoism* (New York: New American Library, 1964), jacket, pp. vii–viii.

18. Ayn Rand, *Capitalism: The Unknown Ideal* (New York: New American Library, 1967), jacket, p. viii.

19. Ibid., p. 65.

20. Ibid., p. 80.

21. Louis Uchitelle, "Caution at the Fed," *New York Times*, 15 January 1989, sec. 6.

Chapter 10. Father Arizmendi Comes to Mondragon

1. The status of the church estates before Henry VIII confiscated them is described in J. Gilchrist, *The Church and Economic Activity in the Middle Ages* (London: Macmillan, 1969).

2. Richard H. Tawney, *Religion and the Rise of Capitalism* (New York: Harcourt, Brace & Co., Mentor Books, 1955), pp. 119–20.

3. For the classic account of the enclosure movement see Richard H. Tawney, *The Agrarian Problem in the 16th Century* (New York: Harper Torchback, 1962, intro. Lawrence Stone; also his *Religion and the Rise of Capitalism*. For a more contemporary account, see Michael Turner, *English Parliamentary Enclosures* (England: Dawson & Sons, Archon Books, 1980).

4. Tawney, *The Rise of Capitalism*, p. 120.

5. Ibid., p. 217.

6. Stone in Tawney, *The Agrarian Problem*, p. vii.

7. Ibid., p. 407.

8. Rajani J. Kanth, *Political Economy and Laissez-Faire* (Totowa, N.J.: Rowman & Littlefield, 1986), p. 71, n. 9.

9. Karl Polanyi, *The Great Transformation* (Boston: Beacon Press, 1959), p. 81.

10. Kanth, *Laissez-Faire*, p. 75, n. 31.

11. Jeremy Bentham, *Jeremy Bentham's Economic Writings*, ed. W. Stark, 3 vols. (London: George Allen and Unwin), p. 428, as quoted in Kanth, *Laissez-Faire,* p. 54.

12. Smith, *The Wealth of Nations*, book 1, chap. 8, p. 83.

13. Pierre J. Proudhon, *What is Property?* (New York: Howard Fertig, 1966), p. 117; first published in 1840.

14. Quoted in Daniel Fusfeld, *Age of the Economist*, 3rd ed. (Glenview, Ill.: Scott, Foresman and Co., 1977), p. 95. For a further account of Catholic social doctrine, see Gregory Baum & Duncan Cameron, *Ethics and Economics* (Toronto: James Lorimer & Co., 1984).

15. In *National Catholic Reporter* 27 May 1988.

16. For an account of the life of Father Arizmendi and the development of Mondragon see Mark A. Lutz and Kenneth Lux, *Humanistic*

Economics: The New Challenge (New York: Intermediate Technology Development Group [Bootstrap], 1988), chap. 12; William F. Whyte and Kathleen K. Whyte, *Making Mondragon* (Ithaca, N.Y.: Cornell University Press, 1988); and Henk Thomas and Chris Logan, *Mondragon: An Economic Analysis* (London: George Allen & Unwin, 1982).

17. For a review of the history of cooperatives as well as a contemporary account of their practice, see Frank T. Adams and Gary B. Hansen, *Putting Democracy to Work* (Somerville, Mass.: The Industrial Cooperative Association, 1987).

18. Quoted in Lutz and Lux, *Humanistic Economics*, p. 258.

Chapter 11. Textbooks of the Temples

1. The relative income gap and welfare support of the U.S. as compared to other industrialized societies can be found in any comparative economics textbook, such as Martin C. Schnitzer, *Comparative Economic Systems*, 4th ed. (Cincinnati: South-Western Publishing Co., 1987), pp. 154–57, 497.

2. Crime rates are noted by Franklin E. Zimring in his review of *Seductions of Crime, New York Times Book Review,* 20 November 1988; and Seymour Wishman in his review of *Crimes of Justice, New York Times Book Review,* 17 April 1988.

3. The drug problem statistics are from a federal study, as noted in the *New York Times,* 10 December 1989, sec. 3; the anthropologist's statement is in the *New York Times,* 12 November 1989, sec. 6.

4. *New York Times,* 4 November 1988, sec. 4.

5. Lena Williams, "It Was a Year When Civility Really Took It on the Chin," *New York Times,* 18 December 1988, sec. 1.

6. Christopher Lasch, *The Culture of Narcissism* (New York: W. W. Norton, 1979).

7. Martin Seligman, "Boomer Blues," *Psychology Today,* October 1988; and "Me Decades Generate Depression," *American Psychological Association Monitor,* October 1988.

8. Quoted in the *New York Times,* 18 December 1988.

9. 1 Tim. 6:10.

10. James Buchanan, "The Constitution of Economic Policy," Nobel Prize acceptance address, *American Economic Review,* June 1987, pp. 243–50.

11. For an account of the *liar's paradox,* see John Eccles and Daniel N.

Robinson, *The Wonder of Being Human: Our Brain and Our Mind* (New York: The Free Press, 1984), chap. 4.

12. This usage of the term *economic imperialism* was first put forth by Kenneth Boulding in his presidential address to the American Economic Association in 1968. See his *Economics as a Science* (New York: McGraw-Hill, 1970), p. 131.

13. Elizabeth M. Landes and Richard A. Posner, "The Economics of the Baby Shortage," *Journal of Legal Studies* 7 (1978): 339.

14. Richard B. McKenzie and Gordon Tullock, *The New World of Economics* (Homewood, Ill.: Irwin, 1975), pp. 51–52.

15. Herman E. Daly, ed., *Economics, Ecology, Ethics: Essays Toward a Steady-State Economy* (San Francisco: W.H. Freeman, 1980), p. 19. For a recent expansion on these themes, see Herman E. Daly and John B. Cobb, Jr., *For The Common Good: Redirecting the Economy Toward Community, the Environment, and a Sustainable Future* (Boston: Beacon Press, 1989).

16. Philip Glass and Constance DeJong, *Satyagraha* (text adapted from the *Bhagavad-Gita*), chap. 4, verses 7–8.

INDEX

Age of the Economist, 1, 3, 5, 52
Amabile, Teresa, 132–133
American Psychologist, The, 27
Amour, Philip, 63
Anacortes Plywood, 183
Anticombination Laws, 177
Appleman, Philip, 46
Aquinas, Thomas, 128–129, 130
Aristotle, 112, 145, 155
Arizmendi, Father Don José
    Maria, 179–183, 189–190
Aveling, Richard, 146

Barron, C. W., 69, 72
Basic Economics (Field), 165–
    166
Basic Economics Concepts (Sichel
    and Eckstein), 153
Bayle, Pierre, 116
Beecher, Henry Ward, 148
Benevolence, 104–105, 123, 191
  in commercial economic
    sphere, 94
  economic gains and, 97
  in economics, 80
  economy and, 81–82
  See also Morality; Virtue
Bentham, Jeremy, 43, 54, 163–
    165, 175
Benton, Thomas Hart, 57
Bhagavad Gita, 204–205
Blake, William, 55
Bork, Robert, 2, 202
Brandeis, Louis D., 75
Bright, John, 51

Brown, Lester, 44
Browne, Thomas, 113
Bryan, William Jennings, 73
Buchanan, James, 161, 201–202
Burke, Edmund, 1
Business
  fairness, 128–129
  goals of, 128–129
  purpose, 130–132
  values, 130–131
Buvet, Antoin, 201

Caja Laboral Popular, 187–188,
  190
California self, 196
Cannan, Edwin, 86, 123, 125
Canterbery, E. Ray, 147–148
Capitalism, 141–142, 144, 166,
  177
  Catholic social doctrine and,
    179
  economics and, 146
  self-interest and, 26
  See also Self-interest
Capitalism: The Unknown Ideal
  (Rand), 166
Captains of Industry, 63
Carlyle, Thomas, 52, 151
Carnegie, Andrew, 62
Central Pacific Company, 58–60
Charles II (king of England), 29
Chicago Mercantile Exchange
  (the Merc), 76–78
Childeric III, 111, 112
Child Labor Laws, 51

Christmas Carol, A (Dickens),
  48–50
Christian Observer, 39
Civil rights movement, 56–57
Civil War, 55–56
Clapham Evangelicals, 29–30,
  38–39, 118
Clapham Saints, 35
Cole, Don, 217 n. 7
*Common Sense of Political
  Economy, The* (Wicksteed),
  156
Common Sense (Paine), 40
Communism, 144
Competition, 69, 72
  monopolies and, 96
  ruinous, 68
Concentration of Wealth, The
  (Canterbery), 147–148
*Condition of the Working Class
  in England in 1844, The*
  (Engels), 53
Confucius, 92
Cooke, Henry, 64
Cooke, Jay, 64
Cooperative business, 182–184,
  188
  banks, 187–188
  capitalists and, 189
  growth, 186
  individual capital account
    (ICA), 184
  Industrial Cooperative
    Association and, 189
  industrial high technology, 188
  organizational discipline, 185
  Rochdale Cooperative
    Manufacturing Society and,
    183
  socialists and, 189
  in Spain, 188
  supermarkets, 188

See also Mondragon
  cooperatives
Corn Laws, 41, 42, 56
*Costs, Risks, and Benefits of
  Surgery* (Bunker, Barnes, and
  Mosteller), 3
Cowherd, Raymond, 43
Coxey, Jacob, 73
Crash of 1987, U.S. budget deficit
  and, 76
Crédit Foncier, 60–62
Crédit Mobilier, 60–62, 63–64,
  148
Crisis, The, 51
Cromwell, Oliver, 29
Crusoe, Robinson, 161–163
Cumberland, Richard, 18–19, 80
Custer, George Armstrong, 64

Daly, Herman E., 203, 222 n. 15
Darwin, Charles, 145–146, 147,
  149–151
Darwinism, Social, 147, 148
Das Kapital (Marx), 146
Day, Dorothy, 179
Demand, substitutes for, 84–85
Dennis, John, 118
Dickens, Charles, 47–51, 95
Dickey, Lawrence, 107
Division of labor, 22–23, 24–25,
  88, 124–125
  and self-interest, 24–25
  technology and, 23
Douglas, Stephen, 57
Drexel, Anthony, 64–65
Dumont, Louis, 126

Economic
  imperialism, 202
  liberty and laissez faire
    concept, 23
  order of United States after
    Civil War, 55–57

system model, 162
teachings, 199–200
theory, 9, 155
theory and greed, 129–130
Economic Aspects of Law, The
(Posner), 2
Economic downturn of 1893,
"Rich Man's Panic," 73
Economic Man *(Homo
economicus)*, 152, 153–154
Economics, 42, 52, 97
Adam Smith and, 14
business motives and, 132
capitalist, 146
classical, 147–148
conflict of interest and, 133
cross-disciplinary influence of,
2
definition of, 152–153, 173
dehumanization of people,
140–141
denial of needs, 8–9
environment and, 203
equilibrium theory, 153
establishment of, 54
government interference and,
162–163
immorality of, 200
labor, viewpoint of, 140
laws of nature and, 148
meaning of choice, 173
medieval versus modern, 127–
128
moral hypocrisy and, 157–158
self-interest and, 80–85, 133,
197–198
self-interest and political
corruption, 66
short-run focus of, 133–134
society, transformation of, 6–8
sophistry, 156
"unlimited wants" and, 9

versus moralism, 154
See also Invisible hand; Laissez-
faire; Self-interest
Economics (McConnell), 26
Economics of Justice, The
(Posner), 202
Economic Way of Thinking, The
(Heyne), 84–85, 159–161
Economists
commodity of conception and,
202–203
definition of pollution, 85–86
influence of, 1–3
market efficiency and, 128, 177
political systems and, 177
Economy
American merger movement
and, 74–75
benevolence and, 81–82
birth rate and, 44
dependence on poor of, 118
greater, 135–136
self-interest and, 81–82
Egoism, 87, 154
Elizabeth, Queen, 28, 171
Enclosure, 170–171
movement, 18
Engels, Friedrich, 53, 171–172
English social system, 18–21, 99–
101, 102–105
Enlightenment, the, 32, 99, 118–
119
Environment, 203
self-interest and, 84–85
*Essay on the Principle of
Population, An* (Malthus),
32–33, 34–35, 36–38, 42,
146
Evolution, theory of, 145

Fable of the Bees, The
(Mandeville), 116–117, 125

Feudalism, 15–17, 98–99, 171
  liberation from, 174
Field, William, 165–166
Fisk, Jim, 66
Forgotten Man, The
  (Canterbery), 147–148
Fox, Charles James, 28, 31
Frankenstein (Shelley), 138–139
Free riding, 159–161
French social thinkers. *See*
  Physiocrats
Friedman, Milton, 77, 162–163,
  167
Fronde wars, 115–116

Galbraith, John Kenneth, 96
Gandhi, Mahatma, 204
George III (king of England), 21,
  31
Gilded Age, The (Twain and
  Warner), 65
Ginsburg, Douglas, 2
Glass, Philip, 204
Godwin, William, 37
Gossen, Hermann, 153–156
Gould, Jay, 66
Grant, Ulysses S., 59–60, 64
Great Depression, The, 155–156,
  162–163
  self-interest and, 155
  tariffs and, 76
Great Transformation, The
  (Polanyi), 6
Greed, 129
Greene, John, 149
Greenspan, Alan, 166–167

Hammond, Barbara, 52
Hammond, J. L., 52
Harper's Weekly, 75
Hazlitt, William, 36–37

Heilbroner, Robert, 6, 9–10, 15,
  72
Helmsley, Harry, 129
Helmsley, Leona, 129
Helvetius, 139
Hendrick, Burton, 65
Henry VIII (king of England),
  169, 171
Heyne, Paul, 25–26, 84–85
Hill, Christopher, 174
Hirschman, Albert, 91
Historical and Critical Dictionary
  (Bayle), 116
*History of The Standard Oil
  Company* (1925) (Tarbell),
  67
Hobbes, Thomas, 19, 113–114,
  119, 122–123, 139, 140
Homestead Act, 55
Horne, Thomas, 117
Huizinger, Josef, 17
Humanistic Economics (Lutz and
  Lux), 5, 9
Human Side of Enterprise, The
  (McGregor), 95
Hume, David, 14, 32
Hutcheson, Francis, 14, 80, 118–
  120, 123–125
Hyde, Lewis, 135

Individual capital account (ICA),
  184
Industrial Revolution, 23
  English working class and, 51–
  52
Inglis, Brian, 48
*Inquiry into the Nature and
  Causes of the Wealth of
  Nations, An* (Smith). *See
  Wealth of Nations*
In Search of Excellence (Peters
  and Waterman), 95–96

Invisible hand, 25, 82, 96, 155, 203
  self-interest and, 89–90
Italian Renaissance, 112–113

Jansen, Cornelis, 115
Jansenism, 115–116, 117
Jevons, William Stanley, 25, 152–153, 153–155, 156
John Paul, Pope, 179
Johnson, Andrew, 59
Justice
  liberty and, 101–102
  as moderator of self-interest, 86

Keynes, John Maynard, 1, 155
Kohn, Alfie, 217 n. 5

Labor, 174–175
  as commodity, 114, 140
  law of supply and demand and, 31–32
  natural price of, 175
  theory of value, 141
Labor unions, 177
Laissez-faire, 23, 40–41, 52, 54–55, 154, 178, 200–201
  absolute, 84
  conflict with public good, 104
  radical, 146, 167
  transcontinental railroad and, 57–60
  United States economy and, 70, 78–79
La Rochefoucauld, 107, 200
Lasch, Christopher, 195
Latimer, John, 171
Law of Settlement, 29
Laws of Human Relations, The (Gossen), 154
Lawson, Thomas, 65

Leo XIII, Pope, 178–179
Lerner, Max, 10
Letter to Samuel Whitebread (Malthus), 36
Leviathan (Hobbes), 19, 114
Levine, Dennis, 129
Lincoln, Abraham, 55–56, 57
Louis XIV (king of France), 115
Luther, Martin, 112
Lutz, Mark, 5
Lux, Kenneth, 5

McGregor, Douglas, 95
Machiavelli, Niccolo, 112–113
McKenzie, Richard, 203
McKinley, William, 74
McVicker, John, 148
Malthus, Daniel, 32
Malthus, Thomas, 25, 32–46, 54, 91, 99, 114, 140, 142, 154, 174–175
Malthusian approach, 172
Mandeville, Bernard de, 107, 116–118, 119, 120, 155
Marshall, Alfred, 152
Martel, Charles, 111
Marx, Karl, 53, 141–144, 145–146, 171–172
Maurin, Peter, 179
Maximes (La Rochefoucauld), 107
Mellon, James, 63
Mercantalism, 21
Middle Ages, 14, 15–18
Mill, John Stuart, 155, 183
Mintzer, Irving R., 86
Mohan, Robert Paul, 196
Mondragon cooperatives, 182–187
  Caja Laboral Popular, 187–188
  finance of, 183–184

growth of, 186
independent school, 180–181
management of, 184–186
Monopolies, 72, 162–163
  competition and, 96
Moody, John, 72, 73–74
Moralists, 35, 118, 154
Morality, 37, 38, 39, 164, 172–
  173
  betrayal of, 111–112
  in business, 95–96
  Darwin's theory and, 149–150
  fairness and, 128–129
  human nature and, 20
  immorality and, 92–93
  as moderator of self-interest,
    86, 89
  motives and, 133
  pursuit of wealth and, 107
  religious conception of, 81
  science and, 139, 173
  self-interest and, 83
  utilitarian theory of, 149–150
  vice and, 33, 36
  See also Benevolence; Virtue
Moral philosophers, 81
Moral philosophy, 14, 20–21
More, Thomas, 169–170
Morgan, J. P., 63–65, 72, 75, 89,
  148
Morgan, Junius, 63, 78–79
Motivation, 175–177
  effects of extrinsic rewards on,
    132–133
  selfishness versus moral
    sentiments, 80–81
Motives
  human behavior and, 106

National Labor Relations Act of
  1935, 73
National Monetary Commission,
  75

Natural law reformers, fallacy of,
  43–44
New Columbia Encyclopedia,
  111–112
New Deal, 148
Newsweek, 77
New Testament, 200
Newton, Isaac, 14, 138, 139
New York Times, 76, 129, 194,
  196
Nineteen Eighty-four (Orwell),
  92
Nontuism, 156–157, 158
Norris, William C., 95
Nozick, Robert, 2

Objectivism, 166
Oliver Twist (Dickens), 47
Olympia Veneer Company, 183
On the Laws of Nature
  (Cumberland), 18–19
Origin of Species (Darwin), 145–
  147
Orwell, George, 92
Other People's Money, 75

Paine, Thomas, 39–40
Panic of 1873, 65–66
Panic of 1909, 75
"Panopticon," 43
Parloff, Robert, 26–27, 163, 166,
  197
Paternalism, 98–99
  welfare of serfs and, 102–103
Peale, Norman Vincent, 96
Pepin the Short, 111, 169
Peters, Tom, 95–96
Philadelphia Ledger, 64
Physiocrats, 21–22, 23
Pioneer, The, 50
Pitt, William, 31–32

Plato, 109
Polanyi, Karl, 6, 174
Political economists, 38, 174–175
  failings of early, 44–45, 52–53
Political economy, 25
Political philosophers, 1
Poor Law Reform Bill, 42–43,
  46–48, 140
Poor Laws, 28–29, 31, 34, 35,
  39, 42, 54, 174
Population
  effect on economics, 172
  problem of, 34
Porter, Glenn, 66–67, 74–75
Posner, Richard, 2, 202
Poverty, 28–29, 34–35, 36–37
  birth rates and, 44
  reasons for, 172
  social reform and, 30–31
Poverty of Philosophy, The (Marx
  and Engels), 172
*Power of Ethical Management,
  The* (Peale), 96
Principle of Population, 42, 45,
  46
  English working class and, 51–
  52
Principles, self-interest and, 204
Principles (Ricardo), 41
Principles of Political Economy
  (Malthus), 41
Production, and land, capital,
  and labor, 140–141
Proudhon, Pierre Joseph, 171–
  172, 174, 175–178
Pujo, Arsene, 75
Pusateri, Joseph, 72–73

Rae, John, 94–95
Rand, Ayn, 26–27, 155, 166–
  168, 197
Rawls, John, 2

Religion, 144
  waning of in Western society,
  197
*Religion and the Rise of
  Capitalism* (Tawney), 6, 170
Rerum Novarum (Leo XIII), 178–
  179
Ricardo, David, 25, 40–42, 99,
  114, 142, 175
Rights of Man, The (Paine), 40
Robber Barons, 63
Robbins, Lionel, 156–159
Robinson, Joan, 86
Rochdale Cooperative
  Manufacturing Society, 183
Rockefeller, John D., 66–69, 71,
  72, 73, 96
Roman Empire, 98–99
Roosevelt, Franklin D., 79, 148,
  155
Roosevelt, Theodore, 65, 72, 75
Rosenberg, Nathan, 99
Rousseau, Jean Jacques, 32, 100

Samuelson, Paul, 11
Sartor Resartus (Carlyle), 151
Satyagraha (Glass), 204–205
Savings and loan (S&L) failure,
  77
Scalia, Anthony, 2, 202
Schwartz, Barry, 217 n. 5
Schweitzer, Albert, 163
Science
  cost of, 150–151
  fairness in, 161
  humanity and, 138–139, 145
  morality and, 139
  social change and, 144
  society and, 143
Scientific sociology, 146
Self-interest, 24–26, 33, 70, 79,
  119, 169, 198–199, 203

benefits for the poor of, 35–36
civility and, 196
competition and, 83–84
consequences of, 84–85, 140–141
definition of, 80–85, 152, 155, 161
economics and, 94–95, 155, 197
employer side of, 54–55
enlightened, 163–165
environment and, 84–85
greed and, 129–130
immorality of, 92–93, 110–112, 200
incompatible motives and, 158
invisible hand and, 25
moderators of, 86–87, 98
morality and, 161
need for temperance of, 198–199
philosophy, 192–193
political corruption and, 66
power and money and, 112
redefined, 156–159
selfishness and, 160–161, 191
social good and, 81–83, 88–90
society and, 195
underlying all social sciences, 202
United States economy and, 55–57
versus moral control, 154
See also Invisible hand
Seligman, Martin, 195
Shaftsbury, Lord, 119–120
Shelley, Mary, 138–139
Sherman, John, 70–71, 84, 120
Sherman Antitrust Bill, 70–71, 74
Sinclair, Upton, 65
Sismondi, Jean C. L., 155
Smith, Adam, 9–11, 28, 31, 45,
46, 70, 97–108, 109–110,
120–127, 199–201
childhood and education of,
13–14
changing social system and, 17
French social thinkers and, 21–22
invisible hand and, 83–84
laissez-faire concept and, 23
the "mistake" and, 88–93, 169
moral philosophy and, 19–21
natural price of labor and, 175
science and, 139–141, 146
self-interest doctrine and, 54–55, 80–81, 94–96, 158
Theory of Moral Sentiments, The, 20–21
Wealth of Nations, 22–25
Smith, Sydney, 47–48
Socialism, 142–143, 144, 178–179
Catholic social doctrine and, 179
Socialism: Utopian or Scientific (Engels), 142
Socialists, 141–142, 177
Social reform
change and, 143–144
civilized society and, 52
poverty and, 30–31
science and, 144–146
welfare provisions for, 177
Social science, 45
Society
basis of, 120
economic transformation of, 7–8
effect of virtue on, 117
human interactions and, 192–195
social reforms and, 52
Society for Bettering the Condition of the Poor, 39

Socrates, 163
Sollicitudo Rei Socialis (Paul), 179
Solzhenitsyn, Alexander, 144
Sorcerer's Apprentice, The, 138
Spencer, Herbert, 146–147
Standard Oil, 66–70, 71–72, 73
Stigler, George, 161
Stone, Lawrence, 172–173
Sumner, William Graham, 147

"Tale of the Long Spoons," 136–137
"Tale of the Technological Father," 133–134
Tarbell, Ida, 67
Tawney, Richard Henry, 6, 170, 172
Ten Hour Bill, 51
Theory of Moral Sentiments, The (Smith), 20, 80–81, 87, 98, 105, 106–107, 109, 119, 120–123, 126
Tilden, Samuel J., 78–79
Townshend, Charles, 21, 22
Townshend Acts, 22
Transcontinental railroad
holding companies and, 60–62
private enterprise and, 57–66
scandals, 62–63
Transvaluation, 92–93, 113, 155, 166
Treatise on Human Nature (Hume), 14
Tullock, Gordon, 203
Turgot, Robert, 94
Twain, Mark, 65

Ulgor, 182–187
Union Cerrajera, 180
Union Pacific, 58–60
United States
culture, 194–196

economic order of, after Civil War, 55–56
economy, laissez-faire, and self-interest, 78–79
economy and crime, 192
self-interest doctrine and, 55–57, 191–192
United States Plywood Corporation, 183
Universities, supplanting Church, 197
Utilitarianism, 163–165
Utility, 152–153, 154
diminishing marginal, 8
Utopia (More), 170
Utopian thought, 142

Values, 130–131, 135
Veblen, Thorsten, 155
Vice, 120
morality and, 33, 36
Viner, Jacob, 19
Virtue, 109
economic value of, 95–96
effect on society of, 117
as force limiting self-interest, 98
See also Benevolence; Morality
Virtue of Selfishness, The (Rand), 166

Wachtel, Paul, 7
Walrus, Leon, 153
Warner, Charles, 65
Waterman, Robert, 95–96
Wealth
pursuit of, 6–7
Wealth of Nations (Smith), 9–10, 14, 39, 54, 99–105, 107–108, 110–111, 121, 123–125, 141, 176
British Parliament and, 28

Geneva High School Library
DISCARD

changed view in, 98
self-interest and, 80–81, 152
writing of, 22–25
What Is Property? (Proudhon),
    171–172
Whitebread, Samuel, 28, 30–32,
    36
Whitebread's bill, 28, 30, 32
Whitman, Walt, 63
Wicksteed, Phillip, 156–159

Wilberforce, William, 29–30, 39,
    56
Wolfe, Tom, 77
Work, self-realization and, 180
Worldly Philosophers, The
    (Heilbroner), 6, 72

Young, Arthur, 38

Zacharias, Pope, 169, 178